Hispanic and Latino New Orleans

LOUISIANA STATE UNIVERSITY PRESS

BATON ROUGE

Hispanic and Latino NEW ORLEANS

IMMIGRATION AND IDENTITY SINCE THE EIGHTEENTH CENTURY

ANDREW SLUYTER

CASE WATKINS

JAMES P. CHANEY

ANNIE M. GIBSON

Foreword by Daniel D. Arreola

Published by Louisiana State University Press
Copyright © 2015 by Louisiana State University Press
All rights reserved
Manufactured in the United States of America
LSU Press Paperback Original
First printing

DESIGNER: Michelle A. Neustrom
TYPEFACE: Sina Nova

All maps and other figures not otherwise credited were created
by Andrew Sluyter and Case Watkins.

LIBRARY OF CONGRESS CATALOGING-IN-PUBLICATION DATA

Sluyter, Andrew, 1958–
    Hispanic and Latino New Orleans : immigration and identity since the eigh-
teenth century / Andrew Sluyter, Case Watkins, James P. Chaney, and Annie M.
Gibson ; foreword by Daniel D. Arreola.
        pages cm
    Includes bibliographical references and index.
    ISBN 978-0-8071-6087-9 (pbk. : alk. paper) — ISBN 978-0-8071-6089-3 (pdf) —
ISBN 978-0-8071-6090-9 (epub) — ISBN 978-0-8071-6091-6 (mobi) 1. Hispanic
Americans—Louisiana—New Orleans—History. 2. Hispanic Americans—Ethnic
identity—History. 3. Latin Americans—Louisiana—New Orleans—History. 4.
Immigrants—Louisiana—New Orleans. 5. New Orleans (La.)—Emigration and
immigration—History. 6. Latin America—Emigration and immigration—History.
I. Watkins, Case, 1976– II. Chaney, James P., 1977– III. Gibson, Annie McNeill. IV.
Title.
    F379.N59S758 2015
    305.9'06912076335—dc23

                                                                        2015020503

We dedicate this book to our families:

Carina Giusti de Sluyter and Sophia and Nicole Sluyter
Kristin N. Wylie
Hulet and Joyce Chaney
Gail, McNeill, and Joshua Gibson

CONTENTS

FIGURES AND TABLES

TABLES

FOREWORD

IN HIS HIGHLY ACCLAIMED 1976 BOOK *New Orleans: The Making of an Urban Landscape,* geographer Peirce F. Lewis concluded a short discussion about the Crescent City's Latin American influence by noting, "In sum, New Orleans found its Latin connection an agreeable one, both profitable and colorful. And in their turn, it is said, Latin Americans enjoy New Orleans, if for no other reason than the Spanish appearance of the Vieux Carré, which they find familiar and comfortable" (p. 51). During the 1970s, New Orleans was a city of few people with Latino-Hispanic ancestry—perhaps 30,000 depending on who was counted and how counts were made, yet likely representing less than 4 percent of all residents. Latino New Orleans then comprised a series of small and scattered neighborhoods created over many generations and populated chiefly by more affluent and bilingual assimilated residents from only a few Latin American–ancestry groups.

Almost four decades later, New Orleans's Latino population has more than doubled. Today, the diversity of Hispanic-ancestry residents has been enhanced with immigrants from many parts of Latin America, and these new Latinos reside in many different quarters across the city. *Hispanic and Latino New Orleans: Immigration and Identity since the Eighteenth Century,* by Andrew Sluyter, Case Watkins, James P. Chaney, and Annie M. Gibson, chronicles the fascinating evolution of Latino populations in this often-proclaimed most distinctive of all American cities. The story moves from a broad, contextualizing introduction that compares New Orleans' Hispanics to Latinos in other American cities through specific chapters that unveil the creation of the oldest and newest Hispanic and Latino communities in the Crescent City. The narrative is organized chronologically by time periods, from colonial to nineteenth century to twentieth and twenty first centuries. Through this temporal framing, the authors demonstrate how different circumstances have shaped the influence of Hispanic and Latino groups at different times.

The work is grounded in historic and contemporary accounts and statistical measurements from censuses, city directories, and ship manifests and supplemented with interviews of local residents to give an active voice to the story. A major strength is the effective way the authors contextualize each Latino population group. For example, we learn how the urban geographies of Cubans and Hondurans in New Orleans are infused with a lived past that connects them to ancestries in Cuba and Honduras. This enriches our understanding, developing a historical context that sheds light on how Cubans and Hondurans came to the Crescent City, and how connections to homeland economies in the past and the present shape the cultural geographies of those who now reside there. Detailed maps enhance the human geographies and enable comparison of the various groups and their residential locations at different time periods. The authors are especially adept at explaining how those geographies change through time as population groups develop tenure and economic viability in the evolving city.

This study will be significant to many fields that study Hispanic and Latino communities in the United States. Its many findings make it one of the most informed analyses of Hispanic and Latino populations for any city in the country. Its comprehensive framework informs how Hispanic and Latino cultures have inhabited and made their places in the Crescent City, and its presentation will prove a model for those who might develop similar studies of these cultures in other American cities where a diversity of Hispanic and Latino populations has emerged in the last several decades.

Daniel D. Arreola

ACKNOWLEDGMENTS

WE OWE AN ENORMOUS DEBT TO many New Orleans Hispanics and Latinos, so many of whom welcomed us into their homes and opened up their personal lives in order to share their experiences, opinions, and dreams concerning New Orleans. We hope the publication of this book repays them by widely sharing what they taught us. Specific individuals who helped with the project and do not wish to remain anonymous include the following, although the views expressed and conclusions reached remain our own: Martín Gutíerrez, Romualdo "Romi" González, Alexey Martí Soltero, Javier Olondo, Aurelio González, Sr., Leticia González, Aurelio González, Jr., Javier Olondo, Natalia Aristizábal Uribe and family, Pedro "Piki" Mendizábal, Anna Frachou, Rafael Delgadillo, Alexis Martínez, Eliza Llewellyn, Angie Ivette Becerril Delgado, Pablo Reyes, Roger Velásquez, Cristobal Maldonado, Robert M. Landry, Ana L. Menes, and Ueliton Barbosa Teixeira.

Librarians and archivists of many institutions assisted in recovering the Hispanic and Latino pasts of New Orleans. We especially thank those of the Louisiana State University Libraries, New Orleans Notarial Archive, New Orleans Public Library, Louisiana State Archives, Louisiana State Land Office, University of New Orleans Libraries, and Tulane University Libraries.

We also thank the funding agencies that made this project possible. The Louisiana Board of Regents and LSU Graduate School provided an Economic Development Assistantship grant for 2009–13 that funded much work on this project. In addition, the LSU College of Humanities and Social Sciences awarded Andrew Sluyter a Manship Summer Grant in 2014 to finalize the manuscript.

Dan Arreola kindly wrote a foreword, which is fitting since all of us have been reading his eloquent books and articles on Latinos and their places since we were graduate students.

Finally, as this project comes to fruition, we thank the editors and others at LSU Press who guided it through the many stages of publication. Alisa Plant was always enthusiastic about the approach we took. The anonymous reviewers provided sage feedback that helped to improve on our efforts. The production phases, from copyediting through indexing and cover design, received the utmost attention from Lee Sioles, Catherine Kadair, freelance editor Jo Ann Kiser, and indexer Victoria Baker.

Hispanic and Latino New Orleans

INTRODUCTION

[New Orleans] is one of those Gulf cities that all seem like sisters, but very large, very developed; Tampico, Veracruz, and Campeche would all fit within it, and it has something of all of them within it, of Veracruz above all.　　　　　　—*Justo Sierra, Mexican writer and politician, 1895*

If you speak Spanish, you are Latino and probably came after Katrina [*laughter*].　　　　　　—*Humberto, interview of June 18, 2010*

NEW ORLEANS, ALSO KNOWN AS THE Crescent City and the Big Easy, has long hidden much of its Hispanic and Latino sides in plain sight. Tourists visiting the French Quarter see the Cabildo, the municipal hall that dates to the period of Spanish colonial rule in the second half of the eighteenth century. History students in Louisiana schools learn about Bernardo de Gálvez, the Spanish governor who sent his militia to help defeat the British in the American Revolution. Various plaques and monuments throughout the city commemorate more recent relationships with Latin America rather than with Spain, most notably the colossal statues of Simon Bolívar, Benito Juárez, and Francisco Morazán Quesada along Basin Street. Other landscape elements such as the Spanish-language signage that proliferates along Williams Boulevard in North Kenner might be more mundane, but they manifest the dynamic Latino communities that helped create the city before the devastation of Hurricane Katrina in 2005 and reconstruct it afterward.

Yet anyone searching the bookstores for a comprehensive account of Latino and Hispanic New Orleans will—until now—have gone home empty-handed. This book provides the first study of how diverse Hispanic and Latino communities have helped to create the Crescent City as a distinctive place. It also, more broadly, contributes to the literature on ethnic change in the United States and thereby informs the escalating debates about immigration and national identity.

We first realized, albeit individually at the time, the need for such a book after Hurricane Katrina flooded much of New Orleans in 2005. As residents left, reconstruction workers arrived, many of them Latinos from elsewhere in the United States or directly from Latin America. The reactions by many in southern Louisiana displayed an astounding ignorance of the long, complex history of the city and the roles of Hispanics and Latinos in creating it. Politicians predictably engaged in hyperbole, variously bemoaning being "overrun by Mexican workers" or celebrating that the city might become "a future San Antonio."[1] The media mainly parroted the representation of Latinos and Hispanics as newcomers, undocumented, and a threat to established social relations that focused on a black-white binary. Some academics proved just as prone to ignoring long-term historical processes and distinctions among Hispanic and Latino communities with extremely different origins. Instead they fixated on the immediate post-Katrina moment, disregarded diversity, failed to acknowledge the extraordinarily unique circumstances, and purveyed the exaggerated claim that New Orleans was "just catching up with a trend that's happening in every other city in the country." We often had to remind our colleagues at Louisiana State University (LSU) and Tulane University of the distinctions among Hispanic and Latino communities that had extremely diverse, long-term relationships with the city and had contributed to making it such a distinctive place.[2]

When we subsequently came together to write this book, we shared that perspective but each of us added a distinct emphasis. One of us, Andrew Sluyter, was engaged in research at LSU on eighteenth-century Louisiana and had a keen awareness of how Spain had controlled the city for nearly four decades and settled thousands of Hispanics in southern Louisiana, many of them Isleños from Spain's Canary Islands. Moreover, since Sluyter is married to an Argentinean, a number of his friends in Baton Rouge are Latinos who grew up in New Orleans, the children or grandchildren of immigrants from the Caribbean and Latin America who had come in the twentieth century, long before Katrina. Any nuanced understanding of the post-Katrina influx of Latino reconstruction workers thus seemed to demand a solid understanding of the origins of the pre-existing Hispanic and Latino communities. Each of them interacted in distinct ways with the post-Katrina newcomers because each had geographically and historically diverse origins that have resulted in different residential geographies within the city and different connections with other places and communities beyond and within the city. Only a detailed historical geography of those long-standing communities can provide a rigorous basis for understanding their current and future roles in the creation of New Orleans.[3]

Another one of us, Case Watkins, grew up in Louisiana and went to Texas State University, where he completed a master's thesis on spatial variation in Katrina flooding and its relations to urban patterns of race and class. When he returned to Louisiana to enroll in the doctoral program at LSU, he applied his skill at using census data and geographic information systems (GIS) to map how residential geographies of Hispanics and Latinos have changed over the past half century and were differentially impacted by Katrina. He subsequently combined GIS with ethnography and archival research to connect historical processes and migration flows with contemporary residential patterns, cultural change, and the formation of identities in New Orleans.[4]

James Chaney completed a dissertation at LSU on the social networks that connect various places in Mexico and Honduras to New Orleans and other cities in the American South. The personal relationships he established with Mexican and Honduran residents of New Orleans while conducting his research allow us to understand how migrant workers were able to use social networks to travel so far to participate in the post-Katrina reconstruction.[5]

Annie Gibson reacted to the rhetoric about Latinos that followed Katrina by interviewing the Brazilians who relocated to New Orleans to participate in the reconstruction. By virtue of coming from Latin America but speaking Portuguese rather than Spanish they are able to shift their identities between Latino and non-Latino. A faculty member in the Center for Global Education and the Stone Center for Latin American Studies at Tulane, Gibson employs an ethnographic approach that permits us to understand how this liminal, Latino/non-Latino community has created a distinct community in the city and contributes to its uniqueness as a place. Gibson also works as resident director for Tulane's fall study-abroad program in Havana, Cuba. She has conducted interviews both on the island and in New Orleans, and her connections to the Cuban community, as well as her work on the processes of identity formation among Brazilian and Cuban immigrant communities, have provided an interdisciplinary lens of analysis.[6]

OUR USE OF THE TERMS "Hispanic" and "Latino" signals appreciation for the distinct but related origins of those communities while acknowledging the inherently subjective character of such categories. Ultimately, any individual decides whether to self-identify as Hispanic, Latino, neither, or both. In the general terms necessary to a study such as this one, however, "Hispanic" designates those groups unified through their Spanish-language heritage, whether from the Canary Islands and other places in Spain or from places in Latin America and the Caribbean as different as Mexico and Cuba. "Latino," more restrictively, designates those Hispanics with origins in Latin America and the Caribbean rather than Europe. Yet "Latino" can also refer to non-Spanish speakers from Latin America, and therefore non-Hispanics: for example, Brazilian speakers of Portuguese, the other major Romance language of that region, and Garínagu, from the Caribbean coast of Central America, unified by the Garifuna language but also fluent in Spanish if from Guatemala, Honduras, or Nicaragua and in English if from Belize—sometimes in all three.[7]

Moreover, although this study focuses on Hispanic and Latino communities defined by national origin, such as Hondurans and Cubans, each community contains great diversity along various dimensions. These include class, gender, generation, age, religion, subnational place of origin, year of arrival, residency status, and others. Many of the statistics used in this study, for example, derive from the question on the US decennial census that asks respondents if they identify as ethnically Hispanic or Latino and to specify their national origin. Another census question then asks if they identify as racially white, black or African American, American Indian or Alaska native, Asian, or native Hawaiian or other Pacific Islander. Moreover, the Census Bureau explicitly states that a Hispanic or Latino can be, according to its categorization, "of any race." In contrast, self-categorization by some Hispanics or Latinos might prioritize their racialized identity over national origin and construct a community that overlaps several of those based on national origin. For example, a person might self-identify primarily as a black Cuban and feel more affinity for those who self-identify as black Hondurans and African Americans than with those who self-identify as white Cubans. Self-categorization might even entirely reject concepts such as ethnicity and race or, conversely, combine them into a single taxonomy in which Hispanic or Latino becomes a racial category distinct from black or white. More than a third of those who identified ethnically as Hispanic or Latino on Census 2010, in fact, selected "other" for the race question because, according to Census Bureau surveys and focus groups, they feel that they do not fit into the census categories. Instead, some think of Latino as a hybrid category, a multiracialized ethnicity defined by mixed parentage due to the highly ramified white, black, and indigenous ancestries of many people from Latin America and the Caribbean.[8]

That relationship between ethnicity and racialized categories has particular relevance in New Orleans. Relations between whites and blacks have long dominated the city's politics, with the category African American complicated by the malleable term "creole." "Creole" derives from the Spanish *criollo* or Portuguese *crioulo,* which both denote birth in the colonies and, because so many born in the Americas had various combinations of European, African, and indigenous parentage, also connote ethnic, racial, linguistic, and cultural mixing. For example, Haitian Creole is the dialect of French spoken in Haiti, a dialect that is based on eighteenth-century French and incorporates African, indigenous, and Spanish elements. Social context, however, strongly modulates the meaning of the term. To illustrate, during the independence movements in Spanish colonies that began in the late eighteenth century, the label "criollo" excluded those with African origins and became reserved for whites born in the Americas, as a way to differentiate them from those of Spanish birth who typically held all of the positions of power in the colonies and were loyal to Spain. Similarly, "creole" applied to whites and blacks alike in colonial Louisiana, but after the Louisiana Purchase of 1803 whites descended from French and Spanish colonists used it specifically to distinguish themselves from the English-speaking Americans who began to flood into the city. The thousands of free and enslaved refugees from the Haitian Revolution who arrived in New Orleans during the first decade of the nineteenth century nonetheless also referred to themselves as creoles, most having been born in Saint-Domingue or Cuba. Nearly doubling the city's population, they were of French, African, or mixed parentage. The Jim Crow era further complicated use of the term as people of mixed European and African descent who had been free already before the Civil War began to use the term to distinguish themselves from the descendants of slaves, many of pure African descent, freed by the war. Currently, "creole" indicates most clearly a mix that is purely New Orleanian. Creole cuisine thus derives from the colonial and subsequent mixing of French cooking with Spanish, African, and other influences but is decidedly urbane and does not include rural, Cajun French cuisine. And creole, sometimes "black creole," as a racialized category signifies people whose families have lived in New Orleans for many generations, back to the colonial period or influx from Saint-Domingue, of mixed French and African parentage and heritage, neither white nor African American, an identity unique to New Orleans.[9]

As a further complication, places, situations, and social relations strongly modulate the emergence of community and individual identities. Newcomers typically redefine the identity they arrived with in order to integrate with the established categories of their new place. The process of negotiating such new identities in order to function socially can yield distinct outcomes for the same ethnic group in different places. For example, Garínagu tend to have a hybrid identity that reflects their mixed African and indigenous ancestry. This ancestry ultimately derives from expulsion of the so-called Black Caribs from the island colony of Saint Vincent in 1797 and relocation to British and Spanish colonies along the Caribbean coast of Central America. Yet in New York City, Garínagu from Honduras tend to emphasize the African aspects of their identity because their residential concentrations make them the neighbors of many African Americans in Harlem and the Bronx.[10]

Such processes become particularly complex for transnational communities, a concept that emerged in the 1990s to capture what seems to be a new type of immigration. Rather than the sort of permanent relocation from one country to another or seasonal migration that characterized the nineteenth and twentieth centuries, transnational migrants create persistent social relations between places in different countries. Transmigrants, then, are those "migrants whose lived experiences transcend the boundaries of nation states," maintaining "familial, economic, social, organizational, religious, and political relationships across international lines and borders."[11] While some have argued that transnational qualities also characterized, to one degree or another, migration during the nineteenth and early twentieth centuries, technologies that have increased the pace and ease of international travel and communication have nonetheless facilitated more and larger transnational communities during the late twentieth and twenty-first centuries. "Economic and cultural umbilical cords now permanently connect hundreds of Latin American and Caribbean localities with counterpart urban neighborhoods in the United States. To the extent that the sending communities have become fully integrated into the economy of the immigrant metropolis as their own nation-state (a process that some researchers call *Nortenización*), they are the *de facto* 'transnational suburbs' of New York, Los Angeles, Chicago and Miami. Indeed, they transform our understanding of the contemporary big city."[12] Critically, those transnational communities and the transmigrants that construct them can exhibit specific identities associated with each of the places in the community as well as with the transnational spaces of mobility that interconnect the nodes.[13]

The communities based on national origin that organize this study, therefore, do not reflect everyone's experience or self-identity. Each such constructed community displays degrees of internal solidarity and division that vary over time and from place to place. So although we pragmatically use constructs such as "the Honduran community of New Orleans" to organize this book, we argue that social relations are in reality much more complex, dynamic, and "messy" than the isolated, homogenous communities implied by shared national origins that readers might infer from our table of contents.

THIS BOOK THEREFORE ADDRESSES THE heterogeneity and social relations within each such national-origin community as well as among different ones to make a substantial contribution to the long-standing but quite minuscule literature on the Hispanic and Latino communities of New Orleans. Louisiana genealogists have certainly scoured early censuses and passenger lists to compile surnames of Spanish origin but with the purpose of understanding particular families rather than entire communities. Graduate students at Louisiana's universities have produced relevant theses and dissertations but on highly specialized aspects of only some of the Hispanic and Latino communities of the Crescent City. The few books published on the topic provide fuller, more accessible accounts but nonetheless focus on individuals such as Bernardo de Gálvez or on particular communities such as the Isleños. Or, conversely, they treat a broader range of Hispanics and Latinos across all of Louisiana so that New Orleans becomes but one place among many, none studied in depth or detail.[14]

In contrast, we endeavor to provide a comprehensive understanding of the city's diverse Hispanic and Latino communities. This book covers the built-up, urbanized areas of Orleans, Jefferson, St. Bernard, and Plaquemines parishes (fig. 1). These areas straddle the Mississippi River south of Lake Pontchartrain, their focal point at the French Quarter, which Jean-Baptiste Le Moyne, Sieur de Bienville, founded in 1718 as Nouvelle-Orléans and which four years later became the capital of the French colony of La Louisiane.[15] The study begins with existing research by genealogists, graduate students, amateur historians, and professional scholars. It builds on that foundation using interviews, census statistics, landscape observations, oral histories, and archival documents. And it results in an understanding of the roles of the varied but related spectrum of Hispanic and Latino communities in the ongoing creation of New Orleans before and after the impact of Hurricane Katrina in 2005.[16]

More broadly than a book about another aspect of New Orleans, though, it is also part of a growing literature on the complex relationships of such Hispanic and Latino communities with US society more generally and the associated debates about immigration policy and national identity. That literature has grown in size and significance together with the increasing proportion of

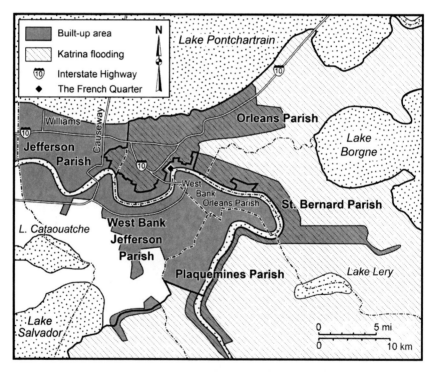

FIG. 1. Map of the city of New Orleans showing the built-up, urbanized areas of Orleans, Jefferson, St. Bernard, and Plaquemines parishes in relation to flooding in the aftermath of Hurricane Katrina in 2005.

Hispanics and Latinos in the US population. Census 1990 enumerated 22.4 million residents of the fifty states and District of Columbia who self-identified as Hispanics and Latinos, 9 percent of the total population. By Census 2000, the count was 35.3 million, a 58 percent increase over 1990 and nearly 13 percent of the entire population. And in 2010, the census counted 50.5 million, a 43 percent increase over 2000 and 16 percent of the US population. Their proportion in such cities as Los Angeles has dramatically increased together with that in the United States as a whole, and they now constitute the majority in such places as Miami and San Antonio.[17]

The prominence of the South in that dramatic shift in US ethnic composition has prompted some to coin the term "New Latino South." The South, not including Florida, did not attract many Hispanics and Latinos during the twentieth century before the 1990s, but between 1990 and 2000 their population in the Atlanta metropolitan area grew from 55,045 to 268,851, an increase of 388 percent. Other southern cites had even higher growth rates that decade, albeit on lower bases. Six states that formed the core of the New Latino South had growth rates of greater than 200 percent in their Hispanic and Latino populations: Alabama, Arkansas, Georgia, North Carolina, South Carolina, and Tennessee. The trend continued over the next decade, with a 57 percent increase in the Hispanic and Latino population of the South between 2000 and 2010, substantially higher than the national growth rate of 43 percent.[18]

Such demographic changes will clearly have broad social and cultural impacts, whether perceived as "Challenges to America's National Identity" or a multicultural "Remaking the American Mainstream." Scholars have developed theories about the general processes involved. Some believe, for example, that immigrants are most likely to assimilate to a national identity if they live in neighborhoods that are integrated with the broader society, resulting in greater interaction, intergroup mutual respect and cooperation, accumulation of social capital, and a shared prosperity that encourages assimilation to a national identity. Others believe the opposite, namely, that close interaction results in greater social competition and conflict, actually inhibiting assimilation to a national identity.[19]

While contributing to that general understanding about immigration and national identity, rather than dwelling on such theories, books such as this one explicate how real people living in actual communities participate in the creation of specific places over the long term. Many places already have comprehensive literatures on their Hispanic and Latino communities, and they inform local and national debates about immigration and assimilation. Los Angeles and San Antonio have well-developed literatures on their Mexican communities, for example, New York on its Puerto Ricans and Dominicans, and Miami on its Cubans. So do smaller cities like Santa Fe, where the descendants of the Hispanics who settled the northern frontier of the colony of New Spain in the seventeenth century call themselves Hispanos. And similar literatures exist for broader regions such as southern Texas and the US-Mexico border-lands more broadly. While the Hispanic and Latino communities of the New Latino South cannot compare in size and influence to the more-established ones of Los Angeles, San Antonio, Miami, and so on, interest in southern cities has also begun to generate a substantial literature, from statistical overviews to field studies of distinctive places that Latinos have created in particular neighborhoods.[20]

New Orleans had until now not received much attention in that literature. The city had simply not participated in the New Latino South over the 1990s. Census 2000 enumerated 51,102 Hispanics and Latinos in Orleans, Jefferson, Plaquemines, and St. Bernard parishes, not even 5 percent of their total population of 1,034,126. Moreover, the number of Hispanics and Latinos in those four parishes had increased only about 5 percent over the 1990s, an order of magnitude lower than the national rate of 58 percent and two orders of magnitude lower than other major cities across the South. Lack of economic opportunity in New Orleans due to the decline of the oil industry and Port of New Orleans over the 1980s seems to explain the Crescent City's isolation from the New Latino South. New Orleans had, in fact, become a net exporter of population, with the four parishes losing nearly 6 percent of their residents over the 1980s and an additional 2 percent or so over the 1990s.

THE SEGREGATION OF NEW ORLEANS from the surging Hispanic and Latino population of the New Latino South and the United States as a whole changed suddenly when the Crescent City suffered extensive flood damage in the aftermath of Hurricane Katrina, attracting many workers to participate in the cleanup and reconstruction effort. Katrina made landfall on the morning of August 29, 2005, and tracked northward across Lake Borgne as a category-three hurricane (fig. 2).[21] Levee breaches and overtopping flooded extensive areas of

Orleans, St. Bernard, and Plaquemines parishes to depths of more than four meters (thirteen feet). Northern Jefferson Parish and areas west of the Mississippi River experienced some wind damage and localized, short-term flooding due to heavy precipitation but did not suffer the breached levees that resulted in persistent inundation. For some neighborhoods in Orleans, St. Bernard, and Plaquemines parishes, however, the floodwaters lasted through much of September, exacerbated when Hurricane Rita struck near the Louisiana-Texas border on September 24 and caused a storm surge that reflooded parts of the city. With their homes and workplaces destroyed, a large proportion of the city's residents relocated to other places. The Census Bureau has estimated that

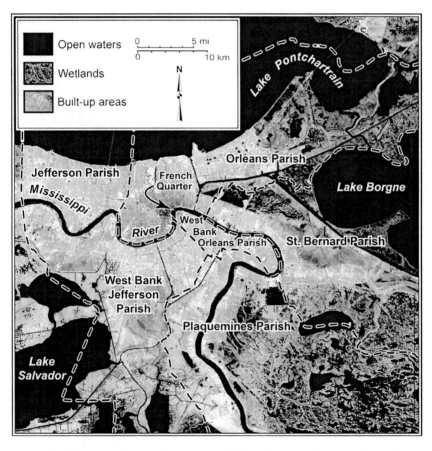

FIG. 2. Satellite image showing built-up area of New Orleans and surrounding wetlands and lakes.

between July 2005 and January 2006 the population of the four parishes de-clined by 42 percent, from 1,013,193 to 593,183.[22]

As residents left and reconstruction workers arrived, many noted the pre-ponderance of Hispanics and Latinos among the newcomers but drew conclu-sions that largely ignored the long, complex ethnic history of the city. Some complained and others celebrated that Mexicans were, by their accounts, over-running the city. New Orleans seemed, to many, to have become part of the New Latino South and to be finally "catching up" with ethnic changes that had long affected many other cities.

The decade that has passed since Katrina struck has somewhat tempered the hyperbole. Census 2010 revealed that the population of the four parishes had rebounded to 835,320, a nearly 41 percent increase over the immediate post-Katrina estimate of 593,183 but still a decline of just over 19 percent relative to the 1,034,126 of Census 2000. Meanwhile, the Hispanic and Latino propor-

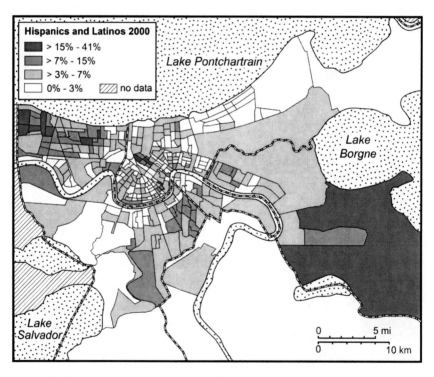

FIG. 3. The Hispanic and Latino population of New Orleans as a proportion of the total popu-lation of each census tract in 2000.

tion of the population had nearly doubled, from nearly 5 to just over 9 percent. Those gross statistics seem, at least on their surface, to support the predictions common immediately after Katrina: the Hispanic and Latino population grew from 51,102 to 76,129, an increase of 49 percent and therefore, admittedly, substantially lower than the 57 percent for the South as a whole but, nonetheless, somewhat higher than the 43 percent for the entire United States. Perhaps most tellingly, when mapped by census tract, Hispanics and Latinos not only had a greater presence in many neighborhoods by 2010 than they did in 2000, up to 41 percent of the total population of some census tracts, but they had become established much more broadly across the city (figs. 3 and 4).[23]

Closer scrutiny of Census 2010, however, suggests that judicious use of such statistics demands detailed understanding of the historically and geographically diverse origins of the city's Hispanic and Latino communities. To illustrate, St. Bernard and Plaquemines parishes had the largest increases in the

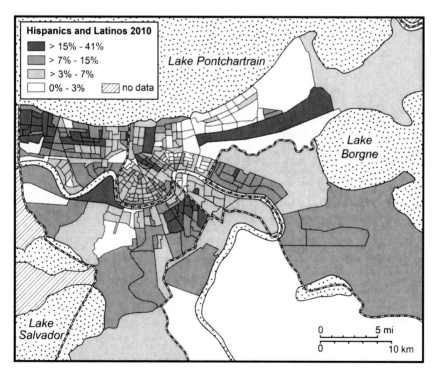

FIG. 4. The Hispanic and Latino population of New Orleans as a proportion of the total population of each census tract in 2010.

proportion of Hispanics and Latinos between 2000 and 2010, respectively from 5.1 to 9.2 percent and from 1.6 to 4.6 percent. Those two parishes also share another notable characteristic: a large proportion of their Hispanics and Latinos claimed Spanish rather than a Latin American or Caribbean heritage in Census 2010, 19.0 percent in the case of St. Bernard Parish and 7.2 percent for Plaquemines Parish. Since few contemporary immigrants to the United States originate in Spain, the Spanish-born comprising only 0.21 percent of all foreign-born residents in 2010 and 0.27 percent in 2000, the statistics for St. Bernard and Plaquemines parishes suggest that at least some of the people contributing to the apparent surge in the city's Hispanic and Latino population came to Louisiana long before Katrina. The most notable such community derives from Hispanics who came from Spain's Canary Islands in the eighteenth century, namely the Isleños, and certainly does not correspond to the rhetoric of a city being "overrun by Mexican workers," "a future San Antonio," or "catching up with a trend that's happening in every other city in the country."[24]

THIS BOOK, THEN, ALTHOUGH CATALYZED by the hyperbolic rhetoric and misconceptions about the city's Hispanic and Latino communities in the aftermath of Katrina, necessarily begins more than two centuries before that devastating hurricane—with the arrival of the Isleños—and explicates the subsequent historical process. We have long known the broad outlines of that history, such as that the Isleño settlement of New Orleans related to Spain's sovereign control of Louisiana in the eighteenth century. Immigration from Spain to New Orleans, however, steadily declined over the nineteenth and twentieth centuries. Census 1850 records just how few Hispanics settled in New Orleans during the early nineteenth century: the 1,171 residents of the four parishes who claimed birth in Spain comprised less than 1 percent of the total population. By the turn of the century, for the period 1899 through 1910, the United States admitted only 51,051 immigrants from Spain, half a percent of all immigrants. Moreover, 16,278 of them declared their destination as New York and 11,355 as Florida. Only 1,074 planned to settle in Louisiana. Consequently, Census 1930 enumerated only 492 residents of Spanish birth in Orleans, Jefferson, St. Bernard, and Plaquemines parishes, less than half as many as in 1850.[25]

In contrast, the Louisiana Purchase of 1803 and emergence of independent republics throughout the Spanish colonial empire initiated greatly increased interaction between New Orleans and Latin America over the nineteenth century. Until surpassed by Houston in the mid-1900s, New Orleans became the major metropolis on the Gulf Coast. Through much of the nineteenth century and into the twentieth, New Orleans served as the self-proclaimed gateway to Latin America (fig. 5). That relationship took many forms, including trade, embarkation port for military expeditions, and home to political exiles such as Benito Juárez, who later became president of Mexico. Products, people, ideas,

FIG. 5. Early twentieth-century pamphlet distributed by the New Orleans Conventions and Tourist Bureau, showing New Orleans as the Latin American gateway. Image from a pamphlet titled *The Convention City for the Tourist*, item F379.N53 N432 1900zx, T. P. Thompson Collection, W. S. Hoole Special Collections Library, University of Alabama. Reproduced courtesy of University Libraries, Division of Special Collections, The University of Alabama.

and invasive biota consequently flowed between New Orleans and ports such as Veracruz, Mexico, and Havana, Cuba. A series of Spanish-language periodicals turned the Crescent City into a northern outpost of Latin American literary culture, beginning in the early nineteenth century with *El Misisipi* and continuing through *El Mercurio* and *El Lucero Latino* in the early twentieth century. Latin American travelers in the United States invariably arrived or departed through the Crescent City and reflected on its liminal personality: in their view, one side of the city represented a vision of the possibilities for the modernization of their own republics while the other side represented a contaminated version of modernity, corrupted through lengthy contact with the ports of the Gulf of Mexico, Caribbean, and South Atlantic.[26]

Three commodities—sugar, coffee, and bananas—came to dominate the networks that emerged to link New Orleans to Latin America and the Caribbean over the nineteenth century and into the twentieth. And one firm, the United Fruit Company, exemplified the types of relationships created with the so-called banana republics. In 1933, a Moldavian immigrant named Samuel Zemurray acquired the United Fruit Company of Boston, moved its headquarters to New Orleans, and proceeded to run what became known throughout Latin America as La Frutera or, more derisively, El Pulpo. The first appellation, meaning "The Fruit Company," referred to its control of the US banana supply through vertical integration of subsidiary companies such as International Railways of Central America, the Tropical Radio and Telegraph Company, and the Great White Fleet of banana freighters. The second nickname, meaning "The Octopus," referred to its paternalistic control of many aspects of its employees' lives and the politics of entire countries through corruption and force. At its peak, United Fruit controlled through lease and purchase some 1.4 million hectares (3.5 million acres) in Central America, the Caribbean, and South America. Zemurray died in 1961, his company disappeared soon thereafter through mergers, and by the 1970s New Orleans was no longer central to the banana trade and Latin American politics. The Sicilian Vaccaro family ran another banana company based in New Orleans, the Standard Fruit and Steamship Company, but it never achieved the scale or influence of United Fruit and moved its operations to Gulfport, Mississippi, in the 1960s.[27]

Coffee, especially from Central America and Brazil, also became a major commodity linking New Orleans to Latin America. The city became and continues to be a larger importer of coffee than any other US port. The networks created between New Orleans coffee companies and places in Central and South America paralleled those of the banana trade. Unlike the case with bananas, though, none of the dozens of relatively small coffee companies ever achieved the dominance, power, and infamy of United Fruit.[28]

Sugar linked New Orleans to Cuba more than to any other place in Latin America or the Caribbean. The Audubon Sugar Institute at LSU became an international leader in sugar research and education, and LSU's football team traveled to Havana to compete in a series known as the Bacardi Bowl. Cuban producers, including LSU alumni and United Fruit subsidiaries, shipped millions of tons of raw sugar to refineries along the lower Mississippi River. And hundreds of thousands of tons of food, lumber, and other products flowed to Cuba through the port of New Orleans. The Cuban Revolution of 1959 and the US trade embargo that followed radically transformed that relationship but did not end it.[29]

The commercial networks linking New Orleans to Latin America and the Caribbean brought Latinos as well as commodities, people who in various ways created communities and participated in shaping the landscapes and other characteristics of the Crescent City. In terms of landscape, the most obvious vestiges remain various plaques and statues throughout the city, notably the colossal monuments erected between 1957 and 1966 along Basin Street to honor the heroes of the nineteenth-century revolts against European rule in South America, Mexico, and Central America. Other relevant landscape elements include Tulane's Center for Latin American Studies, largely funded by the Zemurray family; the cabs of the White Fleet taxicab company, their door emblems echoing the pennant of United Fruit's fleet of banana freighters; and the company headquarters building still standing at 321 St. Charles Avenue, the ornate pilasters flanking its entrance surmounted by three cornucopia spilling bananas and other tropical fruits.

Census 1970 first began to generate spatially precise statistics on national origin, revealing how Cubans and others who arrived via the commodity networks came to form a large proportion of the Hispanic and Latino communities of New Orleans in the twentieth century, despite the dominance of Mexican immigrants in the United States as a whole (fig. 6).[30] The 1970 census was the first to include a question on Hispanic and Latino origins, asking whether the respondent's "origin or descent" was Mexican, Puerto Rican, Cuban, "Central or South American," or "other Spanish." That question, however, appeared

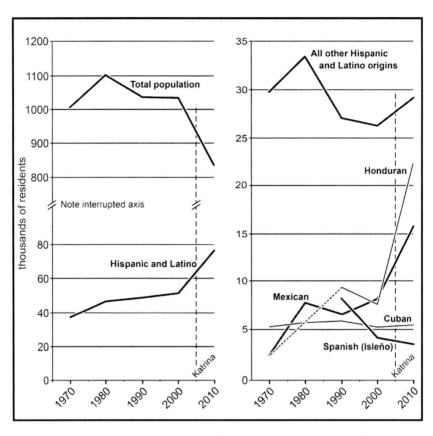

FIG. 6. Comparison of the total population of New Orleans; the population of Hispanic and Latino origin; and the populations of Spanish (mostly Isleño), Cuban, Honduran, Mexican, and "All Other Hispanic and Latino Origins," 1970–2010. The pre-1990 Honduran population estimate is even more imprecise than the others because it derives from regional- and state-level statistics, as discussed in chap. 3.

only on the "long form," sent to a 5 percent sample of households. Census 1980 first included a question on Hispanic and Latino origins as part of the "short form," distributed to all households, asking whether the respondent self-identified as "of Spanish or Hispanic origin or descent" and then more specifically as of Mexican, Puerto Rican, Cuban, or "other Spanish/Hispanic" origin. Census 1990 modified that question on both the short and the long forms by adding a write-in box to allow people to specify what they meant by "other Spanish/Hispanic," providing "Argentinean, Colombian, Dominican, Nicaraguan, Salvadoran, Spaniard, and so on" as examples of possible responses. The Census Bureau, however, coded the responses to the write-in box only for the long form and because of the small sample size could produce only parish-level estimates for most groups, with estimates at the census-tract level possible for only the largest groups. Census 2000 added the term "Latino" to the question, asking whether respondents identified as "Spanish/Hispanic/Latino"; removed the examples of national origin for the write-in box; but coded the responses for the short form and therefore generated statistics on specific origins for all groups at the level of census tracts. Census 2010 included a similar question on the short form, asking if respondents were "of Hispanic, Latino, or Spanish origin"; left the more specific categories as Mexican, Puerto Rican, and Cuban; and again provided examples of other national origins for the write-in box, the same ones as for Census 1990.[31]

Undercounting of Hispanics and Latinos limits, to some degree, the accuracy of such statistics. One of the main reasons for undercounts involves lack of immigration or visitor documentation, which might cause people to avoid census takers because of the perceived possibility of arrest and deportation. The other involves the mobility of migrant workers, which might cause census takers to miss them. Each possibility impacts some national-origin groups more than others. For example, Mexicans in the United States include a higher proportion of undocumented residents than do Cubans, at least until the mid-1990s. Puerto Ricans, meanwhile, are US citizens by virtue of the 1917 Jones-Shafroth Act and are unaffected by that particular undercounting bias. At the same time, the inclusion of Cubans, Mexicans, and Puerto Ricans as explicit categories in the census question results in a relative undercount of other groups such as Hondurans because a large percentage of those who indicate the "other" category choose to forgo writing in a more specific origin or write in a word that the Census Bureau does not code as a specific nationality, resulting in their inclusion in an "Unspecified" category. Moreover, that particular bias has changed in degree over time because of changes to the census form. Census 1990 provided examples of how to fill in the write-in box that followed the check boxes for Mexican, Cuban, and Puerto Rican. Census 2000 replaced them with a blunt "print group," resulting in a failure by many to print anything and a national inflation of the "Unspecified" category. With restoration of the examples in Census 2010, the "Unspecified" category deflated as dramatically as it had inflated in 2000. From 1970 through 2000 that category consistently exceeded 50 percent of the total Hispanic and Latino population of New Orleans. With Census 2010, however, that category fell to 38.4 percent of the total Hispanic and Latino population, seemingly because of the rapid growth in the number of residents of Mexican origin, a group with its own check box and therefore not subject to that particular undercounting bias, as well as because the question again provided examples of national origin for the write-in box.[32]

With those issues related to undercounts in mind, Census 2000 revealed that of the 51,102 Hispanics and Latinos in New Orleans five years before Katrina, 15.9 percent claimed Mexican origin, 14.7 percent Honduran, and 10.2 percent Cuban. That distribution in part reflected the predominance of Mexicans in the national growth of the Hispanic and Latino population ever since the Bracero Program began to bring flexible farm labor from Mexico to the United States in the mid-twentieth century. Nationally, 58.5 percent of the Hispanics and Latinos enumerated in Census 2000 claimed Mexican origins. In New Orleans, however, relative isolation from the New Latino South and the existence of commodity networks that established relationships with particular places in Latin America and the Caribbean allowed Hondurans and Cubans to form proportions of the Hispanic and Latino population that approached the proportion of Mexicans. After those three dominant communities, the next largest were an order of magnitude smaller and had origins in Puerto Rico, at 5.7 percent; Nicaragua, 4.6 percent; Guatemala, 3.0 percent; Colombia, 1.7 percent; El Salvador, 1.4 percent; and the Dominican Republic, 1.2 percent.[33]

Katrina differentially impacted those communities of varied origins, not only directly but through the subsequent influx of Latino reconstruction workers. The Isleños were concentrated in St. Bernard Parish, which was nearly entirely flooded, on the eastern side of the city. The Honduran, Cuban, Mexican, and other Latino communities were concentrated on the western side of the city, many in Jefferson Parish, which largely escaped persistent flooding. As the reconstruction effort began, an influx of Latino workers drove a visible proliferation of Spanish-language signage, taco trucks, Mexican and Central American money-wiring services, advertisers on Radio Tropical Caliente, an Azteca America television station, English classes for Spanish speakers, demand for bilingual employees, and the numbers of Spanish-speaking patients at health clinics. Studies in the immediate aftermath of Katrina characterized the newcomers as largely male, undocumented migrant workers of Mexican and Central American origin. Those newcomers have had a significant impact on the pre-existing Mexican, Honduran, Cuban, and other Latino communities of New Orleans as well as on their relationships with each other and with the Isleños.[34]

THE FOLLOWING CHAPTERS EXAMINE several of those communities in detail, their pre-Katrina roles in the creation of New Orleans, the impact of Katrina, and their post-Katrina roles. While Katrina looms large in that story, others have already provided focused studies of Latinos during the reconstruction, their struggles amid unhealthy working conditions, inadequate housing, discrimination, and wage theft. This book, in contrast, explicates the historical processes and hemispheric networks that have long brought Hispanics and Latinos to New Orleans—before and after Katrina. Chapter 1 begins with the Hispanic Isleños in the eighteenth century. Chapters 2 and 3 treat two Latino communities that became established in New Orleans during the nineteenth century and have played major roles in some of the city's neighborhoods: Cubans and Hondurans. Chapter 4 examines how Mexicans long formed a less prominent community in the city but have steadily increased in number and influence, especially since the mid-twentieth century and, even more so, since Katrina. Chapter 5 deals with a smaller community that nonetheless raises conceptually significant issues: the Brazilians became prominent only after Katrina but play a notable liminal role, negotiating the borderlands between Latino and non-Latino identities. Chapter 6 briefly addresses a constellation of other communities including Garínagu, Dominicans, Argentineans, and others—none numerically large but each of interest intrinsically and in relation to the more populous groups covered in greater detail in the other chapters. Each of those chapters combines historical narrative, interviews, and graphs to explain the changing residential geography of a particular group and its relationship to Katrina flooding, interweaving a demographic narrative with political, economic, and cultural ones. The concluding chapter compares those communities and considers their interactions, broader relationships, and the implications for general debates about immigration and national identity.[35]

1. ISLEÑOS

Some Spanish names and a few Spanish families are still to be found in
New Orleans; but these are not sufficient to make one suppose that it
was ever a Spanish town.   —*E. Bunner,* History of Louisiana, *1855*

And we've had several people who said, "I always thought I was Italian"
or "You know it's strange, I never thought about it before, but my grandmother spoke Spanish." And I tell people when I speak to groups that
even though you're a Broussard or an Hebert or a Thibodaux, your great-
grandmother or your grandmother probably was a Hernandez or a Suarez
or a Falcon. *—John Hickey, 2011, quoted in Perez,* The Isleños of Louisiana

THE FRENCH FOUNDED NEW ORLEANS in 1718, but in the wake of the Seven
Years' War of 1754–63, known as the French and Indian War in North America,
Spain incorporated Louisiana into its colonial empire and encouraged renewed
immigration to secure its new frontier with British North America (fig. 7). The
Acadians, who in the nineteenth century became known as Cajuns, remain the
most recognizable of the groups to settle in Spanish Louisiana, serve as frontier
militia, and establish identifiable communities. While governor from 1777 to
1785, however, Bernardo de Gálvez also recruited three large groups of Hispanic
settlers. Some five hundred Andalusians from Málaga, the ancestral home of
the Gálvez family, arrived in 1779 to found New Iberia about two hundred kilometers (125 miles) west of New Orleans. Another hundred Andalusians arrived
from Granada in 1778, but their settlement failed and most returned to Spain
between 1781 and 1784. Between 1778 and 1783, Gálvez also brought nearly two
thousand Isleños directly from the Canary Islands, where his father had served
as governor, and settled them in four villages to guard the approaches to New

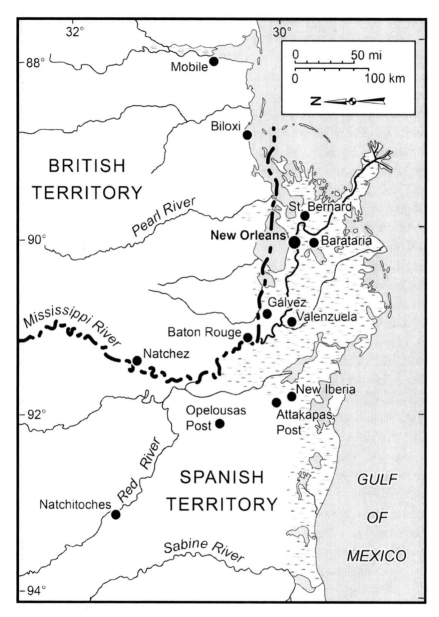

FIG. 7. Spanish and British colonial territories and their principal settlements along the lower Mississippi River.

Orleans: St. Bernard, Villa de Gálvez, Barataria, and Valenzuela. Those 2,500 or so Spanish settlers seem few, but they amounted to around 15 percent of the total population of Louisiana at the time and nearly a third of the free population. The strategy of encouraging Spaniards from the Canary Islands to settle in the Americas became quite general throughout Spain's colonial empire, with that archipelago off the African coast serving not only as a strategic outpost from which to control Atlantic shipping, and as a place to prototype colonial institutions, but also as a convenient source of impoverished farmers willing to settle newly acquired territories and serve as frontier militias.[1]

Gálvez located only two of the four settlements of Isleños, literally "Islanders," in the immediate environs of New Orleans. The other two, Valenzuela and Villa de Gálvez, later Galveztown, were intended to guard the immediate frontier with the British and, when Spain entered the Revolutionary War as an American ally, as staging points from which to attack and occupy Baton Rouge and Natchez. The two Isleño settlements founded in 1779 to guard the southern approaches to New Orleans were just south of the colonial city, now known as the French Quarter, or Vieux Carré. To the west of the Mississippi River, near the shore of Lake Salvador, Gálvez founded Barataria. To the east of the river, he founded La Concepción, later renamed San Bernardo and now known as St. Bernard. Each Isleño family received initial support in the form of food, cloth, tools, and money as well as a land grant of 120 *arpents,* about 41 hectares (101 acres). Within four years hurricanes and floods had forced abandonment of Barataria. St. Bernard, in contrast, thrived and eventually became the Louisiana place, now a parish and suburb of New Orleans, most closely identified with the Isleño community.[2]

By 1788, some 672 people lived in what was to become St. Bernard Parish, an extant census enumerating 18 enslaved blacks and mulattos, 9 free blacks and mulattos, and 645 whites. The vast majority of them were Isleños. Their land grants stretched along the levees of Bayou Tierra de Bueyes, now Bayou Terre aux Boeufs, eastward from the Poydras Plantation on the broad levee of the Mississippi River to where the narrower levees of the bayou virtually disappear downstream of Reggio (fig. 8).[3] The grants of the Primero Población, or First Settlement, centered on the church under construction at St. Bernard, completed in 1791. Those of the Second Settlement extended from those of the First Settlement in a southward arc along the bayou and centered on the village of Benchijigua, later Bencheque and now Reggio. That Second Settlement in-

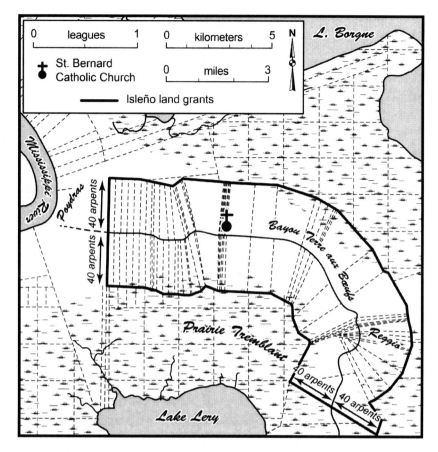

FIG. 8. Eighteenth-century Isleño land grants along Bayou Terre aux Boeufs as based on nineteenth-century claims to private land.

cluded families who had abandoned Barataria together with a group of Isleños who arrived in 1783 after a sojourn of four years on Cuba during the Revolutionary War.[4]

Each Isleño land grant had a bayou frontage of three *arpents* and a depth of forty *arpents,* measuring 176 by 2,340 meters (576 by 7,680 feet) and stretching from the bayou across the levee and into the back swamp. The depth, or length, of each tract corresponded to the ordinance of 1770 by Governor Alejandro O'Reilly, which specified a usual depth for agricultural grants of forty *arpents.* For reasons unknown, however, the width of the grants did not correspond to the 6–8 *arpents* of stream frontage specified in that same ordinance.

Moreover, failure to survey the grants upon initial settlement resulted in such variation in size and conflict over property lines that in 1790 the Isleño community petitioned Governor Esteban Rodríguez Miró, Gálvez's successor, for a survey. The royal surveyor of Louisiana—born Charles Laveau Trudeau but then known as Carlos Trudeau—surveyed at least some of the tracts in 1792 and for each drafted a map that records the lengths and azimuths of the property lines, features such as vegetation and hydrology, and the names of the owner and immediate neighbors. Only fifteen such maps survive in public archives, however, and the General Land Office (GLO) township survey of the early nineteenth century therefore provides the most accurate map of the external boundary of the strip of grants. The property lines internal to that block of Isleño grants would have changed over time through divisions into narrower long lots due to inheritances as well as through mergers into wider long lots due to purchases. The GLO survey nonetheless precisely locates the external boundary of a sizable Hispanic community in the immediate environs of colonial New Orleans.[5]

In the eighteenth century, most of the non-Isleño Hispanics lived in the French Quarter, which at the time comprised the entire city of New Orleans. A 1791 census enumerated 4,816 inhabitants: 2,065 whites, 1,889 enslaved blacks and mulattos, and 862 free people of color. The majority of the whites were of French origin but with substantial Germanic and Hispanic minorities. The Hispanics included the governor, many of the other public officials, the troops, and urban Isleños, possibly "as many as four hundred." The last wills and testaments of some of those Hispanics reveal how they married into and integrated with the majority-French community. As the colonial period drew to a close in the opening years of the nineteenth century and the Spanish authorities and troops withdrew, the Hispanic community established in the city during the last half of the eighteenth century dissipated amid the influx of other groups.[6]

Isleños in the Nineteenth Century

The GLO, founded in 1812, surveyed the descendant boundaries of the original Isleño land grants as part of the process of vetting claims to private land after the Louisiana Purchase of 1803. The federal government considered all of the newly obtained territory to be public land except for those tracts individuals had acquired through grants from the antecedent French or Spanish colonial governments or through purchase from native peoples. The Isleños and others entered claims for their land grants, and the GLO collected copies of grants and associated land surveys, interviewed the surveyors, and deposed witnesses in order to determine the validity of the original acquisitions and their subsequent subdivision and conveyance through sale, inheritance, exchange, or donation. Upon completion of an investigation in a given district, the GLO made recommendations to Congress regarding each claimant's case. Once Congress had confirmed the recommended claims through legislation and the president had signed the act, the GLO surveyed each tract on the ground, placed monuments such as corner posts, and provided the owner with a patent, or deed. Ultimately, as the claim process concluded in a given township, a square measuring six miles on a side and oriented north-south, the GLO produced a connected plat map to demarcate and identify all private and public lands through a system of numbered sections. Within each township, the GLO first assigned sequential numbers to each patented private section and then divided the remaining, public lands into a grid of square sections, each one a mile square with an area of 259 hectares (640 acres). The pre-existing private lands thus became known as irregular sections, were not oriented to the cardinal directions, and where they impinged on the cardinally oriented grid of square sections created fractional sections of public land, each less than the normal 640 acres.[7]

In the case of the Isleños, President Andrew Jackson confirmed their land claims when he signed them into law in 1832. The claimants had initially registered their claims twenty years previously, and in 1812 the GLO submitted a report to Congress summarizing each case. In late 1831, Cave Johnson, a representative from Tennessee and the chairman of the House Committee on Private Land Claims during the Twenty-second Congress, proposed "A Bill for the Relief of the Inhabitants of Terre aux Boeufs." Together with an associated report, the proposed legislation listed the names of each claimant and the acreage involved. The bill passed the House of Representatives on March 28, 1832, and the Senate a few months later, on June 8. The final statute, signed into law by President Jackson on June 25, lists 95 sections, their widths in *arpents* and feet, and their owners. Jackson had some personal familiarity with those particular lands because less than two decades prior he had commanded the US troops that defeated the British at the Battle of New Orleans, which occurred in St. Bernard Parish on January 8, 1815.[8]

In the aftermath of the Louisiana Purchase, St. Bernard remained a rural parish with about eight hundred inhabitants producing sugar, indigo, and cotton for export as well as vegetables, fruit, poultry, eggs, pork, fish, and shellfish for the New Orleans market. Although people of varied origins had settled along Bayou Terre aux Boeufs, Hispanics remained the majority. The surnames of the land claimants provide an indication of that Hispanic dominance. Of the ninety-five sections confirmed as private property in 1832, one went to the Catholic Church. Fifty-five of the remainder, 59 percent, went to people with surnames that appear on the Isleño passenger lists of 1778–83. Nine went to people with other Spanish surnames, five of them to Manuel and Juan Solís. Another twenty-nine went to those with French surnames. And the last went to Augustin Reggio, the creole grandson of an Italian officer in the French military who had arrived in Louisiana in the 1750s.[9]

Even by midcentury, Isleño descendants remained a large proportion of the population of St Bernard Parish. The 1850 Federal Census was the first to attempt a complete enumeration of the free population, recording the name, age, birthplace, and occupation of every free member of every household as well as the numbers and ages of the enslaved population. The previous six decennial censuses, 1790–1840, had recorded only the names of the heads of households, anonymously enumerating other household members by age groups. Census 1850 counted a total population of 3,802 for St. Bernard Parish, including 1,406 whites, 73 free persons of color, and 2,323 enslaved residents. Of the whites, 553 had Hispanic surnames, comprising 37 percent of the free population. Of the Hispanic surnames, 411 appear on the Isleño passenger lists, 28 percent of the free population and 74 percent of the Hispanics. Seven people listed the Canary Islands as their birthplace, but only four were old enough to have been part of the voyages of 1778–83 and only two of them coincide with names on the passenger lists. While the other two might also have sailed on those voyages, their surnames must have changed through marriage to non-Isleños. Similarly, of the eight who listed Cuba as their birthplace, only one was old enough to have come with the Isleños who arrived in 1783 after a sojourn of four years on Cuba, namely Santiago Rodríguez; a young boy with that name does in fact appear on the passenger list of the frigate *Margarita*.[10]

A scattering of Isleño and other Hispanic names also occurred in the other three parishes in 1850 but many fewer in both absolute and relative terms than in St. Bernard Parish. With the Louisiana Purchase, the population of Orleans

Parish began to grow exponentially, and its Hispanic minority, including Isleños, became inconsequential in terms of size as well as political and cultural influence relative to the French, African, Saint-Domingue creole, Anglo, German, and Irish communities. The population of what at that time constituted the city proper more than doubled in the first decade, from around 8,000 in 1803 to 17,242 in 1810. By 1850, the 116,375 people who lived in New Orleans made it the fifth most populous city in the nation. Orleans Parish, which included the city, had a population of 119,460: 91,431 whites, 9,961 free blacks and mulattos, and 18,068 enslaved residents. Jefferson and Plaquemines parishes, more dominated by plantation agriculture, had much lower populations as well as much higher proportions of enslaved residents. Jefferson Parish had a population of 25,093, about 25 percent of it enslaved; and Plaquemines Parish had a population of 7,390, with 65 percent enslaved. The 1850 census lists only 1,171 inhabitants across the four parishes who claimed birth in Spain, less than 1 percent of the total population of 155,745: 68 in St. Bernard Parish, 18 in Plaquemines, 1,022 in Orleans, and 63 in Jefferson. Outside of St. Bernard Parish, only four were old enough to have arrived by 1783, with the Isleños, and only three of them had surnames that appear on the Isleño passenger lists, a Pérez and a Sánchez in Jefferson Parish and a Hernández in Orleans Parish. That urban Isleño population represented those who upon arrival had elected to stay in the city rather than settle in its environs, those who had abandoned rural settlements like Barataria, and their descendants.[11]

In the aftermath of the occupation of St. Bernard Parish by Union troops during the Civil War, Isleños participated in the establishment of settlements beyond the cores of the First and Second Settlements. Some moved to the banks of the Mississippi River in neighboring Plaquemines Parish, including the parents of Leander H. Perez, a controversial Isleño politician of the twentieth century. Others moved to West Bank Jefferson Parish, such as the family of Luis H. Marrero, another notable Isleño politician. Mainly, however, Isleños established new villages at Delacroix, Shell Beach, and Yscloskey in the coastal marshes that rim the eastern margin of St. Bernard Parish. Those who sold their farms in the First and Second Settlements to trap muskrat and fish along the isolated coast sometimes referred to themselves as the true Isleños and applied the term "Torneros" to those who remained behind and became more integrated into the broader New Orleans community. That appellation refers to the English Turn, the dramatic meander bend of the Mississippi River adjacent to the most urbanized portion of the parish. Except among the plantations along the broad levee of the Mississippi River directly downstream from Orleans Parish, then, Isleños dominated St. Bernard Parish through the nineteenth century but became virtually imperceptible in the other three parishes.[12]

New Orleans became a major immigrant reception port of the nineteenth century, second only to New York City, and some of those who disembarked were, of course, Spaniards. Passenger lists for ships arriving in New Orleans record that about eight thousand people with Hispanic surnames, many from Spain, disembarked between 1820 and 1865. Most, however, were in transit for other destinations, either upcountry within the United States or to ports in Latin America and the Caribbean. Comparison of those passenger lists with city directories for 1842, 1851, and 1861 reveals that only 7–15 percent of the eight thousand stayed in New Orleans, the uncertainty being related to common or otherwise ambiguous surnames. The analysis of the 1850 census also demonstrates how few Spaniards settled in New Orleans during the early nineteenth century, the 1,171 residents of the four parishes who claimed birth in Spain comprising less than 1 percent of the total population. They also made up less than 1 percent of the populations of Orleans, Jefferson, and Plaquemines parishes. Even in St. Bernard Parish, which seems to have disproportionately attracted Spanish immigrants because of the Isleño community, the sixty-four Spanish-born, non-Isleño residents amounted to only 1.7 percent of the total population.[13]

The 1850 census also lists 1,330 people who claimed birth in Latin America or the Caribbean as resident across the four parishes: 22 in St. Bernard, 11 in Plaquemines, 48 in Jefferson, and 1,249 in Orleans Parish. With the origins of the term "Latin America" and the idea of a pan–Latin American identity emerging in the mid-nineteenth century, those residents could be considered incipient Latinos as well as Hispanics. Their low proportion in the population and distribution across the four parishes echoes that of the Spanish-born population. More than half of them generically list the West Indies as their birthplace, their surnames suggesting that many came from the French and English as well as the Spanish Caribbean. Cubans and Mexicans made up the only identifiable, relatively large groups. The Cubans numbered 289: 250 in Orleans, 23 in Jefferson, and 8 each in Plaquemines and St. Bernard parishes. The 241 Mexicans numbered slightly fewer but with a similar distribution across the parishes: 219 in Orleans, 13 in Jefferson, 9 in St. Bernard, and none in Plaquemines.

Only in St. Bernard Parish, then, did non-Isleño Hispanics and Latinos make up anything approaching a noticeable proportion of the population. Those born in Spain, Latin America, and the Caribbean comprised slightly more than 2 percent of the total population in 1850. The majority of them claimed birth in Spain, but the group also included eight Cubans and nine Mexicans. Besides those who claimed foreign birth, another 52 parish residents had been born in Louisiana but bore Hispanic surnames not on the Isleño passenger lists. The 1832 confirmation of land claims illustrates how the non-Isleño Hispanics and Latinos of the parish, whether foreign born or not, tended to be tightly integrated into the majority Isleño community. Of the nine sections of land that went to people with Hispanic surnames that do not appear on the Isleño passenger lists, five went to Manuel and Juan Solís. They were the grandsons of Manuel Solís, who in 1771 had come to Louisiana from Cuba with his family, just as the Spaniards were establishing effective control under Governor Luis de Unzaga y Amezaga, Gálvez's immediate predecessor. Their father, Joseph Solís, had been born in Cuba and arrived in Louisiana while a teenager, married an Isleña named Antonia Pérez, established a sugar plantation along Bayou Terre aux Boeufs, and by the 1790s had become one of the most notable molasses and tafia rum producers of Louisiana. While neither Manuel nor Juan appears in the 1850 census for St. Bernard Parish, seven others with the Solís surname do occur, ages four to fifty-five.[14]

Isleños in the Twentieth Century

As the population of St. Bernard Parish grew over the twentieth century, Isleños became a smaller proportion of the total, although still a significant minority and even the majority in rural areas and some villages. People of other origins, principally Irish and Italian, moved into the parish along the Mississippi River. They settled in towns such as Arabi and Chalmette that were becoming industrialized suburbs of New Orleans, built on land formerly occupied by sugar plantations. Much of that development hinged on building levees, shipping channels, and oil and gas exploration canals that disrupted the patterns of water flow, salinity, and sedimentation on which the rural livelihoods of St. Bernard Parish had long depended. Agriculture, fishing, shrimping, oystering, hunting, and trapping all declined at the same time that vulnerability to catastrophic floods increased. Before Katrina, the most notorious were the

1927 Flood and Hurricane Betsy. The 1927 intentional dynamiting of the Mississippi levee at Caernarvon, near Poydras, flooded much of St. Bernard Parish in order to spare New Orleans from inundation by unusually high river levels. In 1965, Hurricane Betsy again inundated most of the parish. The storm surges that funneled up the Mississippi River Gulf Outlet ship canal (MR-GO, also known as Mister Go) and the Intracoastal Waterway (ICWW) during Katrina have become even more infamous than the 1927 Flood or Betsy, flooding nearly the entire parish.[15]

The number of surnames from the Isleño passenger lists that appear in censuses has become a more and more meaningless guide to the size of the Isleño community with each decade since the initial settlement of the eighteenth century. Isleños and other Hispanics increasingly dropped the diacritics from their names, although not the ñ in Isleño, so that Solís, Núñez, Pérez, and González became Solis, Nunez, Perez, and Gonzalez. Others adopted French versions of their surnames, changing Caballero into Chevalier, Dominguez into Domingue, and Rodríguez into Rodrigue. Distinctively Isleño surnames such as Nunez and Perez nonetheless remained common in southwestern Louisiana through the twentieth century, especially in St. Bernard Parish. Review of telephone directories and the decennial censuses through 1930, the most recent year for which the schedules that identify individuals are available, demonstrates that concentration of Isleño surnames. Yet intermarriage with non-Isleños over more than two centuries has introduced many other surnames into the community at the same time that successive generations have established themselves among neighboring communities and no longer necessarily self-identify as Isleños.[16]

Isleños nonetheless continued to form an identifiable community rooted in St. Bernard Parish through the twentieth century. In 1983, one of their leaders estimated that some ten thousand Isleño descendants lived in the parish and that about five hundred of them spoke Spanish. Moreover, despite the increasingly non-Hispanic population of the parish and devastating floods, the Isleño community has managed to maintain its local political power, Spanish dialect, folklore, and place names. In the 1970s, a period of cultural revival and community pride began, marked by the establishment of the Los Isleños Heritage and Cultural Society in 1976. Tensions that in some ways reflected the old Isleño-Tornero distinction eventually led to a split in that social organization and the formation, in 1996, of the Canary Islands Descendants Association. Through such organizations, the community established the Isleños Heritage and Multi-Cultural Park, a museum, the annual Los Isleños Fiesta, and a role in the parish's annual Irish-Italian-Isleño Parade.[17]

Census 1990 and Census 2000 provided direct estimates of how many residents of New Orleans, whether living in St. Bernard Parish or any of the other three parishes, self-identified as Isleños. While Census 1970 first included a question on Hispanic and Latino origins on the long form, only in 1990 was a write-in box added that allowed residents to self-identify as being of Spanish origin (table 1).[18] As detailed in the Introduction, although both the short and long forms contained the write-in box for Census 1990, the Census Bureau coded only the sample responses and therefore could not provide estimates for spatial units smaller than parishes. Nonetheless, as shown in figure 6, Census 1990 reveals that an estimated 8,283 residents of New Orleans considered themselves to be of Spanish origin. Starting with Census 2000, the write-in box responses

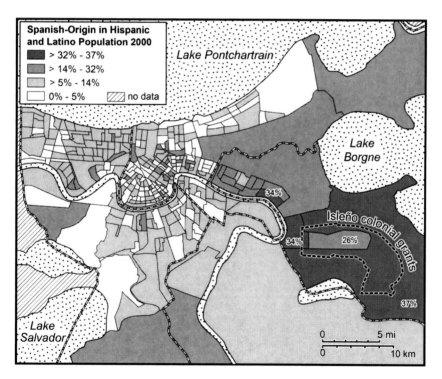

FIG. 9. The Spanish-origin population of New Orleans as a proportion of the total Hispanic and Latino population of each census tract in 2000, with percentages indicated for selected tracts.

TABLE 1. Hispanic and Latino population and Spanish-origin population for selected places, Censuses 1990, 2000, and 2010

CENSUS 1990

Places	Hispanic & Latino (number)	Hispanic & Latino (percent)	Spanish origin (number)	Spanish origin (percent)
United States	22,354,059	9.0	1,057,352	4.7
Louisiana	93,044	2.2	19,313	20.8
St. Bernard Parish	4,183	6.3	2,284	54.6
Plaquemines Parish	590	2.3	250	42.4
Orleans Parish	17,238	3.5	2,106	12.2
Jefferson Parish	26,611	5.9	3,643	13.7
New Orleans	48,622	4.7	8,283	17.0
New Mexico	579,224	38.2	159,644	27.6
Santa Fe County	48,939	49.5	23,229	47.5
Taos County	15,008	64.9	6,316	42.1

CENSUS 2000

Places	Hispanic & Latino (number)	Hispanic & Latino (percent)	Spanish origin (number)	Spanish origin (percent)
United States	35,305,818	12.5	861,911	2.4
Louisiana	107,738	2.4	8,179	7.6
St. Bernard	3,425	5.1	794	23.2
Plaquemines	433	1.6	37	8.6
Orleans	14,826	3.1	1,046	7.1
Jefferson	32,418	7.1	2,178	6.7
New Orleans	51,102	4.9	4,055	7.9
New Mexico	765,386	42.0	94,473	12.3
Santa Fe County	63,405	49.0	11,067	17.5
Taos County	17,370	57.9	3,640	21.0

CENSUS 2010

Places	Hispanic & Latino (number)	Hispanic & Latino (percent)	Spanish origin (number)	Spanish origin (percent)
United States	50,477,594	16.3	1,125,756	2.2
Louisiana	192,560	4.2	10,584	5.4
St. Bernard Parish	3,309	9.2	631	19.0
Plaquemines Parish	1,067	4.6	77	7.2

Places	Hispanic & Latino (number)	Hispanic & Latino (percent)	Spanish origin (number)	Spanish origin (percent)
Orleans Parish	18,051	5.2	904	5.0
Jefferson Parish	53,702	12.4	1,849	3.4
New Orleans	76,129	9.1	3,461	4.6
New Mexico	953,403	46.3	132,567	13.9
Santa Fe County	73,015	50.6	16,090	22.0
Taos County	18,381	55.8	4,782	26.0

from the short form were coded, allowing direct enumeration and mapping at the level of census tracts (fig. 9).[19] Census 2000 enumerated about half as many residents of New Orleans who self-identified with Spanish origin, but the drop to 4,055 from 8,283 a decade before likely relates to differences in data collection rather than a real decline. Not only are the estimates based on sampling in 1990 less accurate than those based on enumeration in 2000, but Census 1990 provided examples of how to fill in the write-in box while Census 2000 did not, resulting in a national inflation of the "Unspecified" category that reversed with restoration of the examples, including "Spaniard," in Census 2010.[20]

Whether Census 1990 and Census 2000 provide accurate estimates of the number of people who self-identified as being of Spanish origin in any particular parish, the relative proportions are revealing. In Census 2000, for example, St. Bernard Parish had a total population of 67,229, some 7 percent of the total population of the four-parish area. It had 3,425 Hispanics and Latinos, 5.1 percent of the parish's total population and 6.7 percent of the 51,102 Hispanics and Latinos across the four parishes. Nearly a quarter of those 3,425 identified their origins as Spanish, Spanish-American, or Spaniard—although within those categories the Census Bureau did not report more specific responses such as Canary Islander, Catalonian, or Andalusian.

Two characteristics of those who self-identified as having Spanish origins suggests they were descendants of and identified with the Isleños and associated Hispanics who settled in New Orleans during, mainly, the eighteenth century. First, much lower proportions of Hispanics and Latinos in the other three parishes identified with Spanish origins: on Census 2000, 6.7 percent in Jefferson Parish, 7.1 percent in Orleans Parish, and 8.6 percent in Plaquemines

Parish. The census tracts in which those who identified themselves as being of Spanish origin made up at least a third of the total Hispanic and Latino population concentrate in St. Bernard Parish, the core of the Isleño community in the eighteenth through nineteenth centuries. Even more significantly, those tracts cluster around the Isleños' colonial land grants along Bayou Terre aux Boeufs.

Second, only other places in the United States associated with Hispanic settlement during the colonial period display similarly high percentages of residents claiming Spanish origins. For the United States as a whole, only 2.4 percent of all the 35.3 million Hispanics and Latinos in 2000 claimed Spanish origins. In contrast, the descendants of the Hispanics who settled the northern frontier of the colony of New Spain beginning in the sixteenth century and now call themselves Hispanos also tend to claim Spanish origins during recent censuses. In 2000, 12.3 percent of the Hispanics and Latinos of New Mexico claimed Spanish origins: among them, 17.5 percent of those in Santa Fe County and 21 percent of those in Taos County, two centers of colonial Hispanic settlement about one hundred kilometers (sixty miles) apart. Those percentages are comparable to the 23 percent identifying with Spanish origins in St. Bernard Parish and an order of magnitude higher than for the United States as a whole, for the state of Louisiana, and for the other three parishes of New Orleans. The Hispanos of New Mexico and the Isleños of Louisiana both comprise communities of Hispanics who settled those places in colonial times, have since become minorities, but retain an identity linked to their Spanish origins. Other such groups include the Tejanos of Texas and the Californianos of California. While the estimates of Census 1990 are not strictly comparable to those of Census 2000, they also display similar patterns of relative proportions at the national, state, and county and parish levels.[21]

Isleños in the Twenty-First Century

Katrina devastated St. Bernard Parish and therefore the core of the Isleño community. While large areas of Orleans and Plaquemines parishes also flooded, only St. Bernard Parish experienced near-total inundation, as illustrated in figure 1. Jefferson Parish went from 448,578 to 411,305 inhabitants, an 8.3 percent loss; Plaquemines Parish from 28,282 to 20,164, a decline of 29 percent; Orleans Parish from 437,186 to 158,353, dramatically losing nearly 64 percent of its population; and St. Bernard Parish from 64,576 to 3,361, a staggering loss of nearly 95 percent. Across the four parishes, Katrina flooded 45 percent of census tracts and 44 percent of the 2000 population of 1,034,126 but only 26 percent of the 51,102 Hispanics and Latinos. However, Katrina flooded all but two of the census tracts of St. Bernard Parish, 90 percent of its total population of 67,229, and 93 percent of its Hispanic and Latino population of 3,425. Meanwhile, in the other three parishes, only 43 percent of census tracts flooded, impacting 41 percent of the total population of 966,897 and 22 percent of the Hispanic and Latino population of 47,677. Moreover, across all four parishes, 37 percent of the 1,493 Hispanics and Latinos who claimed Spanish origins in Census 2000 suffered devastating flooding, 49 percent of them in St. Bernard Parish.[22]

By Census 2010, the population of New Orleans had rebounded to nearly 81 percent of its population in 2000, in part due to the efforts of many Isleños of St. Bernard Parish (fig. 10).[23] Jefferson Parish had recovered to 95 percent of

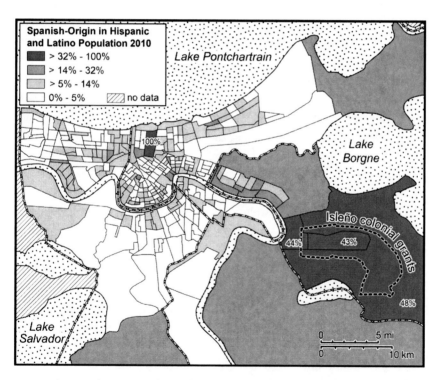

FIG. 10. The Spanish-origin population of New Orleans as a proportion of the total Hispanic and Latino population of each census tract in 2010, with percentages indicated for selected tracts.

its 2000 population; Plaquemines to 86.1 percent; Orleans to 70.9 percent; and St. Bernard to 53.4 percent.

In part the lag in repopulation of St. Bernard relates to destruction of much of the housing stock and in part to a long history of racial discrimination by the parish government that kept blacks out before Katrina and, to some extent, afterward. Leander Perez, who wielded power in St. Bernard and Plaquemines parishes from the 1920s through his death in 1969, was one of the main architects of Louisiana's Jim Crow laws and so vehemently opposed federal desegregation efforts that Governor Earl Long had to remind him that "the feds have got the atom bomb."[24] As a consequence, in Census 2000 the parish was only 8 percent black in contrast to Orleans Parish at 67 percent and Jefferson and Plaquemines at 23 percent each. After Katrina, some blacks from the neighborhoods of Orleans Parish devastated by flooding, such as the Lower Ninth Ward, which borders St. Bernard, tried to move to the three suburban parishes. The St. Bernard Parish Council opposed their efforts by enacting an ordinance to prohibit landlords from renting to anyone other than direct relatives as well as another to stop construction of multifamily housing units, both subsequently ruled violations of federal antisegregation laws. By Census 2010, then, Orleans Parish had become 33 percent white and 60 percent black while St. Bernard had become 74 percent white and 18 percent black. Jefferson Parish had also become somewhat less segregated, at 63 percent white and 26 percent black; while Plaquemines remained much unchanged at 71 percent white and 20 percent black.[25]

At the same time, the number of people identifying with Spanish origins in St. Bernard Parish had declined from 794 in 2000 to 631 in 2010, which equates to a little more than 23 percent of the Hispanic and Latino population in 2000 and 19 percent in 2010. That absolute and relative decline occurred even though Census 2010 restored the examples to the write-in box and, nationally, the number of residents of Spanish origin rebounded. Even so, while the number of Isleños, and their proportion of all Hispanic and Latino residents, in the parish declined, their dominance in the three census tracts that overlap the Isleños' colonial land grants increased, from 26–37 percent in 2000 to 43–48 percent in 2010. While some Isleño descendants did not return to post-Katrina New Orleans, the ones who did have worked hard to reconstruct their homes, workplaces, and communities. Despite additional challenges, like the Deepwater Horizon oil spill of 2010, they have continued the Los Isleños Heritage and Cultural Society, rebuilding its museum and reviving the annual Los Isleños Fiesta.[26]

THE ISLEÑO COMMUNITY PROVED relatively more vulnerable to the devastation of Katrina than Latino communities because of a residential geography focused in St. Bernard Parish. In contrast, the different timing and character of the process through which Cubans settled in New Orleans resulted in a distinct residential geography concentrated on the opposite side of the city. Although the Cuban community, like that of the Isleños, has its origins in colonial times, the principal influx of Cubans took place in the twentieth century and involved neocolonial processes. The resulting focus of the Cuban community in Jefferson Parish spared it from the same prolonged inundation suffered by the Isleños. Indirect impacts associated with an influx of reconstruction workers nonetheless did affect the Cuban community.

2. CUBANS

The effect which a change in the political condition of Cuba and her relations to the United States would have upon the great staple of Louisiana
[sugar] cannot be submitted to the same severe calculation.

—John S. Thrasher, "Cuban Annexation," 1854

But not only that: with the embargo still in effect as of this writing, the
more than forty years of communications blackout between New Orleans and Havana has clouded our memory of how important that link
was, from Spanish colonial times through the 1950s.

—Ned Sublette, The World That Made New Orleans, *2008*

THE NETWORKS THAT BROUGHT Cubans to New Orleans differ in history and
geography from those that brought the Isleños and therefore resulted in a distinct residential geography and different types of impacts on the other side of
the city. The earliest such networks date to French rule during the eighteenth
century, when Louisianians circumvented mercantilist prohibitions on trade
with ports in Spanish colonies. That contraband trade grew into a much larger
flow of products, people, and ideas when Louisiana also became a Spanish colony and a province in the Capitanía General de Cuba, of which Havana served
as the capital. As a US city in the nineteenth century, New Orleans became the
major port of the Gulf Coast and the North American gateway to northern Latin
America and the Caribbean. While those eighteenth- and nineteenth-century
networks established the nucleus of a Cuban community in New Orleans, the
Spanish-American War of 1898 (known in Cuba as the Cuban War of Independence) began a new, neocolonial phase of the relationship between Havana and
the Crescent City. After midcentury, however, that relationship increasingly

declined as Houston surpassed New Orleans in population and became the dominant metropolis of the Gulf Coast and as the United States implemented a trade embargo in the aftermath of the Cuban Revolution. Even so, while Miami became the principal community of Cuban expatriates in the States, some did settle in New Orleans. Those Cubans, settling in the city since the mid-twentieth century, have greatly expanded and altered the small Cuban community established during colonial times.[1]

Cubans in the Eighteenth and Nineteenth Centuries

Despite prohibitions on commerce with Spanish colonies, the French traded with the ports of New Spain, Florida, Hispaniola, Puerto Rico, and Cuba during the early eighteenth century. That contraband trade proved so essential to the establishment of New Orleans and profitable to its residents that the official records probably obfuscate the nationality of many vessels entering the Mississippi River. Even so, those records do indicate that between 1735 and 1763 at least 40 percent of all vessels calling at New Orleans had a Spanish port as their origin, destination, or both.[2]

While that early commerce between the French and the Spaniards might have resulted in some flow of people from Cuba to New Orleans, the number increased dramatically soon after Louisiana became a province in the Capitanía General de Cuba. The first Spanish governor, Antonio de Ulloa, arrived in 1766 with fewer than a hundred troops. The popular revolt of 1768 that ousted him prompted a much larger influx of soldiers from Cuba, however. The second governor, Alejandro O'Reilly, sailed from Havana in 1769 at the head of a fleet that transported about 2,600 troops to New Orleans. They doubled the city's population.[3]

That political and demographic transformation had various consequences that increased the flow of people, materials, and ideas between New Orleans and Havana. In 1787, for example, the Catholic Church created the Diocese of San Cristobal de la Habana, which included Louisiana along with Cuba and Florida. Only in 1793 did the mainland become a distinct diocese. The Spaniards also legalized trade between New Orleans and Havana, albeit with restrictions that favored Cuban tobacco producers and others. By 1802, therefore, as the United States was about to acquire the Louisiana Territory, 40 percent of all the non-US vessels that entered New Orleans originated in Spanish colonies, nearly three-quarters of them in Havana and other Cuban ports. As a consequence of that political, commercial, and cultural relationship, the town council and other residents of New Orleans increasingly looked to Havana for ideas to develop the colony. For example, the streetlight system of Havana provided the inspiration and model for that of New Orleans near the end of the period of Spanish rule.[4]

Consequently, people of Cuban birth made up a significant proportion of the Hispanics of New Orleans in the early nineteenth century. In St. Bernard Parish they constituted a minority of Hispanics that, as detailed in the previous chapter, integrated thoroughly into the majority Isleño community. The ancestors of some, like the Solís family, had been born on Cuba and come to New Orleans near the beginning of Spanish rule in Louisiana. Others were the children of Isleños, born on Cuba during their sojourn of four years on the island during the Revolutionary War. Others had arrived after the Isleño settlement, part of the flow of people between Cuba and Louisiana established during the eighteenth century. Manuel Pérez, for example, claimed on Census 1850 that he had been born on Cuba in 1795, and therefore he could have arrived before the Louisiana Purchase. Given the surname and the significant role that Isleños played in the settlement of Cuba as well as Louisiana, his ancestors may also have originated on the Canary Islands. Census 1850 records three others of Cuban birth in St. Bernard Parish who, like Pérez, were old enough to have arrived before the Louisiana Purchase. Yet others were born in St. Bernard Parish into the Isleño community but with one or more parents or grandparents of Cuban birth, like the seven residents of 1850 with the surname Solís, ages four to fifty-five. The 1850 Census also records twenty-four others of Cuban birth scattered throughout the city and old enough to have arrived before the Louisiana Purchase: twenty-two lived in Orleans Parish and one each in Jefferson and Plaquemines parishes.[5]

The transfer of Louisiana to the United States in 1803 only increased trade with Cuba and the influx of immigrants from that island. During the first decade, more than nine thousand refugees from the Haitian Revolution arrived via Cuba to nearly double the population of New Orleans. The revolt against slavery and French rule in the colony of Saint-Domingue lasted from 1791 until 1804, and refugees initially fled across the narrow channel that separates the islands of Hispaniola and Cuba. When Napoleon Bonaparte occupied Spain in 1808 and initiated the Peninsular War, however, the Spaniards expelled all

French citizens from Cuba. The exiles from Saint-Domingue thus fled once again, many to the United States. French privateers, including Pierre and Jean Lafitte, transported thousands of them to New Orleans. They included whites as well as mulattos and blacks, both free and enslaved, who brought ideas, skills, and capital that consolidated the dominance of the city's Francophone community. The enslaved refugees alone, allowed to enter the United States by virtue of a waiver of the 1807 federal Act Prohibiting Importation of Slaves, numbered more than three thousand. Most had been born on Saint-Domingue, but others had been born during the period of exile on Cuba.[6]

After the end of the Napoleonic Wars in the second decade of the nineteenth century, and especially after the War of 1812, trade through the port of New Orleans grew exponentially, much of it with Spain and its colonies. The immigrants from Saint-Domingue might have augmented the city's Francophone community, but during their years on Cuba they had become involved in the commercial networks of the Spanish Caribbean and northern Latin America. By 1816, ships flying the Spanish flag accounted for 78 percent of all the foreign vessels that entered New Orleans. As the city's Hispanic population grew along with increasing integration into those Latin American networks, so did its Spanish-language press, beginning with the newspaper *El Misisipi* in 1808.[7]

One of the most profound results of the Haitian Revolution, however, involved the conversion of both New Orleans and Cuba into major sugar exporters, catalyzing a new type of relationship focused on that commodity. The revolt in the archetypal sugar colony of Saint-Domingue so reduced the sugar supply and inflated its price that by 1810 Cuban planters had doubled their production relative to the 1780s. To provide the labor for the plantations, Cuban slave imports increased to about 656,000 between 1811 and 1867, compared to some 122,500 in the preceding three centuries. The illegality of the trade after 1820 precludes precise estimates, but the flow of slaves into Cuba during the nineteenth century alone represents about a third of the total for all of the Spanish Americas over the fifteenth through nineteenth centuries and some 6 percent of the entire Atlantic slave trade, estimated to involve more than 10 million Africans. By 1867, Cuban slave imports had ended but the island's enslaved inhabitants numbered more than 370,000, some 40 percent of them working on sugar plantations and directly producing 41 percent of the world's cane sugar. The expansion of sugar plantations deforested Cuba to such an extent that sawmills in the cypress swamps around New Orleans became a major supplier of lumber, posts, shingles, and sugar boxes for Havana merchants. On the return voyage to Louisiana, Cuban coffee filled the holds of the vessels that sailed between New Orleans and Havana.[8]

Louisiana experienced a concurrent boom in sugar production, which turned New Orleans and Havana merchants into competing producers of that commodity in addition to tobacco but at the same time stimulated many types of interactions. The Cuban-born Joseph Solís numbered among the few sugar producers in Louisiana in the early 1790s, using the crop from his plantation along Bayou Terre aux Boeufs to produce molasses and low quality, tafia rum. Only in 1794, however, did another New Orleans planter, Etienne De Boré, hire two Cuban sugar masters to help him become the first producer of granulated sugar in Louisiana. The Haitian Revolution so reduced supply of that commodity that prices rose high enough to motivate other Louisianians to follow his example, hire Cuban experts, intensify production, increase quality, and line the levees of the lower Mississippi River with sugar plantations. In part the planters of New Orleans sought models among the planters of Havana because of the existing networks that had connected those two places for, by then, several generations. And in part their motivation derived from the similar climates and commercial networks of Louisiana and Cuba. The plantations up- and downriver from New Orleans therefore adopted Cuban technologies such as ox-driven sugar mills rather than the wind- and watermills prevalent in the French Caribbean.[9]

Over the first half of the nineteenth century the relationship between Louisiana and Cuba intensified to the degree that filibusters operating out of New Orleans attempted to annex the island to the United States. As one independent republic after another emerged in Latin America, US support for a Cuban revolt grew under the rubrics of the Monroe Doctrine and Manifest Destiny. Spanish acknowledgment of the independence of the new republics of Latin America in 1836 only served to focus US attention on ending Spain's control of its last remaining American colonies, Cuba and Puerto Rico. Such political sentiments combined with commercial interests to impose punitive tariffs on the Cuban sugar and tobacco trades. A populist annexation movement followed, exemplified in John S. Thrasher's 1854 letter in the *New Orleans Picayune,* reprinted in the *New York Times,* that urged southern planters to finance mercenaries to undertake private military expeditions and overthrow Spanish rule in Cuba. In New Orleans, filibuster regiments paraded down St. Charles Avenue waving Cuban flags to the tune of *Yankee Doodle* and vandalized the Spanish consulate. Narciso López, an expatriate Cuban, became the most famous of the filibuster leaders. He led two invasions of Cuba from New Orleans: the first, in 1850, resulted in retreat; and the second, in 1851, ended with his capture and execution. Other filibuster expeditions to Cuba, such as the one led by Francisco Estrampes y Gómez in 1854, met the same end before the Civil War overtook all attempts to annex Cuba.[10]

By then New Orleans had become one of the two principal Cuban communities in the United States. The 1850 Census recorded 1,056 US residents who claimed Cuban birth. Nearly a third of them lived in Louisiana, mainly in New Orleans. Orleans Parish had 250 Cuban-born residents; Jefferson Parish had 23, and Plaquemines and St. Bernard parishes had eight each. Only a small proportion had been born before 1803 and therefore could have arrived before the Louisiana Purchase. The vast majority had arrived afterward, during the intensification of interactions between New Orleans and Havana related to their concurrent booms in sugar production. The only other US place that rivaled the New Orleans Cuban community in size in 1850 was New York City, with 211 residents of Cuban birth.

The relationship that developed between New Orleans and Havana over the first half of the nineteenth century also catalyzed musical innovations that became an essential characteristic of the Crescent City's sense of place, its *genius loci*. The role of the pianist Louis Moreau Gottschalk illustrates the process. Born in New Orleans in 1829, Gottschalk traveled regularly to Cuba and innovated with Afro-Cuban rhythms in such midcentury songs as "Creole Eyes," entitled "Ojos Criollos" in Spanish and "Danse Cubaine" in French. The musical styles that dominated later in the century incorporated Gottschalk's syncopated two-handed piano riffs, from minstrel show tunes, ragtime, and cakewalks in New Orleans to *habanera, rumba,* and *son clave* in Havana. The same styles persist in the second-line parades still common in New Orleans and the *congas* of Cuba.[11]

The Civil War interrupted the connection between the two ports, but during Reconstruction and its aftermath New Orleans merchants and others not only renewed the relationship but vastly expanded their networks throughout Latin America and the Caribbean. By then, independent republics rather than Spanish colonies dominated Central and South America, facilitating trade, investment, immigration, and political alliances and interventions. New technologies such as steamships and submarine telegraph cables further increased the flows of products, people, and ideas between New Orleans and ports such as Havana. By 1884, as host to the World's Industrial and Cotton Centennial Exposition, the city's business community could brand New Orleans as the "Gateway to the Americas."[12]

Cuba and Puerto Rico remained notable exceptions among the newly independent republics, the last remaining Spanish colonies in the Americas and the focus of a recalibrated Monroe Doctrine. Using the sinking of the battleship USS *Maine* in Havana's harbor on February 15, 1898, as justification, the United States intervened in the insurrection that José Martí had begun three years earlier. New Orleans became one of the major troop assembly ports in the ensuing Spanish-American War. It ended Spanish colonialism in the Americas and ushered in a century of US neocolonialism in Latin America and the Caribbean. Troops from the United States, including the Second Louisiana Regiment, occupied Cuba until 1902. The conditions of withdrawal under the Platt Amendment included a permanent US military base at Guantánamo Bay as well as preferential terms of trade and investment.[13]

Cubans in the Twentieth Century

That new, neocolonial relationship between Cuba and the United States reversed the previous roles of Havana and New Orleans. Havana had dominated New Orleans during Spanish rule of Louisiana and into the nineteenth century, during the initial sugar boom. But thereafter, New Orleans increasingly dominated the relationship, a subjugation made exceedingly clear when the Second Louisiana Regiment marched into Havana in 1898 to raise the state's Pelican Flag alongside the Stars and Stripes.[14]

Louisiana, for example, took the lead in industrializing sugar production technology during the twentieth century. Louisiana State University's Audubon Sugar School, later the Audubon Sugar Institute, became an international leader in research and education. Cuban students came to LSU to study, and in 1907 the LSU Tigers football team went to Cuba to play la Universidad de Havana in the Bacardi Bowl on Christmas Day, winning 56 to 0. Tulane University followed two years later, playing on New Year's Day and losing 11 to 0. Julio Lobo became the most prominent Cuban involved in that academic relationship. The son of an affluent Cuban sugar planter, Lobo arrived in New

Orleans in 1915 to spend four years studying new techniques at the Audubon Sugar School, at that time located in the city's Audubon Park. After graduation he returned to Havana to work in his father's business, eventually becoming Cuba's wealthiest tycoon and self-styled "Sugar King." Not only LSU's Audubon Sugar Institute but the bilingual *Manual de la Industria Azucarera Cubana/The Cuba Sugar Manual,* published in New Orleans from 1927 through 1942, helped to consolidate the dominance of the Crescent City over Havana.[15]

By the late 1950s, the relationship between Cuba and Louisiana as well as other US ports had reached its zenith. In 1958, the value of US-Cuba trade amounted to 57 percent of Cuba's gross national product. A third of the exports that shipped out of New Orleans went to Cuba: 269,000 tons, half of it food products such as flour, grains, vegetables, and animal feed. In return, more tonnage imported through New Orleans came from Cuba than from any other country: 1.2 million tons, 80 percent of it unrefined sugar and another 19 percent molasses. Seven of the seventeen largest US sugar companies had refineries in and around New Orleans, and large proportions of their raw sugar came from the Cuban plantations of Lobos and other LSU alumni. Although US corporations profited greatly from Cuba's imports of food and exports of unrefined sugar, they also expanded their interests to other products, for example, a nickel mine on the island that shipped ore to a processing plant in Plaquemines Parish. During Prohibition in the 1920s, Cuban contraband alcohol also arrived via New Orleans, with Isleños such as Leander Perez becoming wealthy rum-runners and powerful in local politics.[16]

Despite the continuation of the long-standing relationship between New Orleans and Cuba, not many Cubans settled in the city during the first half of the twentieth century. In the immediate aftermath of the Spanish-American War, from 1899 through 1910, the United States admitted 9,555,698 immigrants— but only 44,211 from Cuba. Moreover, 29,332 of those Cubans listed Florida as their destination and 11,481 New York. Louisiana, destination for a mere 736, ranked a distant third among the states. Consequently, Census 1930 enumerated only 299 residents of Cuban birth in Orleans, Jefferson, St. Bernard, and Plaquemines parishes, only ten more than a century before, in 1850. Also similar to 1850, the Cuban community remained concentrated in Orleans Parish, home to 294 of those who claimed Cuban birth in 1930. Nationally, US residents of Cuban birth had increased from 1,056 to 19,992 between 1850 and 1930. But New Orleans had fallen from the principal Cuban community in the

United States, home to a third of all US residents born on Cuba, to a minor one over those eight decades. New York and Florida, particularly New York City and Tampa, had become the most populous Cuban communities in the United States, each with nearly a third of the Cuban-born population compared to the less than 2 percent living in New Orleans.[17]

The relationship between New Orleans and Cuba nonetheless continued to catalyze musical innovations as significant as those of the antebellum nineteenth century. New Orleans musicians, including Willie Cornish and John Baptiste Delisle, fought on Cuba during the Spanish-American War and brought back musical elements that helped transform ragtime into jazz during the early twentieth century. On returning home they played in the seminal Onward Brass Band and Buddy Bolden's Band. Others who played with the Onward Brass Band included Joe "King" Oliver, mentor to Louis Armstrong, and Manuel Perez, likely of Isleño descent. Some of those originators of jazz, most notably Ferdinand "Jelly Roll" Morton, explicitly credited the "Spanish tinge" as the essential "seasoning" of the new style. New Orleans rhythm and blues progenitors also incorporated Cuban elements, as in Professor Longhair's 1949 "Blues Rhumba" and Art Neville's 1954 "Mardi Gras Mambo."[18]

The Cuban Revolution largely ended that neocolonial relationship—although not right away. In the immediate aftermath of the overthrow of Fulgencio Batista's dictatorship in January of 1959, Louisianians worked to preserve the commercial relationship. The mayor of New Orleans, DeLesseps Story "Chep" Morrison, led a delegation of 152 representatives to Havana in May 1959. They staged a Mardi Gras parade complete with elaborate regalia, three floats from the Krewe of Rex, walking heads, tiny cars, and a city council member on horseback who portrayed Narciso López, the filibuster leader of a century before. The parade culminated with a presentation of the Cuban flag to Manuel Urrutia Lleó, the first president of the revolutionary government. Neither Urrutia nor the goodwill lasted, however. By the end of the year Fidel Castro had exiled Urrutia, and relations with the United States had deteriorated to the point that the Central Intelligence Agency began to plot a coup. New Orleans corporations, their Cuban sugar plantations expropriated by the revolutionary government, lobbied President Dwight D. Eisenhower to invade and restore their property. United Fruit even provided the use of its banana ports in Central America to support the attempted invasion of Cuba at the Bay of Pigs in 1961. Ultimately, the Missile Crisis and President John F. Kennedy's implementation of the trade embargo in 1962, known as El Bloqueo among Cubans, ended any hope that commerce between New Orleans and Cuba would be quickly restored.[19]

Counterintuitively, however, while the thriving commercial relationship between Cuba and New Orleans suddenly ended with the embargo, the flow of Cuban immigrants to the city actually increased. Thousands of Cubans fled their island home for the United States over the half century following the revolution. Many settled in Florida, especially Miami, including Lobo, by then the ex–Sugar King of Cuba. Others such as the deposed president, Urrutia, chose New York City. But still others came to New Orleans and vastly increased the size of its Cuban community.

Cuban exiles opposed to the revolutionary government began arriving in the United States in 1959. The initial exodus of 1959–62 numbered approximately 250,000, roughly the same number of Cuban immigrants as over the preceding nine decades. The next wave, another 300,000 or so, came during the period of the Freedom Flights, which lasted from 1965 through 1973. Most initially arrived in Florida; many stayed there, but the federal government and the Catholic Church helped some resettle in cities across the United States, including New Orleans.[20]

Interviews with Cubans who arrived in New Orleans during that initial period, from the revolution through the early 1970s, reveal a variety of reasons for settling in the Crescent City. Some cite the prevalence of Catholicism, others a climate more similar to Cuba than places like New York City and Chicago, employment opportunities, a general knowledge of the city because of its long-standing relationship with Cuba, or friends and family among the established, albeit small, pre-existing Cuban community.[21]

> I was fooled because I was told that the temperature was like in Havana. But snow fell when I arrived! In the seventh grade, in the textbook, I studied the Mississippi . . . and the city of New Orleans. That stuck in my head, and I said, I'd like to live there because it has something Spanish, because Spain founded the city, with the park and the city government building. Around that [Jackson Square and the Cabildo] lies the city. I would be in a completely Spanish environment. That's why I decided on New Orleans.[22]

And, once settled, they appreciated that the culture of New Orleans had much in common with that of Cuba: "People here work to live well, enjoy life, go to

Carnival. . . . In Miami, there are more Cubans, but the way of life in Miami is like New York. . . . The way of life in Louisiana is like Cuba."[23]

Census 1970, as graphed in figure 6, provided the first opportunity to estimate directly how many residents considered themselves to be of Cuban origin, whether by birth or ancestry, and thereby gauge the impact of the postrevolutionary exodus on the city. That year, 37,324 Hispanics and Latinos lived in the four parishes, about 3.7 percent of the total population of 1,007,449. Among them, the 5,209 who self-identified as being of Cuban origin made up 14 percent of the Hispanic and Latino population. The vast majority lived in Orleans and Jefferson parishes, with nearly three-quarters of them in Orleans and most of the remainder in Jefferson.

Census 1970 does not allow mapping residents of Cuban origin at the level of census tracts, but the map of the proportion of Hispanics and Latinos in the total population of each census tract for that year does reflect the neighborhoods in which interviews reveal that Cuban exiles established themselves during the 1960s: Gentilly, Mid-City, the Garden District, and Uptown (fig. 11).[24] The interviews reveal how, even though Catholic charities and municipal governments helped to establish Cubans in many parts of the city, a few notable concentrations emerged. The first home for many became the St. Thomas Housing Project, an immense, publicly funded apartment complex in the Lower Garden District dating to the 1930s and racially integrated in the 1960s, and the large Park Chester Apartment complex in Gentilly. A third concentration emerged in Mid-City, south of City Park. And those who worked or studied at Tulane University established a fourth concentration in Uptown. Some of the Cubans who concentrated in those neighborhoods opened stores, restaurants, bars, and other businesses to cater to the expatriates. A string of Cuban nightclubs along Magazine Street in the Garden District—El Latin American, El Loco, El Tranvia, Los Mayas, and the Guantanamo Room—attempted to recreate the boisterous nightlife of Havana for those first-generation exiles, places they fondly recalled in several interviews.[25]

Those Cubans also founded institutions to foster a sense of place and community. The Liceo Cubano José Martí and the Club Cubano de Profesionales celebrated Cuban culture through community gatherings, monthly dinners, and annual galas. The Comité Organizador del Festival Latinoamericano hosted a music festival to develop relationships with other communities in the city. To-

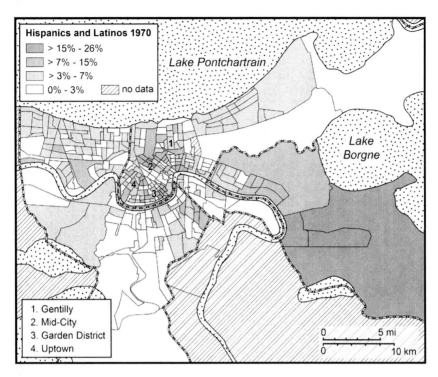

Lake Pontchartrain

Lake
Borgne

1. Gentilly
2. Mid-City
3. Garden District
4. Uptown

0   5 mi
0   10 km

FIG. 11. The Hispanic and Latino population of New Orleans as a proportion of the total population of each census tract in 1970.

gether those institutions provided mutual support and helped to define the identity of the expatriates as simultaneously Cuban and New Orleanian.

The distribution of Cubans, as well as of Hispanics and Latinos more generally, had begun to change significantly by Census 1980 (figs. 12 and 13). The overall Hispanic and Latino population had grown nearly 26 percent, to 46,875, while the Cuban community had grown by only less than 10 percent, to 5,704. At the same time, the proportion of Cubans living in Orleans Parish had fallen from nearly three quarters to a little under half, and the percentage living in Jefferson Parish had increased from just under a quarter to nearly half. Although the original Cuban concentrations in the Garden District, Gentilly, Mid-City, and Uptown remained apparent in 1980, new ones had appeared in the suburbs that began to emerge from the former wetlands of Jefferson Parish in the 1960s. Northern Jefferson Parish, North Kenner and Metairie, particularly north of

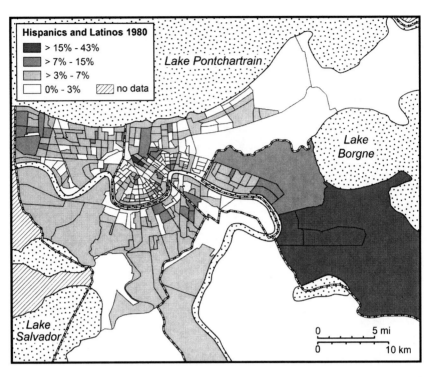

FIG. 12. The Hispanic and Latino population of New Orleans as a proportion of the total population of each census tract in 1980.

Interstate 10, attracted many Cubans. They also settled in Westbank Jefferson Parish, especially in the Terrytown neighborhood. As well, the new suburbs of New Orleans East attracted some Cubans.[26]

That change in the city's Cuban geography reflects both the general flight of the middle class, especially whites, from Orleans Parish to the new suburbs as well as the upward social mobility of many Cubans. Between Census 1970 and Census 2000, New Orleans became increasingly racially segregated at the parish level, with Orleans Parish dominated by blacks and the three surrounding parishes by whites. According to interviews, many who arrived during the initial exodus were middle-class doctors, architects, and so on but lacked the US credentials and proficiency in English to work in their professions. They therefore took blue-collar jobs while taking English courses and studying for professional licensing examinations. Once established, they left the St. Thomas

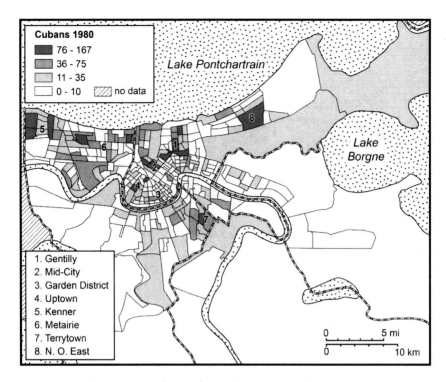

FIG. 13. The Cuban-origin population of New Orleans in 1980.

Housing Project, which over the 1980s became notorious for high levels of poverty and crime, and other parts of Orleans Parish for the suburbs.[27]

Businesses established near the original Cuban concentrations in Orleans Parish remained behind, no longer integral elements of Cuban neighborhoods but equally accessible from the suburbs of Jefferson Parish and New Orleans East. Liborio's Cuban Restaurant provides one example. It was originally established on Magazine Street in the Lower Garden District in 1969 as La Caridad Restaurant. The Liborio family later moved it down the street closer to the French Quarter and changed the name. La Tienda Música Latina, a music store owned by a Cuban established on Magazine Street in Uptown, provides another example of a Cuban business that persists in one of the community's foundational neighborhoods. At the same time, as the movement to the suburbs progressed, other Cubans opened businesses there, such as Churros Cuban Café in Metairie.

The decline in the oil industry during the 1980s prompted a corresponding decline of nearly 6 percent in the city's total population and slowed the growth of the Hispanic and Latino population, including the Cuban component. The movement of the Cuban community to the suburbs continued, however (figs. 14 and 15).[28] Census 1990 enumerated 5,867 people who self-identified with Cuban origins by birth or ancestry compared to the 5,704 in Census 1980. Some 40 percent of them resided in Orleans and a little over 57 percent in Jefferson Parish.

That continued, if modest, growth of about 3 percent in the Cuban population over the 1980s related to the Mariel Boatlift and its aftermath. In 1980, the Cuban government released thousands of political prisoners and urged them to seek exile in the United States. The resulting exodus of about 275,000 Cubans over the 1980s has become associated with the enormous flotilla of small boats that transported many refugees from the port of Mariel on Cuba's north coast to Key West, Florida. Others arrived via a revival of the Freedom Flights, such as

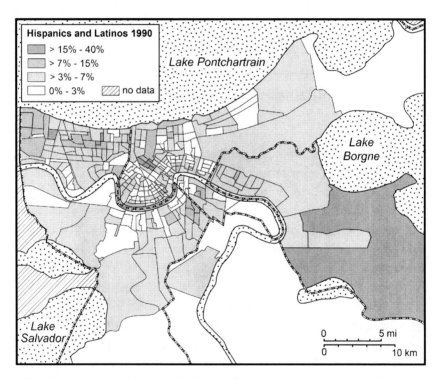

FIG. 14. The Hispanic and Latino population of New Orleans as a proportion of the total population of each census tract in 1990.

the seven charter flights organized by two priests from Grace Episcopal Church in Mid-City to transport 1,100 Cubans, most of them relatives of parishioners, to New Orleans. The same priests purchased a converted World War II submarine chaser, christened it *God's Mercy,* and circumvented a US Coast Guard blockade with another 437 Cubans. No matter the means of transport, however, all became known as Marielitos. While the majority settled in Miami, by far the largest Cuban community in the United States, some went to New Orleans.[29]

Those new immigrants somewhat slowed the shift of Cubans to the suburbs. While many Marielitos settled in Jefferson Parish, some concentrated in the Faubourg Marigny just east of the French Quarter. Teté's Bar, on St. Claude Avenue, became a major social nexus for them. As the city's economy declined, the economic opportunities of Miami and its large Cuban community attracted some of the Cubans who had established themselves in Orleans Parish over the 1960s and 1970s, but the newcomers somewhat compensated for such losses.[30]

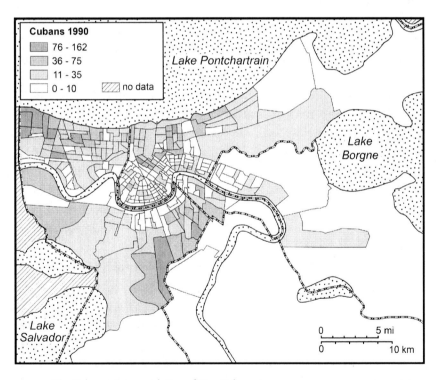

FIG. 15. The Cuban-origin population of New Orleans in 1990.

The newcomers also injected fresh elements into the established Cuban community. While those who had come in the 1960s and 1970s tended to be white, middle-class professionals, those who came in the 1980s had grown up in Communist Cuba and included many more working-class people, political prisoners, and blacks and mulattos. The term "Marielito," in fact, is not only a diminutive but a pejorative when applied to those who came in the 1980s by those who came in 1959–73. Such differences have caused schisms in Cuban communities throughout the United States as well as in New Orleans. One artist and former political prisoner, Guillermo de Bango, attempted to bridge that divide by opening the Cervantes Fundación Hispano-Americana de Arte in North Kenner. Before passing away in 2009, he taught Cuban and other styles of Latin American art, music, and dance to long-established Cubans, their children, newcomers, and anyone else with an interest.[31]

Over the 1990s the New Orleans Cuban community declined by about 11 percent even though Cubans continued their exodus to the United States, including the so-called *balseros*. Those "rafters" arrived not only on makeshift boats to settle in southern Florida but via other means and with other destinations. In all, approximately one hundred thousand Cubans came to the United States during the 1990s, mainly due to economic hardship related to the dissolution of the Soviet Union and its Council for Mutual Economic Assistance (Comecon) in 1991. Some settled in New Orleans and partially offset those Cubans who left for Miami and elsewhere over the 1990s. As Cubans who had established themselves in Orleans Parish left and the newcomers settled in the suburbs, the geographic focus of the community shifted nearly entirely to North Kenner, Metairie, and Westbank Jefferson Parish (fig. 16). By Census 2000, some 65 percent of the 5,196 residents who self-identified as being of Cuban origin lived in Jefferson Parish. Only a little more than 31 percent resided in Orleans Parish.[32]

Between 1959 and 2000, then, the Cuban community of New Orleans went through not only a geographic transformation, but a social one. Middle-class professionals who had grown up in prerevolutionary Cuba dominated the exiles who settled in a few neighborhoods in Orleans Parish during the 1960s. Many of the upwardly mobile among them subsequently relocated to the suburbs, part of the more general exodus by the middle class that transformed the city during that period. The so-called Marielitos and balseros who arrived in the 1980s and 1990s mainly settled among the established Cubans in the suburbs

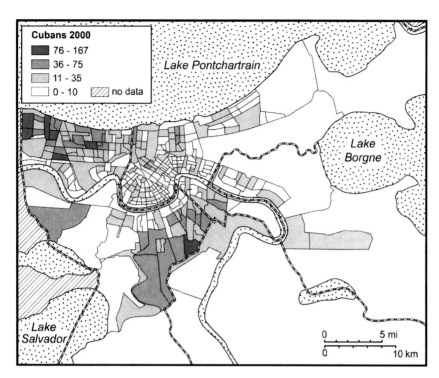

Lake Pontchartrain

Lake Borgne

Lake Salvador

0   5 mi
0   10 km

FIG. 16. The Cuban-origin population of New Orleans in 2000.

but differed greatly in terms of social class, age, and political views. They had grown up in Communist Cuba and more of them were working class, black or mulatto, and former political prisoners. Moreover, the children and grandchildren born and raised in New Orleans over half a century have gradually added even more cultural, political, and social diversity to the community. The Cubans interviewed for this study were all well aware of that diversity within their community.

> Cubans are marked or distinguished by the time that they left Cuba, and by their age more than anything. So, somebody that left in '59 left for different reasons than somebody who left in '91, like I did. We have different political views, different social views, different backgrounds, and I think that maybe affected the cohesion here in New Orleans as a Cuban community. It's very hard to get together a Cuban that came in the '50s or '60s with a Cuban that came in the '90s.[33]

By the late twentieth century the Cuban community had become hetero-
geneous and divided at the same time that its population had begun to decline. The aging memberships of the Liceo Cubano José Martí and Club Cubano de Profesionales continued their efforts but attracted few new members
from among either their own descendants or the newcomers. Over the 1990s
they erected a statue of Martí in Mid-City to commemorate the centennial of
his death. They also placed a plaque to mark the sesquicentennial of Narciso
López's death during his filibuster campaign to annex Cuba to the United
States. Some of the generation that arrived in the 1960s still gathers at Churros Cuban Café to play dominoes and celebrate the anniversary of the birth
of Martí each January, preserving their identity as a Cuban exile community.
They even founded an entirely new social organization in 2000, called Cuba
Centenario. In contrast, their children and those who arrived over the 1980s
and 1990s focus on contributing Cuban elements to the city's pan-Latino community through such organizations as the Cervantes Fundación Hispano-
Americana de Arte, the Carnaval Latino music festival, the Hispanic Chamber
of Commerce of Louisiana, Puentes, LatiNOLA.com, the ¿Qué pasa, New Orleans? television program, Aquí New Orleans magazine, and the local bilingual
newspapers El Tiempo and Jambalaya News. Even the nationalistically named
CubaNOLA Arts Collective, organized in 1999, explicitly reaches out to "explore
the shared histories and lifestyles of New Orleans, Louisiana, Cuba, the Caribbean and Latin America ... to understand the complexity of African and Latino
identity throughout the Americas" rather than focusing on Cuba alone.[34]

The September 8 feast day for La Virgen de la Caridad del Cobre, Our Lady
of Charity, has to some degree bridged the divides within the Cuban community because she has been the patron saint of Cuba since long before 1959, is
dark-skinned, and syncretizes with a Santería deity named Oshún. The virgin
dates to the seventeenth century, when a Spaniard sent three enslaved workers to look for salt along Cuba's northern coast. The trio, a black named Juan
Moreno and two natives named Juan and Rodrigo, discovered a statue of the
virgin floating in the water after a storm, an inscription identifying her as La
Virgen de la Caridad. They placed the statue in their parish church, but it kept
disappearing. Each time they found it atop a hill overlooking the nearby royal
copper mines of El Cobre, its clothing dripping wet. The enslaved blacks who
then worked in those mines integrated the virgin into the emerging Santería
religion, which syncretizes Christian, West African, and native elements. In

Santería, Our Lady of Charity became Oshún, the West African goddess of the rivers and the lakes who received offerings of copper but became sad that so many of her children were enslaved and transported to Cuba. Oshún secured the permission of her mother, Yemanya, the goddess of the sea, to go to Cuba to watch over her children. Yemanya warned Oshún that not everyone in Cuba was black and made her daughter's hair straighter and skin lighter so that she would be able to watch over all Cubans. She thereby became the statue of the virgin floating along the shore, found by three representatives of the oppressed peoples of the colony.[35]

The diverse Cuban community of New Orleans relates to the same spiritual figure in different ways. Those who arrived in the mid-twentieth century revere Our Lady of Charity as the patron saint of Cuba since long before Castro came to power and, therefore, as a link to the prerevolutionary homeland they knew and would like to restore. As one person interviewed remarked, "She is our mother. We take our mother wherever we go. In our cars, in our houses. Cubans can't go back and forth, we have our memories and our mother—La Virgen de la Caridad."[36] Cubans in New Orleans have celebrated the saint's feast day each September 8 since the 1960s at St. Theresa of Avila Catholic Church in the Lower Garden District, near the St. Thomas Housing Project. In 1968 that church began to offer mass in Spanish and still does so every Sunday at noon. Those who arrived in the late twentieth century revere the Santería version of the same saint. The balseros typically affixed an image of Oshún to the helms of their makeshift boats to guide them across the Straits of Florida, a reference to her Atlantic crossing in the seventeenth century to succor her enslaved children during the colonial period. She thereby reflects the character of the Cuban community in general—multiracial, multiethnic, displaced, mobile, and hopeful.

Cubans in the Twenty-first Century

Hurricane Katrina partially reversed the decline in the population of the Cuban community but further increased its heterogeneity. With about two-thirds of the city's residents of Cuban origin living in Jefferson Parish in 2005, the majority escaped the direct impact of persistent flooding. Those living in Orleans Parish did suffer some of the worst flooding, however, with the densest concentrations of Cubans in the devastated neighborhoods of Mid-City, Gentilly, and Lakeview. In the aftermath of Katrina, some relocated to Jefferson Parish while others left New Orleans entirely. At the same time, however, Cubans who had initially settled in Florida began moving to New Orleans to work in the reconstruction effort.

Census 2010 reveals the result of that process (fig. 17). While the city lost 19.2 percent of its population between Census 2000 and 2010, the Cuban-origin population grew 3.4 percent. The 5,322 Cubans of Census 2010 remains well below the peak of 5,867 reached in 1990, but the influx of Cubans from Miami and elsewhere in the nation seems to have begun to reverse the decline. The impact of Katrina also further concentrated the Cuban population, with a little more than 72 percent living in Jefferson Parish in 2010 and only about 24 percent in Orleans Parish. In fact, Cubans have become even more noticeably concentrated in a contiguous block of census tracts in North Kenner and Metairie north of Interstate 10 and west of the Lake Pontchartrain Causeway. Cuban businesses in Mid-City, destroyed by the flood, also relocated to Jeffer-

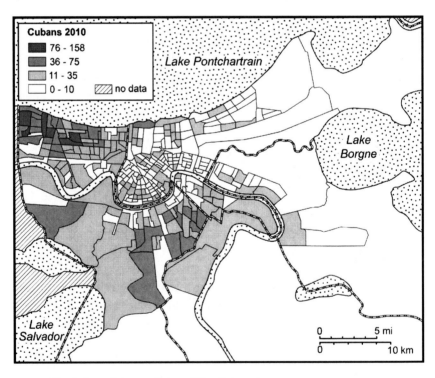

FIG. 17. The Cuban-origin population of New Orleans in 2010.

son Parish. Garcés Restaurant, for example, founded in the 1970s by expatriate Cubans, relocated to North Kenner, although the Garcés family has since reopened the Mid-City location as the Regla Store, named for their old Havana neighborhood, a Cuban grocery store and delicatessen that serves patrons from throughout the city.

Whether that residential concentration will result in greater community cohesion remains uncertain. Some theorists suggest that residential integration of diverse groups, both distinct ones such as Latinos and non-Latinos and more nuanced types of diversity such as the ones that internally divide the Cuban community, results in greater harmony. Proximity supposedly results in greater interaction, increased social capital, more economic opportunity, general prosperity, and broader identification with a single community. Other theorists suggest the opposite, predicting that increased social interaction actually leads to greater conflict. Ultimately, much depends on whether the economic opportunities that resulted from post-Katrina reconstruction diminish, in which case the size of the Cuban community could again begin to decrease and its internal diversity and divisions lessen.[37]

Perhaps more significantly, over the longer term, if political relations between Cuba and the United States normalize, the trade embargo ends, and New Orleans and Havana can reestablish their commercial relationship, the Cuban community could grow in size, influence, and diversity. Since the 1970s, Louisiana's politicians have been conducting trade missions to Cuba and advocating in Washington, DC, to end the embargo, in large part at the behest of the state's rice producers. The United States exports about half its rice harvest, and Louisiana has long been one of the principal producers, accounting for more than 13 percent of the nation's crop in 2010. Moreover, about two-thirds of the US rice harvest comes from Arkansas, Mississippi, and Missouri. And much of it is exported down the Mississippi River through the port of New Orleans. From the perspective of Louisiana in general and New Orleans in particular, therefore, Cuba represents a nearby and potentially lucrative market.[38]

The embargo eased somewhat with the passage in 2000 of the Trade Sanctions Reform and Export Enhancement Act. That federal law cites humanitarian assistance to allow cash sales of limited amounts of food and medicine to Cuba but does not allow imports from Cuba. By 2003, US corporations had used that new law to become the leading exporters of food to Cuba, and Cuba had become the sixth largest importer of US rice. Nonetheless, Louisiana's politicians have continued to lobby for full repeal of the embargo and lead trade missions to Cuba to promote the revival of the old relationship. After reversals during the administration of President George W. Bush (2001–9), the embargo has again eased during the administration of President Barack Obama. In 2010, for example, 566,400 tons of bulk agricultural products shipped from New Orleans to Cuba, nearly twice as much as the total tonnage of goods shipped in 1958. Then, in December 2014, Obama announced a major initiative to normalize relations by opening an embassy in Havana, easing travel and financial restrictions, and eventually negotiating an end to the embargo in exchange for Cuba's release of political prisoners and other social, political, and economic changes. Whether even complete elimination of the embargo would actually revive the old relationship with Louisiana remains unpredictable, however. The location of New Orleans along the lower Mississippi River certainly provides an advantage over other US ports given proximity to Havana and the fact that bulk agricultural products such as grains and petrochemicals transported down the river constitute a large proportion of Cuban imports. Yet New Orleans is no longer the dominant city on the Gulf Coast, as it was for all of the nineteenth century and well into the twentieth. Nor does New Orleans have one of the largest expatriate Cuban populations in the United States, as it did in the nineteenth century. Houston, Miami, and Tampa would compete vigorously with New Orleans for large shares of the Cuban market if the embargo were to end.[39]

Positions on the embargo remain a major issue dividing the Cuban community in New Orleans. Some, such as Romualdo "Romi" González, have been prominent in efforts to lift the embargo. An attorney, he has collaborated with Cuban and non-Cuban civic and business leaders to strengthen the relationship between New Orleans and Cuba. A notable effort followed the relaxation of restrictions on travel to Cuba that began in 2003. González and others succeeded in securing federal authorization for weekly direct flights between New Orleans's Louis Armstrong International Airport and Havana's Jose Martí International Airport that began in March 2012. Others, in contrast, agree with the pro-embargo position of the Cuban-American National Foundation, which wields great political power in Washington, DC.[40]

The easing of travel restrictions to visit family and the direct flights have, nonetheless, reinvigorated the flow of people and ideas between New Orleans and Cuba and made the Cuban community much more transnational than in the twentieth century. The new freedom to visit Cuba frequently has allowed regular incorporations into the New Orleans community of elements of Cuban material culture, idiom, art, cuisine, and so on as they emerge on the island. Transnationalism marks, for example, distinctive Afro-Cuban musical styles emerging among bands such as Los Hombres Calientes, AshéSon, and Urban Minds. The name of the band AshéSon provides an example by combining a Spanish word that designates regional musical styles with one from the Afro-Cuban Santería religion that means something similar to karma. The *timba* dance music, which developed on Cuba over the 1980s, that those bands play provides another example of the ongoing exchange of ideas involved in transnationalism. That sort of musical hybridization recreates the process that began in eighteenth-century New Orleans and resulted in the emergence of jazz in the early twentieth century. Alexey Martí Soltero, a percussionist born in Havana who plays with some of those bands, is one of the Cuban musicians contributing to a revived musical exchange between Cuba and New Orleans: "I say that I live in the same house but in different rooms. Apparently I'm in the US, but I feel I'm in the same house in different rooms. Here there is a musical movement, a cultural experience of parades playing in the streets. In Cuba we have the same thing but only with percussion and a *corneta china*. There it's known as a *conga*. Here it's known as a second line."[41]

THE TIMING AND CHARACTER OF THE processes that established the Cuban community in New Orleans differed greatly from those that established the Isleño community, resulting in much different residential geographies, roles in creating the city, and impact from Katrina. While the Isleños arrived during colonial times and settled in a rural area that would later become part of the southeastern suburban fringe of the city, the Cubans mainly arrived during neocolonial times, many as refugees from a revolution against neocolonialism, initially settled near the city's center, and later relocated to the northwestern suburbs. Katrina devastated the majority of Isleños but only a minority of Cubans. Moreover, the Cubans arrived not only more recently but in a series of mass migrations that resulted in a great deal of social heterogeneity relative to the Isleños. The changing character of the process that brought Cubans to New

Orleans makes their community different from those of other Latinos who arrived during the neocolonial twentieth century. Because of the embargo, the Cuban community did not until recently, with the easing of travel restrictions, develop the same sorts of transnational characteristics as other Latino communities in New Orleans, for example, the Hondurans.

3. HONDURANS

If sugar blended with geopolitics began to shape the relationship between New Orleans and Cuba in the nineteenth century, bananas began to turn the Crescent City into one of the most notable Honduran communities in the United States in the twentieth century. In 1910, Samuel Zemurray, the New Orleans entrepreneur who became known as Sam the Banana Man, bought the Cuyamel Fruit Company and started growing bananas on two thousand hectares (five thousand acres) near the Caribbean coast of Honduras. Within a few years he had gained additional land concessions from the Honduran government and turned Cuyamel Fruit into a major US importer of bananas. Zemurray's commercial success derived from a political alliance with Manuel Bonilla, a deposed Honduran president who had been living in exile in New Orleans since 1907. Zemurray financed the mercenaries who returned Bonilla to power in a 1911 coup and, in return, profited not only from land and tax concessions but from the Honduran army's violent repression of labor strikes on the company's plantations. By 1929 Cuyamel Fruit had grown to control 15 percent of US banana imports, and Zemurray decided to sell it to the United Fruit Company of Boston. As United Fruit's stock prices fell in the wake of the Wall Street crash, however, he changed his mind about leaving the banana business. He bought a controlling interest in the company and proceeded to turn it into the largest grower and shipper of bananas in the world.[1]

By moving United Fruit's headquarters from Boston to New Orleans in 1933, Zemurray placed the Crescent City at the epicenter of the hemispheric banana trade. Bananas from United Fruit's plantations in Honduras and elsewhere in Central America, the Caribbean, and South America arrived aboard the freighters of the company's Great White Fleet at the Banana Wharf at the foot of Thalia Street, were transferred to refrigerated boxcars, and ended up on breakfast tables and in lunch boxes across North America (fig. 18). Zemurray had expanded his original plantation in Honduras to an archipelago of industrialized production that encompassed approximately 1.4 million hectares (3.5 million acres) that he purchased and leased throughout the Caribbean and Latin America. He controlled that neocolonial banana empire from his desk at company headquarters on St. Charles Avenue, just a few blocks away from the Banana Wharf, organizing commercial operations as well as coups in the banana republics. Even between his official retirement in 1951 and death in 1961 he played influential roles in the 1954 coup that ousted Guatemalan president Jacobo Árbenz Guzmán and in the 1961 attempted invasion of Cuba at the Bay of Pigs. In 1970, United Fruit disappeared in the merger that created United Brands, now Chiquita Brands International, and over the ensuing decade the share of US banana imports through New Orleans fell to around 25 percent.[2]

Despite the relatively brief period that New Orleans dominated the banana trade and Honduran politics, from the 1930s through the 1960s, the city's resulting Honduran community developed a reputation as the largest in the United States. New Orleans thereby came to have a strong Honduran sense of place in the same way that Miami has a Cuban one, New York City a Puerto Rican and Dominican one, and Los Angeles and San Antonio a Mexican one. The emergence of that sort of *genius loci* relates, in part, to the number of residents of a particular national origin in both absolute terms and relative to other groups and other places. But sense of place also emerges through the narratives communities construct about their relationship with a place, the landscapes they

FIG. 18. Longshoremen at the New Orleans Banana Wharf in the early twentieth century, transferring bananas from a freighter to a refrigerated boxcar of the Illinois Central Railroad. Photograph from the Frank B. Moore Photograph Collection, Louisiana and Special Collections Library, University of New Orleans, object file name fbm000313. Reproduced courtesy of the Frank B. Moore Collection, Louisiana and Special Collections Department, Earl K. Long Library, University of New Orleans.

create, and other processes through which people form an attachment to their city of residence in which personal identity, ethnic identity, and place identity become intricately interwoven.[3]

In terms of the demographic component of that sense of place, the number of residents of Honduran origin in the Crescent City remained low until the mid-twentieth century. Census 1850 recorded only six residents of Honduran birth in the entire United States. Another twenty-three claimed birth in Central America, and some of them might have been born in Honduras because it had been part of the United Provinces of Central America from independence in 1821 until becoming a separate republic in 1838. But those twenty-three might just as well have been born in any of the other republics that resulted from the dissolution of the United Provinces: Guatemala, El Salvador, Nicaragua, or Costa Rica. And, in any case, none of the twenty-nine US residents born in Honduras or elsewhere in Central America lived in New Orleans. From 1899 through 1910, the nation admitted 10,699 immigrants born in "Spanish-America," meaning one of the former Spanish colonies of Central or South America. While some of those Latinos might well have been from Honduras, few came to Louisiana. Slightly more than half declared their destination to be New York, with only 836 destined for any place in Louisiana.[4]

Hondurans in the Twentieth Century

Census 1930 consequently enumerated only 443 residents of New Orleans, all but four in Orleans Parish, who claimed birth in Honduras; moreover, the majority were not Latinos. Nearly a third of the 443 claimed birth in British Honduras, which was then a colony of Britain, became Belize in 1973, and an independent country in 1981. Many of those 136 were likely the adult children of expatriate Louisianians who had emigrated to British Honduras at the end of the Civil War but returned upon the failure of their plan to recreate an antebellum society in Central America. Only fourteen of the 443 specified their origin as Spanish Honduras, the term for the country of Honduras then used to distinguish it from neighboring British Honduras. If the ratio of Anglo versus Hispanic surnames provides any guide, most of the remaining 293, who claimed Honduran birth without specifying British or Spanish Honduras, were not Latinos and had come from British Honduras. The total number of Latinos of Honduran birth living in New Orleans in 1930, then, must have been fewer than a hundred. In contrast, Census 1930 enumerated 299 residents of Cuban birth in New Orleans, who, as covered in the previous chapter, were also highly concentrated in Orleans Parish.[5]

Although the Honduran community in New Orleans was small in the early twentieth century, it nonetheless constituted the largest one in the United States. It included fourteen of the twenty-three US residents claiming birth in Spanish Honduras and about a third of the vaguer category of Hondurans, including Anglos and Latinos born in either Spanish or British Honduras. Only New York City had even half as many Hondurans, of whatever type, as New Orleans. To again contrast the Cuban and Honduran communities of New Orleans, in both absolute and relative terms, the city had at least three times as many residents of Cuban birth as of Honduran birth; but the Cubans constituted less than 2 percent of all Cubans resident in the United States while the Hondurans constituted at least a third.

Only after Zemurray turned New Orleans into the neocolonial hub of the hemispheric banana trade in 1933, by reestablishing United Fruit's headquarters there, did relatively large numbers of Hondurans begin to move to the city. Various factors prompted them to leave Honduras. Beginning in the 1930s, banana pathogens such as Panama disease and Sigatoka periodically reduced production and therefore employment on the plantations and in the associated company towns, ports, and railroads, thus prompting some workers to emigrate. Political repression during the dictatorship of Tiburcio Carías Andino forced opponents into exile over the 1930s and 1940s. The threat of German submarines in the Gulf of Mexico during the Second World War interfered with shipping, decreased banana exports, and resulted in worker layoffs on the plantations. Hurricanes that devastated the Caribbean coast of Honduras also periodically resulted in widespread unemployment: Hattie in 1959, Fifi in 1974, and Mitch in 1998 remain among the most notable. Several coups and the Soccer War with neighboring El Salvador militarized the country during the 1950s through the 1970s, a process that intensified in the 1980s as civil wars overwhelmed neighboring El Salvador, Guatemala, and Nicaragua. Those conflicts did not directly impact the majority of Hondurans but did result in a large US military presence and the establishment of bases for the Contras who were fighting the Sandinistas in neighboring Nicaragua. The related political repression and endemic violence increased the flow of Honduran refugees to the United States.[6]

In parallel, various factors attracted Hondurans to New Orleans over the twentieth century. The city was for several decades the main destination for the Honduran banana crop, the source of about half of all bananas imported into the United States at midcentury, and many Hondurans had therefore heard of New Orleans. Meanwhile, the Great White Fleet's passenger service provided good transportation connections between the Caribbean coast of Honduras and New Orleans. Other pull factors included environmental and cultural similarities between New Orleans and the Caribbean lowlands of Honduras, notably their warm, humid climates and the dominance of Catholicism. As the size of the city's Honduran community grew, it became large enough to act as its own pull factor, attracting additional Hondurans by providing a familiar cultural context and supportive social network.

None of the decennial censuses from 1940 through 1980 generated statistics on Hondurans that allow mapping their residential pattern or even venturing more than rough estimates of their population during the period that their community became firmly established in New Orleans. The censuses of 1940 and 1950 do not disaggregate residents of Honduran birth from a general Latin America category. Census 1960, and each census since, provides an estimate of the Honduran-born population in the United States as a whole, showing exponential decadal increases from the thousands into the hundreds of thousands over the second half of the twentieth century. Census 1970 reports residents of Honduran ancestry, including those either born in Honduras or with a parent born there, at the level of four broad regions because the estimates derive from questions administered to only a 15 percent sample of households (table 2). Moreover, although nearly half of all those residents of Honduran ancestry lived in the South, that region includes both Louisiana and Florida, and the statistics therefore cannot do more than suggest that by 1970 New Orleans had a Honduran community that numbered in the thousands. Census 1980 presents similar statistics on ancestry and reports them at the state level because they derive from a question administered to a 5 percent sample of households (table 3). Of the estimated 55,565 US residents of Honduran ancestry in 1980, more than three-quarters lived in New York, New Jersey, Florida, California, and Louisiana. Those statistics suggest that the population of the New Orleans Honduran community grew substantially between 1970 and 1980, perhaps doubling, but remained well below ten thousand.[7]

TABLE 2. Honduran-ancestry population by US region, Census 1970

Rank	Region	Honduran population (number)	Proportion of US Honduran population (percent)
1	South	4,839	44.9
2	Northeast	3,333	30.9
3	West	1,850	17.2
4	North-central	760	7.0
	US TOTAL	10,782	100

TABLE 3. Honduran-ancestry population in top-seven US states, Census 1980

Rank	State	Honduran population (number)	Proportion of US Honduran population (percent)
1	New York	14,853	26.7
2	California	11,452	20.6
3	Louisiana	6,813	12.3
4	Florida	6,522	11.7
5	New Jersey	2,835	5.1
6	Illinois	2,256	4.1
7	Texas	2,225	4.0

Only with Census 1990 do the statistics begin to permit more precise estimates of the number of residents who self-identified as being of Honduran origin. At that time the city had the fourth most residents of Honduran origin among all US cities, with 9,700 in the Metropolitan Statistical Area (MSA) as compared to the 9,282 in the four parishes graphed in figure 6 (table 4).[8] The New York–Northern New Jersey–Long Island Consolidated Metropolitan Statistical Area (CMSA) had more than three times as many, about a quarter of all those enumerated. The Los Angeles–Anaheim–Riverside and the Miami–Fort Lauderdale CMSAs followed, each with more than double the Honduran-origin population of the New Orleans MSA.

Census 1990 also permits mapping the Honduran community's residential pattern, which by then only echoed the neighborhoods that oral histories reveal they had concentrated in during the 1930s through 1960s (fig. 19). The community's founders congregated in the Lower Garden District for several decades. That neighborhood had been known as the Irish Channel, but as residents of Irish origin moved out and Hondurans moved in, it became the Barrio Lempira, renamed for the currency that replaced the Honduran peso in the 1930s. Many of those *catrachos,* as expatriate Hondurans refer to themselves, had worked for United Fruit in Honduras and continued to do so in New Orleans. The Barrio Lempira provided them with affordable housing near the Banana Wharf and other, similar employment opportunities along the waterfront and in the adjoining Warehouse District. Some of the Hondurans established restaurants and other businesses and services that catered to their community in the Lower Garden District, especially along Magazine Street. At the nearby St. Theresa of

TABLE 4. Honduran-origin population for six metropolitan areas, Louisiana, and the United States, Census 1990

Rank	Place (MSA or CMSA)[a]	Honduran-origin population (number)	Total population (number)	Hispanic & Latino population (number)	Hondurans in total population (percent)	Hondurans in Hispanic & Latino population (percent)
1	New York–Northern New Jersey–Long Island	33,690	18,087,251	2,704,960	0.19	1.25
2	Los Angeles–Anaheim–Riverside	25,422	14,531,529	4,714,405	0.17	0.54
3	Miami–Fort Lauderdale	19,694	3,192,582	1,055,368	0.62	1.87
4	New Orleans	9,700	1,238,816	51,574	0.78	18.81
5	Houston–Galveston–Brazoria	5,996	3,711,043	759,857	0.16	0.79
6	Washington, DC	3,525	3,923,574	218,256	0.09	1.62
	Louisiana	10,414	4,219,973	90,609	0.25	11.49
	United States	131,066	248,709,873	21,900,089	0.05	0.60

[a]Metropolitan Statistical Area (MSA) and Consolidated Metropolitan Statistical Area (CMSA) are terms the US Census Bureau uses to spatially delimit urbanized areas. See note 8 of this chapter for details.

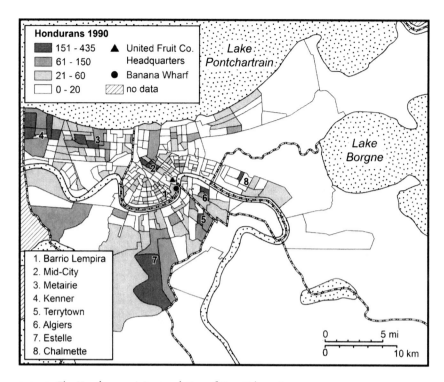

Hondurans 1990
- 151 - 435
- 61 - 150
- 21 - 60
- 0 - 20

▲ United Fruit Co. Headquarters
● Banana Wharf
/// no data

Lake Pontchartrain

Lake Borgne

1. Barrio Lempira
2. Mid-City
3. Metairie
4. Kenner
5. Terrytown
6. Algiers
7. Estelle
8. Chalmette

0   5 mi
0   10 km

FIG. 19. The Honduran-origin population of New Orleans in 1990.

Avila Catholic Church, they celebrated the feast day of the Virgin de la Suyapa, the Honduran patron saint.[9]

Over the 1960s and 1970s, like their Cuban neighbors in the Lower Garden District, upwardly mobile Hondurans moved to middle-class neighborhoods farther from the waterfront. Mid-City, south of City Park, displayed a notable concentration of Hondurans as late as Census 1990. But many others chose the newer suburbs of Jefferson Parish, particularly North Kenner and Metairie north of Interstate 10. New arrivals, in particular, initially moved into the Redwood Park Apartments, a sprawling complex of four hundred low-income units built in 1970 in North Kenner and dominated by Hondurans and other Latinos: "This place [the Redwood Park Apartments] is like a little city on its own. It's a trampoline into the American Dream. . . . People start out here and go on to buy houses in Kenner."[10] Other concentrations of Hondurans developed in the Westbank neighborhoods of Terrytown and Estelle in Jefferson Parish and in

TABLE 5. Honduran-origin population for six metropolitan areas, Louisiana, and the United States, Census 2000

Rank	Place (MSA or CMSA)[a]	Honduran-origin population (number)	Total population (number)	Hispanic & Latino population (number)	Hondurans in total population (percent)	Hondurans in Hispanic & Latino population (percent)
1	New York–Northern New Jersey–Long Island	50,106	21,199,865	3,852,138	0.24	1.30
2	Miami–Fort Lauderdale	30,726	3,876,380	1,563,389	0.79	1.97
3	Los Angeles–Riverside–Orange County	23,669	16,373,645	6,598,488	0.14	0.36
4	Houston–Galveston–Brazoria	14,456	4,669,571	1,348,588	0.31	1.07
5	Washington, DC–Baltimore	11,319	7,608,070	484,902	0.15	2.33
6	New Orleans	8,112	1,337,726	58,545	0.61	13.86
	Louisiana	8,792	4,468,976	107,738	0.20	8.16
	United States	217,569	281,421,906	35,305,818	0.08	0.62

[a]See note to table 4.

Algiers in Orleans Parish. By 1990, Hondurans had also created a concentration in Chalmette, in urbanized St. Bernard Parish.[11]

By 2000, New Orleans had fallen to sixth place among cities with substantial Honduran communities (table 5).[12] New York remained first, with more than six times as many Hondurans as New Orleans, followed by Miami, Los Angeles, Houston, and Washington, DC. In part that fall in rank from fourth to sixth related to a decline of approximately 19 percent in the population of the Honduran community in New Orleans. The downturn in the city's economy explains much of that decline, as well as the parallel declines in the city's total population and that of the Cuban community. Just as some balseros arrived in the 1990s to partially counter the loss of residents of Cuban origin who relocated to other US cities, some Honduran newcomers chose to settle in New Orleans and partially compensated for those who left. Those newcomers were generally economic rather than political refugees, another similarity with parallel trends in the Cuban community. The civil wars in El Salvador, Guatemala, and Nicaragua all came to an end in the 1990s; the Contras abandoned the bases within Honduras from which they had attacked Nicaragua's Sandinista government; and as associated repression in Honduras declined so did the flow of political refugees into the United States. Instead, the Honduran refugees of the 1990s, like the balseros, were escaping economic hardship, not caused by the dissolution of Comecon in 1991 but by Hurricane Mitch in 1998. Flooding and landslides throughout Honduras killed thousands and destroyed the homes and livelihoods of hundreds of thousands more, especially along the Caribbean coast. The US Immigration and Naturalization Service, now the Citizenship and Immigration Service, granted Hondurans temporary protected status to allow non-immigrants already in the country, such as those on student visas, to remain and work while their country recovered from Mitch's devastation. Mitch did not precipitate a surge in legal Honduran immigration to the United States, however. In fact, the number of documented Honduran immigrants declined somewhat in the immediate aftermath of the hurricane before recovering to the levels characteristic through the 1990s, approximately six thousand per year. Honduras, however, has long been one of the major sources of undocumented immigration to the United States, albeit a distant second to Mexico. Although interviews indicate that New Orleans did attract some undocumented refugees from the economic devastation associated with Mitch, the decline in the population of the Honduran community suggests that few had arrived in New Orleans by 2000.[13]

While the decline in the population of the Honduran community over the 1990s could be more apparent than real, a function of the change in Census 2000 that resulted in a massive inflation of the "Unspecified" category, the decline did parallel a similar one in the population of the Cuban community. Moreover, Hondurans underwent a residential shift from Orleans to Jefferson Parish, again similar to Cubans (fig. 20). In 1990, about 38 percent of Hondurans lived in Orleans Parish and 58 percent in Jefferson Parish. By 2000, 26 percent lived in Orleans Parish and nearly 70 percent in Jefferson Parish. Within Jefferson Parish, moreover, Hondurans became extremely concentrated in North Kenner.[14]

Honduran Sense of Place during the Twentieth Century

Despite the relatively few Hondurans living in New Orleans at any one time during the twentieth century, claims of an enormous population became central to the community's sense of place and identity as well as to the self-identities of many of its members. Rene Arturo Bendana, Honduran ambassador to the United States from 1992 to 1994, claimed that "about 100,000 Hondurans" then lived in New Orleans.[15] In 1999, during a debate in Congress about disaster relief related to Hurricane Mitch, US senator Mary Landrieu claimed that "with one of the largest Honduran communities outside Honduras, New Orleans is sometimes referred to as 'the third largest Honduran city.'"[16] In the aftermath of Katrina, some academics naively raised the population estimate to "140,000 to 150,000 Hondurans, the largest Honduran community in the [United States]" and "the second-largest urban concentration of Hondurans in the world."[17]

Such mythic accounts of the size of the city's Honduran population clearly do not match the relatively accurate statistical evidence from Census 1990 and Census 2000. The enumerated population of Honduran origin for the four parishes amounted to 9,282 in Census 1990 and 7,503 in Census 2000, far short of 100,000. Even considering the larger MSA, 9,700 Hondurans in 1990 and 8,112 in 2000 do not make up much of the difference.

Undercounting of residents of Honduran origin does not seem to account for the large difference between these statistics and the assertions of some politicians and academics. The census certainly undercounts Hondurans, probably more so than many other Latino groups. First, Hondurans had to use the write-in box to identify their specific national origin on Census 1990 and Census

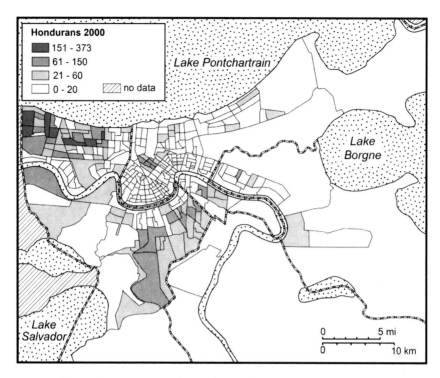

Hondurans 2000
- 151 - 373
- 61 - 150
- 21 - 60
- 0 - 20
- no data

Lake Pontchartrain

Lake Borgne

Lake Salvador

0   5 mi

0   10 km

FIG. 20. The Honduran-origin population of New Orleans in 2000.

2000 rather than simply selecting among the given categories of Cuban, Puerto Rican, and Mexican. Second, like Mexicans, a large proportion of Hondurans is undocumented and might avoid census takers. Third, also like Mexicans, many Hondurans are highly mobile migrant workers and therefore transient residents that might be missed by census takers. Yet logic dictates that undercounting cannot account for the two orders of magnitude that separate the assertions from the statistics because if a hundred thousand Hondurans really lived in New Orleans in 2000 they would have constituted nearly a tenth of the total population and been so extraordinarily noticeable that the census could not possibly have undercounted them to such a degree. Moreover, logic also dictates that any such undercounting would apply in every place in the United States and, therefore, assumptions of an undercount cannot alter the rankings of table 5 and miraculously elevate New Orleans above five other metropolitan areas to become the largest Honduran community in the country.

In fact, although New Orleans did host the largest Honduran community in the United States in 1930, the available statistics suggest that it lost that rank-ing to New York City around 1970. While Census 1980 provides relevant sta-tistics only at the state level, Census 1990 demonstrates that the vast majority of Hondurans in Florida, New York and New Jersey, Louisiana, and California then lived in New York City, Miami, Los Angeles, and New Orleans. The state ranking of table 3, therefore, provides a good proxy for a metropolitan ranking in 1980. It suggests that the Honduran communities of New Orleans and Miami were then roughly equal in population, and that only by 1990 would Miami de-cisively relegate New Orleans to fourth place. Similarly, Census 1970 provided only regional-level statistics, and table 2 therefore cannot resolve the relative sizes of the Honduran communities of Miami and New Orleans because they are both in the South. Nonetheless, given that those two communities were roughly equal in size in 1980 and that relatively few Hondurans lived in the west in 1970, New Orleans likely hosted one of the two largest Honduran communi-ties in the United States in 1970, probably a close second to New York City.[18]

In terms of population size, therefore, New Orleans became the largest Hon-duran city in the United States during the early and mid-twentieth century due to its dominance in the banana trade but thereafter lost that ranking due to re-structuring of the banana industry. The Honduran community in New Orleans was the largest in 1930, albeit with a population of fewer than a hundred. It grew into the thousands by midcentury, but as New Orleans's role in the banana trade diminished over the 1960s, so did the influx of Hondurans. New York overtook it around 1970, followed by Los Angeles in 1980, Miami by 1990, and Houston and Washington, DC, by the end of the century. The surge in Hondu-ran migration that began in the 1980s, due initially to political repression and then to Hurricane Mitch in 1998 and a poor economy thereafter, largely by-passed New Orleans because of its own economic decline. The Honduran-born population of the United States therefore increased nearly fifteen-fold between 1970 and 2000, from the tens of thousands into the hundreds of thousands, but those catrachos went to other places while the Honduran population of New Orleans declined over the 1990s and the community's rank fell to a distant sixth by the end of the century.

A similar analysis demonstrates that New Orleans cannot ever have been "the third largest Honduran city" in the world.[19] Assuming, with some certainty, that the vast majority of people enumerated in Honduran censuses are of Hon-duran origin, those for 1974, 1988, and 2001 reveal that New Orleans would have ranked far down that country's urban hierarchy in any of those years (table 6).[20] In contrast, New York City's Honduran-origin population of 50,106 in 2000 would actually have been a fairly large provincial city in Honduras, about the size of seventh-ranked Comayagua, at the end of the twentieth century. Even an assumption of substantial undercounting of Hondurans in the United States cannot elevate New York, let alone New Orleans, to anywhere near the size of Tegucigalpa, San Pedro Sula, or La Ceiba in 2000 or anytime previously.

Those statistics suggest that the perception of New Orleans as the largest Honduran community in the United States derives more from its being a gateway community than from ever having had a particularly large Honduran-origin population. The passenger service of the Great White Fleet made the city the preferred port of entry for Hondurans arriving in the United States. While many might have stayed only briefly before moving on to opportunities in New York or elsewhere, they remained connected to New Orleans through memories and social networks. Even as the Crescent City's Honduran population went into decline over the 1990s, it remained so much a part of the identity of many catrachos that the Honduran ambassador could ingenuously claim that "about 100,000 Hondurans" lived in the city.[21]

But the statistics also suggest that the perception of New Orleans as the largest Honduran community in the United States derives to some degree from the relative rather than the absolute size of its Honduran-origin population. As tables 4 and 5 show, Hondurans in New Orleans and Miami made up a much higher percentage of the total population than in other cities in the late twentieth century, between six- and eight-tenths of a percent compared to less than half that for any other. Even more tellingly, Hondurans in New Orleans made up a much higher percentage of the total Hispanic and Latino population than in any other city. In 1990 Hondurans made up nearly 19 percent of all Hispanics and Latinos in New Orleans, and in 2000 they made up nearly 14 percent. In both years, the percentage of Hondurans relative to other Hispanics and Latinos reached an order of magnitude higher than for any other city. The runners-up were Tuscaloosa, Alabama, in 1990, with 49 Hondurans making up 5.2 percent of the Hispanic population, and Roanoke, Virginia, in 2000, with 143 Hondurans making up 5.3 percent. While several other cities might have had larger Honduran populations in absolute terms, only in New Orleans were Hondurans highly visible relative to all other Hispanic and Latino groups.

TABLE 6. Population for selected Honduran places in Censuses 1974, 1988, and 2001

Place	1974	1988	2001
Tegucigalpa	273,894	539,590	765,675
San Pedro Sula	150,991	270,804	437,798
La Ceiba	38,788	65,489	114,277
Choloma	9,161	37,194	105,899
El Progreso	28,105	57,198	90,475
Choluteca	26,152	51,887	70,968
Comayagua	15,941	35,453	53,367
Puerto Cortés	25,817	30,082	43,845
La Lima	14,631	27,336	41,490
Danlí	10,825	27,643	40,915
Siguatepeque	12,456	25,993	39,070
Juticalpa	10,075	19,622	30,030
Catacamas	9,134	17,965	29,024
Tela	19,055	22,193	27,990
Villanueva	no data	11,981	27,938
Tocoa	*2,803*	14,079	26,020
Santa Rosa de Copán	12,413	19,680	25,861
Olanchito	7,411	13,581	22,626
San Lorenzo	9,467	15,294	20,653
Cofradía	no data	14,699	18,011
El Paraíso	6,709	13,069	17,412
La Paz	6,811	11,238	15,889
Yoro	4,449	*9,416*	14,069
La Entrada	no data	8,943	13,949
Potrerillos	no data	8,954	13,900
Santa Bárbara	5,883	10,503	13,896
Talanga	4,917	9,062	13,533
Nacaome	6,159	*9,801*	12,972
Santa Rita	no data	no data	12,111
Intibucá	no data	7,291	11,995
Guaimaca	no data	6,289	11,101
Morazán	no data	7,508	10,205
Trujillo	3,961	5,883	*8,541*
Nueva Ocotepeque	4,724	6,667	*8,297*
Gracias	2,299	3,678	6,716
Roatán	1,943	3,774	6,498

Note: Italics indicates places with approximately the same Honduran-origin population as the New Orleans MSA at that time.

Moreover, only in New Orleans was the population of the Honduran community much greater than that of Puerto Ricans and comparable to that of Mexicans and Cubans, the three nationally dominant groups. Even ignoring that Hondurans generally suffer a greater undercount than Mexicans, Cubans, or Puerto Ricans, figure 6 illustrates how the Honduran and Mexican communities vied for second place behind Cubans in 1970. That decade, as the Cuban population remained relatively stable, Hondurans caught up and Mexicans took the lead. Over the 1980s, the city's total population and Mexican population declined, the Cuban population remained stable, and the Honduran population increased to become the largest among the Hispanic and Latino communities. Census 1990 enumerated 48,622 Hispanics and Latinos in the four parishes, of whom approximately 19 percent were of Honduran origin, 13 percent Mexican, and 12 percent Cuban. Over the following decade, however, Mexicans increased and Hondurans decreased until they were nearly equal by Census 2000: of the 51,102 Hispanics and Latinos about 16 percent claimed Mexican origin and 15 percent Honduran, followed by 10 percent Cuban. Given the proportionately smaller undercounts for the Cuban and Mexican communities than for the Honduran community as well as the use of only somewhat commensurable ancestry statistics for 1970 and 1980, Figure 6 likely underrepresents the relative population of the Honduran community across the breadth of the graph. As the city's Honduran population grew through mid-century in concert with the banana trade, it probably caught up with that of the Cuban community over the 1930s, surpassed it in the 1940s, and then fell behind again during the Cuban influx of the 1960s before again surpassing it around 1980.

Relative dominance in particular neighborhoods and the associated creation of distinctive landscapes has also contributed to the Honduran community's vigorous sense that New Orleans is their city in comparison to Cuban Miami or Puerto Rican New York City. Census 2000 reveals not only the concentration of Hondurans in particular parts of the city, as mapped in figure 20, but their dominance relative to other Hispanic and Latino groups in some of those neighborhoods (fig. 21). North Kenner, in particular, had a dense concentration of Hispanics and Latinos in 2000, as illustrated in figure 3, and Hondurans dominated in many of that neighborhood's census tracts to a higher degree than they did in the city as a whole. While only about 15 percent of Hispanics and Latinos were of Honduran origin across the city, in North Kenner they

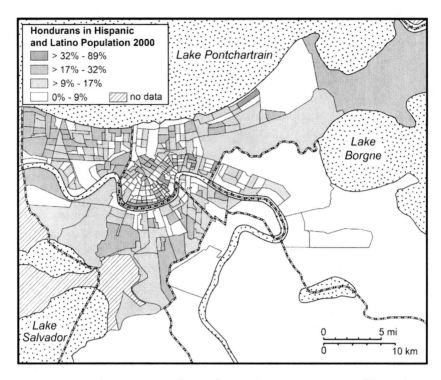

FIG. 21. The Honduran-origin population of New Orleans as a proportion of the total Hispanic and Latino population of each census tract in 2000.

comprised between 17 and 32 percent in a majority of census tracts. Hondurans dominated to an even greater degree in some other census tracts, up to 89 percent of all Hispanics and Latinos, but those tracts occurred scattered across the city rather than in a large contiguous block.

That concentration and dominance in a particular neighborhood has allowed Hondurans to create a landscape that both reflects and reinforces their sense of place. With the residential shift from the Barrio Lempira to the suburbs, the landscape elements essential to sense of place disappeared from the Lower Garden District but reemerged along the Williams Boulevard corridor in North Kenner (fig. 22).[22] The *supermercados*, meaning Latino supermarkets, provide a primary example. They sell the ingredients for Honduran and other Latino cuisines but also offer services such as international money transfers and telephone calls. Some have a lunch counter or restaurant section. Many other types of Latino businesses and services also occur in the corridor, either

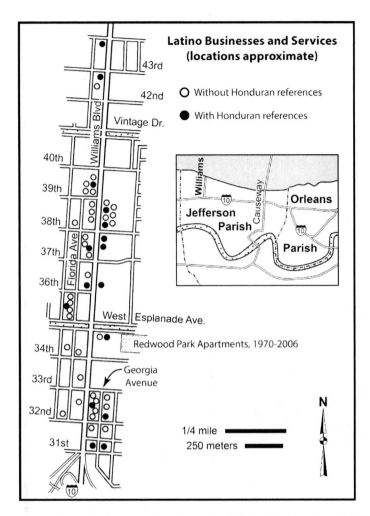

FIG. 22. Latino businesses and services in the Williams Boulevard corridor, North Kenner.

directly on Williams Boulevard or on Florida and Georgia avenues, narrower streets a block to the west and east: restaurants, lawyers, money exchange and transfer offices, hair and nail salons, religious bookstores, churches, and so on. In all, based on signage, fieldwork identified fifty-two such places. They either explicitly identify as Latino through the use of adjectives such as Honduran, Cuban, and Mexican or use signage with Spanish words such as *abogado* (lawyer), *comida* (food), *belleza* (beauty), *dinero* (money), and so on.

Some of those businesses and services reinforce the Honduran sense of place with various landscape elements. Fixed-feature landscape elements such as architecture tend to be in the same generic commercial style as in many US suburbs. But sixteen of the fifty-two Latino businesses and services use semi-fixed landscape elements to help create a Honduran sense of place (fig. 23). They use signage with nationalist imagery such as the entire Honduran flag or one of its elements such as its five stars and deep, cerulean blue. Others use the adjective Honduran or its Spanish version, *hondureño*. One uses the adjective Ceibeño, meaning a person from La Ceiba, the third-largest city in Honduras and largest on the Caribbean coast. A few of the other thirty-six Latino businesses and services display Mexican, Cuban, and Brazilian semi-fixed landscape elements, but most are generic. Such everyday landscapes provide not only visual reminders of a substantial Honduran presence but spaces in which

FIG. 23. Montage of Honduran semi-fixed landscape elements in the Williams Boulevard corridor. The grayscale image cannot convey the deep, cerulean blue that dominates the color schemes, evoking the Honduran flag. Photographs by A. Sluyter, 2007–12.

Hondurans can foster social capital critical for developing and maintaining attachment to place. In contrast, formal, institutional, fixed landscape elements such as the colossal statue of Francisco Morazán Quesada on Basin Street and the United Fruit Building on St. Charles Avenue do more to evoke the historical depth of the relationship between New Orleans and Hondurans than directly relate to the everyday lives of most Hondurans.[23]

Interviews provide further understanding of the processes through which a strong Honduran sense of place emerged in New Orleans. Some concern key actors such as employees of the Honduran consulate and community leaders who have played pivotal roles in that process. Others concern Latinos inside and outside of the Honduran community who have participated in the process through the countless thoughts and acts of everyday life.

The interviews indicate that the inflated estimate of a Honduran population of a hundred thousand derives from speculation by the Honduran consulate in New Orleans, seemingly motivated by self-preservation. The standard response by consular staff to inquiries from the media, politicians, and the public has long been, since at least the 1980s, that about a hundred thousand people of Honduran origin live in New Orleans. Consular officials admitted, however, that they based that estimate on speculation rather than on census statistics or any type of systematic survey. They generally thought the estimate might be somewhat inflated, with one official venturing that perhaps *only* about eighty thousand Hondurans lived in the city and another that *only* fifty thousand lived in the consulate's entire territory, which includes all of Louisiana and southern Mississippi.[24] They also admitted that they had noted a decline in the number of passport renewal applications over the 1990s, concluded that the number of Honduran residents in New Orleans was decreasing, and discussed the possibility that the consulate might be closed. The consulate nonetheless remained open and its staff continued to disseminate the estimate that some one hundred thousand of the city's residents were of Honduran origin. One of the reasons for the commitment to maintain a consulate in Louisiana through the decline of the 1990s might have been that the Honduran president from 1998 through 2002, Carlos Roberto Flores, had completed two degrees at LSU and his wife, Mary Flake Flores, had been born in Louisiana. Louisiana also sent several thousand National Guard troops to Honduras to assist with the recovery from the devastation of Hurricane Mitch in the late 1990s, prompting further goodwill by the Honduran government toward its consulate in New Orleans.

That official narrative that New Orleans is a *ciudad hondureña,* a Honduran city, is reflected in and reinforced by the collective narratives of many Honduran families. One, recounted by a second-generation Honduran woman resident, illustrates.

> Hondurans new and old in New Orleans share a common belief that New Orleans has been a Honduran city, at least as far as Hispanics go, for a long time because we arrived here on the banana boats, stayed, and brought our families. It is kind of our heritage. This is the history of many here. The majority of Hondurans here have at least one family story that they love to tell about a parent, grandparent, aunt or uncle that was the first to arrive here through the fruit company. We got here through my uncle who worked on the docks. My best Honduran friend's family has been here even longer. Her grandparents immigrated here. I think that was in the forties.[25]

Another Honduran, a man, expresses just how deeply his community believes that New Orleans is a Honduran city in the same sense that Miami is a Cuban one: "There is history between Honduras and New Orleans, because here is where the banana companies imported their bananas from Hondurans. We are the majority here, like Cubans in Miami. For us, it is the best place to live in the US. I feel great here. To me, it is like being in Honduras."[26]

The focus group made up of pre-Katrina Latino residents of Honduran and non-Honduran origin universally expressed disbelief when presented with Census 2000 statistics that enumerated more residents of Mexican than of Honduran origin. They tended to favor their own observations over census statistics, argued that it was common knowledge that New Orleans was the third-largest Honduran city in the world and that anyone could plainly see how it was a Honduran city. They also rationalized that the census vastly undercounted Hondurans and that many second-generation Hondurans, especially those who had only one Honduran parent, chose not to identify themselves as Latinos of any type.

Non-Honduran Latinos offered key insights into the process through which the Honduran community and its sense of place became so dominant. Most believed that while many Mexicans, Guatemalans, and Salvadorans might live in New Orleans, Hondurans dominate the social hierarchy and therefore appear more numerous than their actual population. Non-Hondurans believe that Hondurans own most of the Latino-oriented businesses and preferentially hire other Hondurans. They believe that Hondurans dominate employment in bilingual positions in the private and public sectors as well as charities and churches. And they believe that Hondurans are thereby able to mediate interactions between non-Honduran Latinos and the broader society in ways that perpetuate Honduran dominance, such as limiting the employment opportunities and access to public services of non-Honduran Latinos.

In one example, a Salvadoran woman expressed her belief that Honduran ownership of the supermercados limited the ability of Salvadorans to make, sell, and promote their traditional cuisine, the ability to do so being key to establishing a sense of place related to ethnic origin. The lunch counters of the supermercados sell *pupusas,* she explained. Pupusas are a traditional dish of El Salvador that consists of a thick corn tortilla filled with some combination of cheese, pork, and beans. While they also occur in Honduras and Guatemala, especially along the frontiers with El Salvador, only Salvadorans consider them part of their national cuisine and therefore a key element of their ethnic identity. Reina expressed a twofold frustration with the pupusas available at the supermercado lunch counters. She believed that the Honduran owners and employees made inauthentic pupusas. And she believed that Salvadorans could not open authentic *pupuserías,* meaning stores that make pupusas, because they could not compete with the larger, established supermercados: "There are a lot of Latinos who like to buy pupusas in New Orleans, but there really are no Salvadoran pupuserías. So you have to go to Honduran places to buy them. That means if you are a Salvadoran lady who wants to make and sell pupusas, you would probably have to deal with a Honduran business owner."[27]

A Mexican man provided another example that emphasizes both the importance of cuisine to sense of place and the belief that Hondurans dominate control of Latino cuisine and other elements of sense of place. "It is difficult to find real Mexican food in New Orleans. All the Latino restaurants serve Honduran food.... New Orleans is a Honduran city, unlike Houston. There everyone is Mexican, and you can get real Mexican food."[28] In the case of the Honduran community, then, residential concentration in Jefferson Parish together with other Latino groups has resulted in intragroup coherence but intergroup conflict. Concentration in a cluster of census tracts in North Kenner has facilitated greater interaction among Hondurans, their accumulation of social capital, and increased economic opportunity. In turn, the community's prosperity has attracted more Hondurans and further increased its population, strengthened community solidarity, and built a durable sense of place interwoven with ethnic, family, and personal identity. In contrast, the dominance of the Honduran community, both in terms of population and social capital, over other Latino communities with residential concentrations in North Kenner has resulted in intergroup conflict.

Hondurans in the Twenty-First Century

Katrina reversed the apparent decline in the population of the Honduran community, similarly to the Cuban community but much more dramatically. With more than two-thirds of the city's residents of Honduran origin living in Jefferson Parish by 2005, the majority escaped the direct impact of persistent flooding. Only 23 percent of the 7,503 Hondurans enumerated in Census 2000 resided in census tracts inundated in 2005, about half the proportion of the city's total population directly impacted by Katrina. Many of those living in Orleans Parish, however, had been concentrated in Mid-City and lost their homes and businesses, including a supermercado, restaurant, nightclub, and others near the intersection of South Carrollton and Tulane Avenues. Some Hondurans in Jefferson Parish also lost their homes to wind damage, the most notable case being the Redwood Park Apartments near the intersection of Williams Boulevard and West Esplanade Avenue. Strong winds ripped off roofs and broke windows to such a degree that the complex became uninhabitable. After much controversy over the lack of affordable housing and ethnic discrimination, the Redwood Park Apartments were demolished in 2006, part of a long-standing effort across the city to reduce the availability of low income housing and thereby reduce the options for poor people, especially blacks, to live in the city, draw on social services, and vote in elections. The site remained a large vacant lot in 2012, a missing landscape element that through absence reminded many Hondurans of their family and community narratives. Some Hondurans who lost their homes relocated within New Orleans while others left the city entirely.[29]

Katrina also had a significant indirect impact on the Honduran community because many of the reconstruction workers came from Honduras, either directly or via other places in the United States. Those newcomers had long-standing knowledge of and social connections with the New Orleans Honduran community. Such transnational social networks of friends and families already established in New Orleans assisted newly arrived catrachos to establish themselves, from locating housing and employment to overcoming culture shock and starting small businesses. In discussing such transnational social capital, one Honduran woman who arrived after Katrina exemplifies many of the interviews. "I am from a small village near San Pedro [Sula]. I have always known about New Orleans. There have always been people from my village living or working in New Orleans. In fact, many people in my village even celebrate Mardi Gras."[30]

At the same time, push factors have continued to encourage Hondurans to move to the United States. In part those factors are economic, but political turmoil and an increase in violent crime have also encouraged Hondurans to leave. Murders related to narcotics trafficking plague San Pedro Sula, the largest city of the Caribbean lowlands once so central to the banana plantations of United Fruit and therefore intimately involved in the social networks of many catrachos in New Orleans. As the drug trade has escalated, the national government has militarized the lowlands with US involvement.[31]

Census 2010 reveals the dramatic result of Katrina's direct and indirect impacts, as illustrated in figure 6. Between 2000 and 2010, the city's enumerated population of Honduran origin grew from 7,503 to 22,335, a threefold increase. Some of that increase might be due to the restoration of the examples of "another Hispanic, Latino, or Spanish origin" to the write-in box on the census form, but a Honduran consular official recounted how the associated increase in the number of passport-renewal applications ended all discussion of closing the consulate.

Honduran residential geography continued to change during that population boom. Like Cubans, Hondurans also became more concentrated in Jefferson Parish: a little over 76 percent lived there in 2010 compared to about 70 percent a decade earlier; only some 20 percent lived in Orleans Parish compared to 26 percent in 2000 (fig. 24). Because Hondurans constituted the single largest Latino-origin group attracted to New Orleans to work in the reconstruction effort, however, many of the newcomers had to settle elsewhere than North Kenner and Metairie because of limitations on the availability of affordable housing. The loss of the Redwood Park Apartments, home to some 1,800 people before Katrina, contributed significantly to that lack of housing. The newcomers therefore rebuilt the Honduran presence in Westbank Jefferson Parish lost over the 1990s, namely in Estelle and Terrytown but also in Harvey and Marrero.

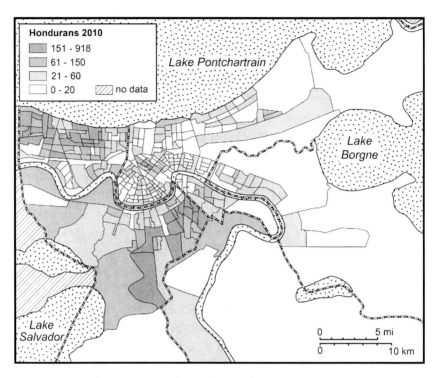

FIG. 24. The Honduran-origin population of New Orleans in 2010.

Moreover, even though not a large percentage of Hondurans lived in Orleans Parish, they did make up a large proportion of the Hispanic and Latino residents of some census tracts, most notably in Mid-City but also in Central City, Algiers, Gentilly, New Orleans East, and Village De l'Est (fig. 25).

While most of the Orleans Parish neighborhoods in which Hondurans became dominant after Katrina had a history of Latino residence, Village De l'Est had instead been central to the Vietnamese community. In particular, the neighborhood in Village De l'Est known as Versailles had been a concentration of Catholic Vietnamese immigrants since the 1970s, political refugees from the Vietnam War. Residents of Vietnamese origin so dominated Versailles, both in terms of population and business ownership, that the neighborhood became known as Little Vietnam. Many semi-fixed landscape elements, from store and restaurant signage to a famers' market each Saturday morning that featured the ingredients of Vietnamese cuisine, reinforced the community's sense of

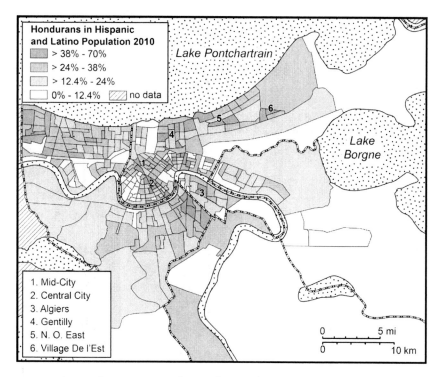

Honced in image:

Hondurans in Hispanic and Latino Population 2010

> 38% - 70%
> 24% - 38%
> 12.4% - 24%
0% - 12.4%   no data

Lake Pontchartrain

Lake Borgne

6
5
4
1
2
3

1. Mid-City
2. Central City
3. Algiers
4. Gentilly
5. N. O. East
6. Village De l'Est

0 ⎯ 5 mi
0 ⎯ 10 km

FIG. 25. The Honduran-origin population of New Orleans as a proportion of the total Hispanic and Latino population of each census tract in 2010.

place. After Katrina, Honduran and other Latino reconstruction workers began to live in the neighborhood. Village De l'Est and nearby neighborhoods in northern St. Bernard and eastern Orleans parishes had suffered some of the worst flood damage in the city, making for many employment opportunities. As a consequence of the influx of reconstruction workers, Vietnamese stores began to stock Latino food items as well as Latin American phone cards and money transfer services. Latinos attended the Mary Queen of Vietnam Catholic Church, which accommodated the new parishioners by offering a mass in Spanish alongside the long-standing one in Vietnamese. A family of Mexican origin from Houston moved into the neighborhood to open a restaurant called the Taquería México. The same family operates taco trucks, known as *loncheras,* to serve the demand from Latino reconstruction workers. And semi-fixed landscape elements with Latino elements began to occur among the dominant Vietnamese ones (fig. 26).[32]

FIG. 26. Sign of the Taquería México restaurant in Little Vietnam, Village De l'Est. Photograph by A. Sluyter, February 22, 2007.

The dramatic increase in the city's Honduran-origin population did not, however, improve its rank from the sixth-largest Honduran community in the United States (table 7).[33] The Honduran population of the New Orleans-Metairie-Kenner MSA was higher than for the four parishes, 25,112 compared to 22,335, but not enough to pass even Washington, DC, for fifth place. Between 2000 and 2010, the Honduran-origin population of New Orleans had increased threefold but so had that of the United States as a whole, from 217,569 to 633,401. Many Honduran newcomers had gone to New York, Miami, Los Angles, Houston, and Washington, DC. Hondurans also increased their proportions of the Hispanic and Latino as well as the total populations in each of those cities and nationally, from 0.62 percent in 2000 to 1.26 percent for the United States as a whole. But in New Orleans, Hondurans made the greatest gains in their relative dominance of the Hispanic and Latino population, increasing from nearly 14 percent in 2000 to a little over 27 percent in 2010. While New Orleans remained the sixth most populous Honduran community in the

TABLE 7. Honduran-origin population for six metropolitan areas, Louisiana, and the United States, Census 2010

Rank	Place (MSA or CMSA)[a]	Honduran-origin population (number)	Total population (number)	Hispanic & Latino population (number)	Hondurans in total population (percent)	Hondurans in Hispanic & Latino population (percent)
1	New York–Northern New Jersey–Long Island	97,854	18,897,109	4,327,560	0.52	2.26
2	Miami–Fort Lauderdale–Pompano Beach	74,357	5,564,635	2,312,929	1.34	3.22
3	Houston–Sugar Land–Baytown	53,598	5,946,800	2,099,412	0.90	2.55
4	Los Angeles–Long Beach–Santa Ana	46,044	12,828,837	5,700,862	0.36	0.81
5	Washington, DC–Arlington–Alexandria	37,665	5,582,170	770,795	0.68	4.89
6	New Orleans–Metairie–Kenner	25,112	1,167,764	91,922	2.15	27.32
	Louisiana	30,617	4,533,372	192,560	0.68	15.90
	United States	633,401	308,745,538	50,477,594	0.21	1.26

[a]See note to table 4.

nation, that community's relative dominance over the city's other Latino communities had doubled. Katrina, in that sense, certainly consolidated the status of New Orleans as the Honduran capital of the United States.

CREATING "THE THIRD LARGEST HONDURAN CITY" in the world out of a few thousand Honduran residents seems like "magical urbanism," but in reality various mundane processes interacted to create the prominent Honduran side of New Orleans.[34] The banana trade made the city the US gateway for Honduran immigration during the mid-twentieth century and thereby New Orleans, despite being overtaken in the 1970s by several other cities in terms of Honduran-origin population, remained prominent in the national catracho narrative. Honduran residential concentration in North Kenner resulted in social cohesion, dominance over other Latino-origin groups, and a landscape that reflected and reinforced the belief in New Orleans as a Honduran city: "Honduras es New Orleans."[35] While in absolute terms the Honduran population remained modest and even declined in the late twentieth century, Katrina combined with Hondurans' transnational linkages to the city and their strong sense of place to increase their relative dominance to at least a quarter of the total Latino population. Considering that the census undercounts Hondurans even more than Cubans and Mexicans, their actual proportion of the Latino population might be substantially higher, approaching a third. Moreover, Hondurans are at least that dominant in contiguous blocks of census tracts across large areas of the city.

As figure 6 illustrates, the Mexican-origin population of New Orleans also surged dramatically after Katrina, although not as much as for the Honduran community. Yet the city's history of connections to Mexico differs greatly from that of Honduras, Cuba, and Spain's Canary Islands. The Mexican community therefore had its own distinct residential geography, and Katrina has impacted that community differently than other Hispanic and Latino groups.

4. MEXICANS

Poor Mexico—so far from God, so close to the United States.
—Anonymous, nineteenth century (sometimes attributed
to Porfirio Díaz, president of Mexico, 1876–1911)

How do I ensure that New Orleans is not overrun by Mexican workers?
—Ray Nagin, mayor of New Orleans, quoted in Campo-Flores,
"A New Spice in the Gumbo," 2005

WHILE THE EIGHTEENTH- AND nineteenth-century flows of products, people, and ideas from Mexico to New Orleans resembled those from Cuba, subsequent ones did not. In the eighteenth century, a small contraband trade between colonial Latin America and French New Orleans gave way to a larger, officially sanctioned one when Louisiana became a Spanish colony and its commerce greatly increased along with its population. The city's relationship with ports around the Gulf of Mexico further intensified over the nineteenth century when Spanish rule ended in both Mexico and Louisiana, New Orleans grew even more populous, and it became the principal US gateway to northern Latin America.[1]

The Mexican-American War, which lasted from 1846 through 1848, made Louisiana the dominant pole in its relationship with Mexico in the same way that the Spanish-American War would allow New Orleans to dominate Havana half a century later. Filibusters, motivated by the settlement of thousands of US citizens in northern Mexico, especially Texas, actually focused their attention there earlier than on Cuba. Their campaigns culminated in the outbreak of the Texas War of Independence in 1835, defeat the next year of the army of General Antonio López de Santa Ana at the Battle of San Jacinto, and foundation of the Lone Star Republic. Subsequent popular support for "manifest destiny" resulted in US annexation of Texas in 1845 and an ensuing war with Mexico in which New Orleans played a principal role. The city served as the main port for marshaling and embarking troops for the beachheads at Veracruz, Tampico, and Matamoros. Federal funds flowed into the Crescent City to pay military wages, purchase supplies, and hire troop transports. In December of 1846, General Winfield Scott departed New Orleans, landed with ten thousand troops at Veracruz the following March, and occupied Mexico City six months later. As a condition for withdrawal of the occupying army, Santa Ana ceded to the United States a portion of Mexican territory stretching from Texas to California. If the boosters of New Orleans commerce had had their way, the United States would also have annexed southern Mexico and built a canal across the Isthmus of Tehuantepec. New Orleans would have become the hub of a shipping corridor that stretched from New York City through the Erie Canal, the Great Lakes, the Illinois and Michigan Canal, the Mississippi River, and across the Gulf of Mexico, the isthmus, and on to the Pacific and the goldfields of California.[2]

While the annexation of Tehuantepec never occurred, the loss of so much territory in the north fomented such domestic opposition to Santa Ana's continued rule that Mexican exiles established a community in New Orleans to plot the dictator's overthrow. They included Melchor Ocampo, José María Mata, and others who would play notable roles in Mexico's history. Benito Juárez, a Zapotec from a mountain village in Oaxaca and governor of that state from 1846 to 1852, became the best known among them. In the wake of the Mexican-American War he emerged as a critic of Santa Ana and in 1853 had to seek exile in New Orleans. There he joined a Mexican expatriate community that Census 1850 enumerated at 241, nearly as many as the 289 Cubans but only a little more than 1 percent of all 17,291 Mexican-born residents of the United States. While working in a French Quarter cigar factory, Juárez conspired with Mexican and other exiles, like the Cuban nationalist Pedro Santacilia, to establish republics in Latin America. From their base in New Orleans they supplied arms and ammunition to rebel troops, ousting Santa Ana in 1855. Juárez participated in drafting the new Mexican constitution and became president. Then, in the early 1860s, as the Mexican civil war that ensued came to an end and the one in the United States escalated, the French were able to invade and install Maximilian von Habsburg as emperor of Mexico. After the republicans regained power in 1867, however, Juárez resumed the presidency and served until his death in 1872.[3]

Porfirio Díaz, another long-serving Mexican president, briefly also used nineteenth-century New Orleans as a base from which to plot revolt. After several attempted coups, in 1876 he succeeded in overthrowing President Sebastián Lerdo de Tejada, who had succeeded Juárez. The dictatorship that Díaz established would endure for the next thirty-five years, until the Mexican Revolution sent him into exile in Europe in 1911. During his long, autocratic presidency, Díaz did much to industrialize Mexico on the basis of foreign investment. As part of his effort to convince European and US investors that Mexico was a stable, modernizing nation, Díaz financed a large Mexican pavilion at the New Orleans World's Fair of 1884–85, commonly known as the World's Industrial and Cotton Centennial Exposition. He also granted foreign investors terms so favorable that the Guggenheims, Hearsts, Rockefellers, and others were able to acquire enormous Mexican cattle ranches and plantations, mines and smelters, railroads, and oil fields.[4]

One immediate impact on New Orleans involved music. Mexican participation in the city's World's Fair introduced musical elements that proved key to the emergence of jazz. Various Mexican orchestras, folkloric groups, and a military brass band led by Encarnación Payen performed at the fairgrounds, which later became Audubon Park, and thereafter made the city a regular stop on their US tours (fig. 27). Jazz, as it emerged over the next several decades, thereby incorporated Mexican stylistic elements such as plucking the bass violin; instrumentation, especially the saxophone; and compositions, most notably "Sobre las Olas," or "Over the Waves."[5]

Mexicans in the Twentieth Century

Most notably for the long-term future of the Mexican community in New Orleans, Díaz's modernization policies initiated the mass migration of workers from Mexico to the United States. Low wages, extreme concentration of wealth and property, the violent repression of political opposition and organized labor, rural landlessness, rapid urbanization, and associated burgeoning population all encouraged Mexicans to leave during the closing decades of the nineteenth century and the first of the twentieth. Higher wages in the country to the north, social networks produced by companies operating in both countries, new north-south railroad lines, and a relatively open border attracted them northward. The violence of the Mexican Revolution in 1910–20, which overthrew the Díaz dic-

FIG. 27. Mexican military band at the World's Industrial and Cotton Centennial Exposition, 1884–85. Reproduced courtesy of the Historic New Orleans Collection, acc. no. 1982.127.225.

tatorship, and the Cristero War that followed in 1926–29 further encouraged Mexicans to leave. Meanwhile, the First World War depressed European immigration to the United States from 1914 through 1918 and thereby increased demand for Mexican workers. Following the war, the Johnson-Reed Act severely restricted immigration from Asia and southern and eastern Europe, resulting in continued demand for Mexican workers. The number of Mexican-born US residents therefore increased steadily, from 42,435 according to Census 1870 to 639,017 by Census 1930. Over the 1930s, however, the high unemployment rates of the Great Depression resulted in mass deportations of Mexicans, many of them undocumented migrant workers.[6]

The immigration statistics of 1899–1910 reveal the destination states of only those Mexicans who legally entered the United States but nonetheless indicate that New Orleans was a marginal destination during the initial phase of the mass, northward migration of workers. Out of a total of 9,555,698 immigrants during that decade, the United States admitted 41,914 from Mexico. The vast majority, 90 percent, went to the four border states—32,078 to Texas alone—with Louisiana attracting only 123. Census 1930 consequently enumerated only 1,083 residents in the four parishes of New Orleans who had been born in Mexico. Although their population had grown by more than four times since Census 1850, they totaled little more than two-tenths of a percent of the city's population, remained highly concentrated in Orleans Parish, and made up less than two-tenths of a percent of all 669,490 US residents of Mexican birth. Nonetheless, they were the Crescent City's largest community of Latino expatriates. Mexicans therefore dominated organization of the New Orleans Latin American Club and its inaugural event on September 16, 1926—a celebration of Mexican Independence Day.[7]

The entry of the United States into the Second World War in late 1941 revived the northward flow of Mexican workers. In order to meet demand for agricultural labor during wartime, the federal government passed the Mexican Farm Labor Program. That particular legislation, popularly known as the Bracero Program, ended with the peace, demobilization of the troops, and an end to the labor scarcity. A succession of other laws and treaties has nonetheless continued to permit employers to recruit Mexican employees to temporarily work in the United States. The number of such guest workers reached a peak in the 1950s, with nearly half a million admitted each year. Mexican-born residents therefore increased from 377,433 in Census 1940 to 450,562 in Census 1950. They and their US-born children worked predominantly as farm laborers, and the rural focus of that northward flow of labor ensured that it largely bypassed New Orleans.[8]

The isolation from the networks that brought so many rural workers from Mexico to the United States over the mid-twentieth century resulted in not only the relatively small size but also the distinctive character of the city's Mexican community. Interviews in the late 1940s by a graduate student at Tulane University indicate that entrepreneurs, diplomats, and academics rather than guest workers typified the community. Wealthy Mexican families sent their daughters to finishing schools in the Garden District and Uptown. Their brothers studied law at Tulane and Loyola universities. They so dominated the Latin American Club that they renamed it the Mexican Patriotic Committee, thereby thoroughly distinguishing themselves from the vast majority of Mexicans who had come northward because they had so little opportunity to earn a living in Mexico. The

New Orleans Mexican community, in contrast, was made up of members of the elite that controlled businesses and politics in Mexico. They celebrated their patriotism by supporting erection of a colossal statue of Juárez on the Basin Street neutral ground, or median, in 1972 in order to commemorate the historic connections between the city and their country of origin on the hundredth anniversary of his death (fig. 28).[9]

FIG. 28. Monument honoring Benito Juárez on the Basin Street neutral ground, erected in 1972. Photograph by A. Sluyter, January 14, 2007.

Despite the professional character of the city's Mexican community in the mid-twentieth century, literature that featured Mexicans in New Orleans at that time employed tropes more relevant to the rural, impoverished agricultural laborers who then made up the majority of US residents of Mexican origin. In the 1947 play *A Streetcar Named Desire*, for example, Tennessee Williams used a blind Mexican woman who peddled flowers on the street to foretell the demise of the protagonist's desire to recapture the past grandeur of her ancestral plantation. The peddler walks the streets dressed in a dark shawl, carrying brightly painted tin flowers used at funerals, and repeating her call, "Flowers for the dead." The refrain haunts the Southern belle, Blanche DuBois, throughout the play until she goes insane and enters a mental institution in the final act. While the play won a Pulitzer Prize in 1948, the effectiveness of the Mexican character had more to do with US stereotypes of Mexico and Mexicans as indigent and superstitious than with anything related to the urbane Mexican community of New Orleans in the mid-twentieth century.[10]

The end of major guest-worker programs in the 1960s only marked an escalation in the northward flow of Mexicans, both documented and undocumented. Enumerations of residents of Mexican origin increased steadily from Census 1970 through Census 2000: 4.5 million in 1970, 8.7 million in 1980, 13.5 million in 1990, and 20.6 million in 2000. Those figures equate to growth rates of 93 percent over the 1970s, 55 percent over the 1980s, and 52 percent over the 1990s. Between 1970 and 2000, residents of Mexican origin increased from about 2 percent to more than 7 percent of the total population and consistently made up between 50 and 60 percent of all residents of Hispanic and Latino origin. Many of those millions of Mexicans, hundreds of thousands per year, came as immigrants or guest workers. But Mexicans also comprise the single largest group of undocumented US residents. Moreover, the US-born children of those documented and undocumented residents have become an ever-larger proportion of the Mexican-origin population, ensuring that its continued growth will no longer rely on immigration.[11]

New Orleans remained largely isolated from that enormous increase in US citizens and other residents of Mexican origin. As illustrated in figure 6, even considering that the census undercounts undocumented and itinerant residents, New Orleans experienced much more modest growth of its relatively small Mexican community during the late twentieth century than the United States as a whole. Census 1970 enumerated only 2,337 residents of New Orleans who considered themselves to be of Mexican origin, suggesting little growth since Census 1930 had enumerated 1,083 residents of Mexican birth. As the city's economy boomed in the 1970s, the Mexican-origin population did grow at a rate greater than the national one. The increase from 2,337 in 1970 to 7,770 in 1980, in fact, equates to a growth rate roughly triple the national one. Many of those new residents of Mexican origin came from Texas, attracted to employment in the oil industry or related jobs in construction, shipyards, and fabrication shops. Companies actively recruited Mexican employees because of their familiarity with the oil industry and their work ethic, sending recruiters to Mexico to arrange contracts, visas, and transportation. As the price of oil and the city's economy declined over the 1980s, however, so did the size of the Mexican community, to 6,535 by Census 1990, a decrease of nearly 16 percent compared to a national increase of 55 percent. Modest growth occurred over the 1990s, but the 24 percent increase to 8,111 by Census 2000 amounted to less than half the national growth rate of 53 percent and paled in comparison to the even higher rates of increase for Atlanta and other cities in the New Latino South. The dramatic surge in the Mexican-origin population of the United States over the late twentieth century thereby largely bypassed New Orleans. As one consequence, the city's Mexican consulate became so underutilized compared to others in the United States that in 2002 the Secretaría de Relaciones Exteriores closed it despite the historic affinity that Mexicans feel toward New Orleans, especially as a former place of exile for one of their principal national heroes, Juárez. The Houston consulate took over responsibility for Mexicans resident in Louisiana and Mississippi.[12]

Not only did the Mexican community of New Orleans pale in terms of growth compared to the nation as a whole and to the cities of the New Latino South, it lost its early twentieth-century dominance over the city's other Latino communities. The Cuban community had become the largest by 1970, and the Mexican community had to vie with the Honduran one for even second place. That situation had reversed by 2000, with the Mexican and Honduran communities still about the same size but substantially larger than the Cuban one. Despite the greater prominence of the Honduran community, some residents of Mexican origin nonetheless achieved influence in the broader Latino community. One, Jimmie Martinez, ran for and nearly won a position on Kenner's city council in 1982. Another, Carmen Llewellyn, founded the Mexican Cultural Center of the South.

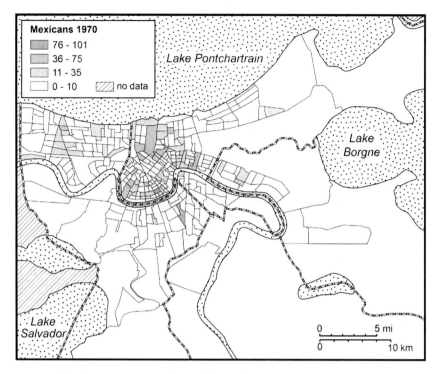

FIG. 29. The Mexican-origin population of New Orleans in 1970.

Figures 29–32 reveal how the residential pattern of the Mexican community changed between 1970 and 2000. In some ways the changes parallel those of the Cuban and Honduran communities. In 1970 the Mexican community was concentrated in the Garden District and the Mid-City and Uptown neighborhoods, with 65 percent resident in Orleans Parish and only 28 percent in Jefferson. Over the 1970s, however, as the Mexican community more than tripled in size, most of that growth occurred in Jefferson Parish. By Census 1980, the Mexican-origin residents of Orleans Parish had more than doubled in number and become established in many of the parish's neighborhoods beyond Mid-City, Uptown, and the Garden District. The suburbs of New Orleans East, in particular, had attracted residents of Mexican origin. But even more rapid growth had taken place in Jefferson Parish: the share of the community living in Orleans Parish had declined to 48 percent while that living in Jefferson Parish had increased to 44 percent. That westward and southward shift in the residential geography of the community continued through its population decline over

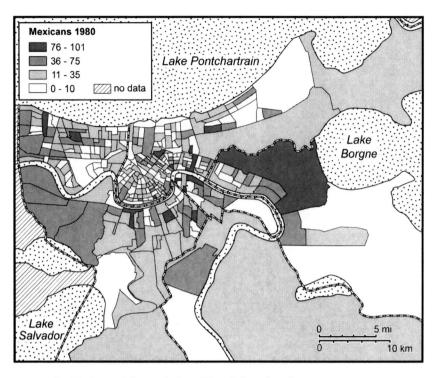

FIG. 30. The Mexican-origin population of New Orleans in 1980.

the 1980s and recovery of the 1990s. By Census 2000 the proportions living in the two parishes had nearly completely reversed relative to those of Census 1970, with 32 percent in Orleans Parish and 60 percent in Jefferson Parish.

Despite that similarity to the changing residential patterns of the Honduran and Cuban communities, the Mexican community displayed a somewhat broader distribution across the four parishes than the others. While many of Mexican origin chose to reside in North Kenner and Metairie north of Interstate 10, together with many of Honduran and Cuban origin, many others chose neighborhoods in eastern Orleans, southern Jefferson, and northern St. Bernard and Plaquemines parishes. Comparison of the Cuban, Honduran, and Mexican residential patterns of Census 2000, when the three communities all had populations between five thousand and nine thousand, reveals that the Mexican community had a greater presence on the eastern and southern sides of the city than the Honduran and Cuban communities. As one measure of that difference, nearly 9 percent of residents of Mexican origin lived in Plaquemines

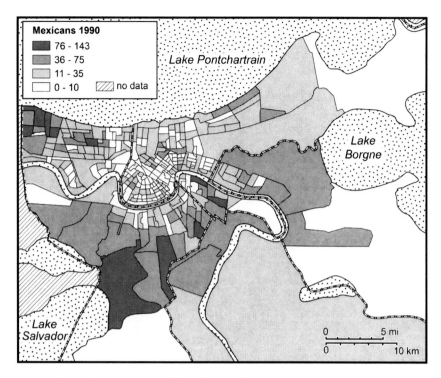

FIG. 31. The Mexican-origin population of New Orleans in 1990.

and St. Bernard parishes while only some 4 percent of residents of Honduran and Cuban origin lived there. That distinct residential pattern has to do with the concentration of petrochemical plants and related shipyards and fabrication shops along the southern and eastern margins of the city. Mexican workers attracted to those businesses beginning in the 1970s chose to reside near their places of employment.

Interviews reveal the sense of place and other aspects of identity that the Mexican community has constructed in relation to other Latino communities, especially the Honduran one. A man from San Luis Potosí who arrived in New Orleans in 1975 remembered how "the number of Hondurans simply seemed to keep growing."[13] Another Mexican, a middle-aged woman from Ciudad Juárez, first came to New Orleans in 1979 and eventually, after periodically moving to various US cities, settled in northern Metairie. She compared that neighborhood to the places she had lived in Texas and California: "Here we were not the majority. If you went to a Hispanic business, the owner was Cuban, Honduran,

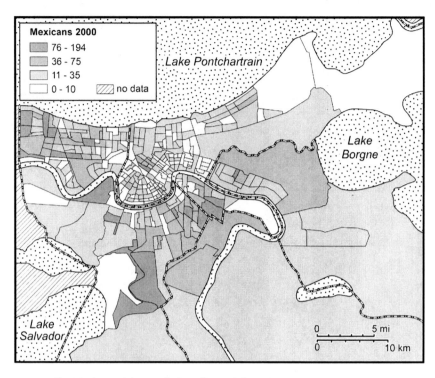

Lake Pontchartrain

Lake Borgne

Lake Salvador

0   5 mi

0   10 km

FIG. 32. The Mexican-origin population of New Orleans in 2000.

or Salvadoran. That was different for us. Even the idiom of Spanish was difficult for me to understand."[14] Despite the Honduran and Mexican communities
growing to a similar size by Census 2000, the deep-seated belief in Honduran
dominance caused many in the Mexican community to question the accuracy
of the statistics: "They don't make sense to me. It seems the majority of Hispanics that I meet here are from Central America, usually Honduras. I mean, I have
Mexican friends and acquaintances, but we are the minority."[15]

In part that perception relates to the different residential geographies of
the Mexican versus the other Latino communities. Although the Honduran
and Mexican communities had approximately similar populations in 2000, the
Honduran one was concentrated in fewer census tracts than the Mexican one.
As a result, the Mexican community could achieve relative dominance over
other Latino groups only in census tracts on the eastern and southern fringes
of the city, establishing restaurants and other landscape elements that strength-

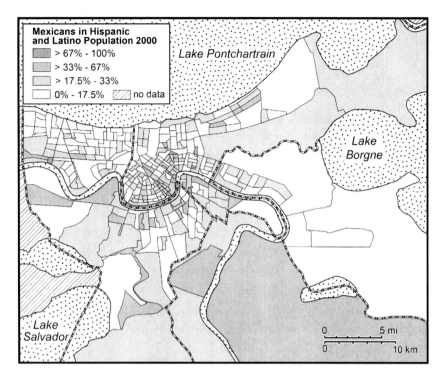

Mexicans in Hispanic and Latino Population 2000
- > 67% - 100%
- > 33% - 67%
- > 17.5% - 33%
- 0% - 17.5%
- no data

Lake Pontchartrain

Lake Borgne

Lake Salvador

0   5 mi
0   10 km

FIG. 33. The Mexican-origin population of New Orleans as a proportion of the total Hispanic and Latino population of each census tract in 2000.

ened their sense of place (fig. 33). As one interviewee recalled, "I think it wasn't until after Katrina that Mexicans became more common here. I mean, when I first moved here [from Oaxaca], I worked in a kitchen in a downtown hotel. Everyone Hispanic was from Central America, and if you went to an authentic Hispanic restaurant, it was probably owned by Hondurans. There were some Mexican places on the West Bank, but not really any in New Orleans."[16]

That residential pattern achieved a degree of segregation between the Mexican and the Honduran communities. Mexicans living on the southern and eastern margins of the city did not experience the same sorts of conflicts with Hondurans as Latino groups concentrated in North Kenner, such as Cubans. Instead, the residential pattern of the Mexican community overlaps more than other Latino groups with that of the Isleño community. Although interviews suggest little interaction between the Isleño and Mexican communities, the concentration of Mexicans on the West Bank did allow them to establish their own supermercados and restaurants, essential elements in building social capital and identity related to place and ethnicity.

Mexicans in the Twenty-First Century

The Mexican community's residential geography also resulted in a greater direct impact by Katrina than suffered by the Honduran and Cuban communities. A relatively larger proportion of the Mexican community, although not nearly as large as the proportion of the Isleño community, lived or worked in inundated neighborhoods in New Orleans East and Plaquemines and St. Bernard parishes.

The greatest impact on the Mexican community as a whole, however, became the influx of reconstruction workers. Surveys in early 2006 suggested that Mexicans made up the majority of the newcomers, many of them male, undocumented, and from Texas. The appearance of taco trucks, or *loncheras*, that set up near the reconstruction job sites seemed to support those surveys, tacos being emblematic of Mexican cuisine (fig. 34). The mayor of New Orleans began to worry that the city would be "overrun by Mexican workers," while representatives of the Mexican community celebrated that it might become as dominant in New Orleans as it already was in San Antonio, not just among other Latino communities but in the city as whole.[17]

By Census 2010, the boom in reconstruction jobs had passed, but those who stayed have nearly doubled the population of the Mexican community compared to Census 2000, from 8,111 to 15,779. Mexican consular officials, community organizations such as Oportunidades NOLA, and census takers all agree that the 2010 enumeration undercounted the actual number of residents of Mexican origin. Even accepting the enumerated population of the Mexican community, however, it experienced phenomenal growth over the first decade of the twenty-first century. In absolute terms, it exceeded the growth in any other decade in the community's history. Moreover, it occurred despite the simultaneous decrease in Mexican immigration at the national scale. An epochal recession in the United States, improvement of employment opportunities in Mexico, greater violence related to narcotics trafficking along the international border, and the militarization of the border jointly resulted in a decrease from approximately 1 million immigrants in 2006 to less than half that in 2010. By 2012 the number of people returning to Mexico at least equaled and perhaps exceeded the number coming to the United States. While the Mexican-origin

FIG. 34. A *lonchera* from Houston, Texas, in Little Vietnam, Village De l'Est. *Photograph by A. Sluyter, February 22, 2007.*

population nonetheless continued to grow, from 20.6 million in 2000 to 31.8 million in 2010, most of that growth has derived from the birth of 7.2 million children to US residents of Mexican origin between 2000 and 2010—not to new immigrants.[18]

The post-Katrina shift in the residential geography of the Mexican community continued the trend of the late twentieth century (fig. 35). Census 2010 revealed that the Mexican community had continued to move its focus from Orleans to Jefferson Parish, attaining a complete reversal from the proportions of Census 1970: 65 percent in Jefferson Parish and 27 percent in Orleans. Many of the newcomers who did settle in Orleans Parish chose the eastern neighborhoods of New Orleans East and Village De l'Est. Others settled in St. Bernard, Plaquemines, and southern Jefferson parishes, maintaining the Mexican dominance over other Latino groups in those parts of the city (fig. 36).

Availability of affordable rental housing in proximity to reconstruction jobs as well as relationships between newcomers and the pre-Katrina Mexican com-

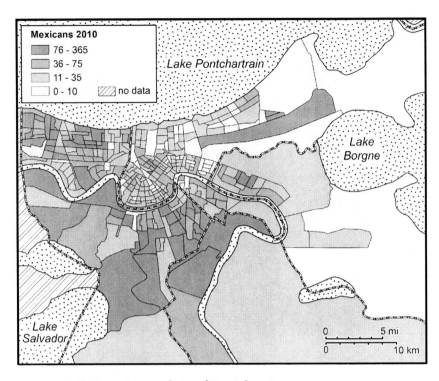

FIG. 35. The Mexican-origin population of New Orleans in 2010.

munity influenced that residential geography. In the first few months after Ka-trina, the supply of affordable rental housing could not meet the demand from incoming reconstruction workers. Jefferson Parish had most of the undamaged rental housing, despite the loss of the Redwood Park Apartments in North Ken-ner. Most of the reconstruction work, in contrast, occurred in Orleans and St. Bernard parishes. The lack of accommodations and the high rents in the four parishes necessitated high-occupancy rates—for example, eight men in a two-bedroom apartment. Interviews reveal that one person would typically hold the lease and then sublease space to the others. While those of Mexican origin would try to stay together, they sometimes shared an apartment with those of Honduran or other origins. Newcomers with social connections to the pre-Katrina Mexican community generally found housing more easily, especially on the eastern and southern margins of the city, closer to much of the reconstruc-tion work. News of employment opportunities and offers of accommodation

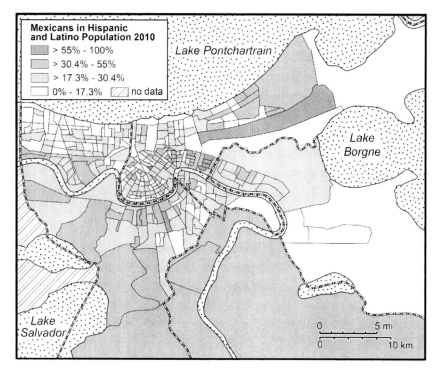

FIG. 36. The Mexican-origin population of New Orleans as a proportion of the total Hispanic and Latino population of each census tract in 2010.

went out over social networks immediately after Katrina, to other places in the United States as well as to Mexico.[19]

As a result, the two largest Latino communities—by far, as illustrated in figure 6—have maintained the same partial residential segregation as before Katrina while both their populations have increased by an order of magnitude. Comparison of figures 25 and 36 illustrates that on the eastern and southern margins of the city, Mexicans have a majority over Hondurans. After Katrina, Mexicans established even more restaurants in that part of the city, as exemplified in figure 26 by the Taquería México in Village De l'Est. Such restaurants provide employment opportunities for a few Mexicans and, even more central to the accumulation of social capital and group cohesion, places to socialize, exchange information about hometowns and employment opportunities, as well as, in general, establish a community identity and sense of place. The taco trucks that follow the reconstruction workers play a similar role, providing not only familiar cuisine but important nodes in social networks. They also visually confirm the presence of a substantial Mexican community in eastern and southern New Orleans that contributes to the emergence of a Mexican sense of place on those sides of the city in contrast to the long-established Honduran sense of place focused on its northwestern side. In neighborhoods like Village De l'Est, for example, many Hondurans also worked in reconstruction but had to eat at Mexican restaurants and taco trucks.

As the size of the Mexican community grew, so did its social capital and sense of place, further encouraging many to stay. With increased demand, the Honduran supermercados of the Williams Boulevard corridor in North Kenner began to stock a broader range of items relevant to Mexican customers, everything from tomatillos to the jerseys of popular Mexican soccer teams. The lunch counters in the supermercados began to serve tacos, *menudo, gorditas,* and *aguas frescas.* Nightclubs began to play Mexican *banda* and *norteña* alongside *bachata, reggaeton,* and *cumbia.* And Latino radio stations such as La Raza increased their Mexican programming. The city's Mexican consulate reopened in the spring of 2008 because the Houston one could not effectively handle the increasing number of arrests of Mexican citizens, documented or undocumented, in Louisiana, nor the inquiries from contractors trying to recruit Mexican guest workers. The presidents of both countries attended the reopening ceremony, and President Felipe Calderón used his speech to emphasize how the participation of so many Mexicans in post-Katrina reconstruction symbolized the historic and essential role of Mexican labor in the US economy. The consulate issued 3,915 identity cards in 2010, with 25 percent of them to people from the states of Veracruz and Guanajuato.[20]

Some Mexicans stayed for other reasons, such as the city's cosmopolitan character, lax immigration enforcement, and less frequent exploitation of undocumented residents than in other places.

> I moved here from a small town in Texas to work in construction. At first [immediately after Katrina] no one was in New Orleans, but after a year the people came back. I know it is not a very big city, but it is a city. I lived in Mexico City before, and I was bored in Texas. Here I go out more, eat in restaurants, or just go dancing. Also, a lot of people are patient with you. Sometimes Mexicans who came here from other cities in the US, say it is easier to live here because people do not get angry if you don't speak English well.[21]

I think there are more opportunities here. It is easier to live here because when you look for a job, employers don't always ask for papers and they pay you well. For example, if you are in New York or San Francisco and you don't have papers, they pay terrible—like four dollars an hour.[22]

The rise of anti-Latino sentiment and legislation in other states certainly has made Louisiana a more attractive place than others to stay for Mexicans and Latinos in general. Arizona, Alabama, Georgia, and South Carolina have all passed legislation that directs state and local government agencies to enforce federal immigration laws. The legislation ranges from requiring police to check the residency status of suspects to denying education, health care, and utility connections to those who cannot document legal residency. Latinos have labeled such legislation "Juan Crow laws," a reference to the racist Jim Crow laws of the South that emerged in the aftermath of the Civil War and persisted for nearly a century, until the 1960s and passage of the federal Civil Rights Act. When nearby Alabama enacted a particularly draconian version of Juan Crow legislation in 2011, the reopened Mexican consulate in New Orleans experienced a surge in clientele that consular officials expect will only continue to grow.[23]

Not only has Louisiana's state government resisted passing similar legislation, but also by 2009 Mayor Nagin had reversed his initial concerns about being "overrun by Mexican workers."[24] Opposition by Latino organizations, the Catholic Church, and others prevented those who attempted to copy the Alabama law from gaining broad support in the state legislature. So has the recognition that Latinos, and especially Mexicans and Hondurans, carried out much of the hazardous, dirty, post-Katrina reconstruction work. Most fundamentally, however, the Louisiana constitution enshrines the "right of the people to preserve, foster, and promote their respective historic linguistic and cultural origins." That provision remains unique among state constitutions and reflects Louisiana's Francophone more than its Hispanic heritage. Nonetheless, the state constitution effectively prohibits English-only legislation. The initial hostility of the city's municipal government toward Latinos included everything from demanding documentation of legal residency to ignoring crimes against reconstruction workers. By 2009, however, Nagin and the police superintendent, Warren Riley, had realized the importance of Latinos to the reconstruction effort and begun to cooperate with community organizations to reduce the kinds of crime Mexican and other workers commonly suffered, from assaults and robberies to exploitation by employers. By then, news reports and public opinion had generally become more positive toward Latino residents.[25]

As the reconstruction effort has declined, some of the Mexicans who initially came to New Orleans have left the city but nonetheless stayed in Louisiana. One indication of that trend is the growth of Louisiana's population of Mexican origin outside of New Orleans. Louisiana's total population grew by 64,396 residents between 2000 and 2010, but its Hispanic and Latino population grew by 84,822, from 107,738 to 192,560, a growth rate of 79 percent. Those of Mexican origin contributed the most to that growth, increasing from 32,267 to 78,643, an absolute increase of 46,376 and a growth rate of 144 percent. Not only do Louisianians of Mexican origin now make up 41 percent of the state's Hispanic and Latino population, only 20 percent of them live in Orleans, Jefferson, St. Bernard, or Plaquemines parishes. In contrast, 73 percent of the state's Honduran-origin population lives in those four parishes. While employment opportunities created by Katrina's destruction might have attracted many people of Mexican and Honduran origin to New Orleans initially, the Hondurans have tended to stay in the city while the Mexicans have increasingly relocated to other places in Louisiana. The Baton Rouge MSA, for example, increased in total population from 602,894 in 2000 to 802,484 in 2010. Many of the new residents relocated from New Orleans after losing home and workplace in 2005. The city's Hispanic and Latino population has also grown, however, from 10,576 in 2000 to 27,357 in 2010. Residents of Mexican origin have contributed the most to that 159 percent growth, increasing from 4,085 to 12,897 between 2000 and 2010. By Census 2010, Mexican-origin residents of Baton Rouge made up the largest proportion, slightly more than 47 percent, of the city's Hispanics and Latinos. Residents of Honduran origin, in contrast, made up only a little more than 9 percent.

That 79 percent growth in Louisiana's Hispanic and Latino population between 2000 and 2010 far exceeded the 16 percent growth between 1990 and 2000, but not by enough for the state to definitively join the New Latino South. The six states that had growth rates of greater than 200 percent in their Hispanic and Latino populations between 1990 and 2000—Alabama, Arkansas, Georgia, North Carolina, South Carolina, and Tennessee—initially defined the New Latino South. Their growth rates fell to between 96 and 148 percent between 2000 and 2010. Two other southern states seem to have clearly joined the New Latino South, with growth rates of greater than 100 percent in their Hispanic and Latino populations between 2000 and 2010: Mississippi with 105.9 percent growth and Kentucky with 121.6 percent growth. The Hispanic and Latino population of the entire South grew by 57 percent between Census 2000 and Census 2010, from 11,586,696 to 18,227,508. The proportion of the region's total population that claims Hispanic or Latino origins consequently grew from 11.6 to 15.9 percent. The New Latino South therefore continued to grow during the first decade of the twenty-first century, albeit not as quickly as during the last decade of the twentieth century. But Louisiana has only begun to contribute significantly to that phenomenon, lagging behind the more rapid growth in Arkansas, Mississippi, Kentucky, Alabama, Georgia, Tennessee, North Carolina, and South Carolina.[26]

Interviews confirm the process by which those of Mexican origin were initially attracted to New Orleans by reconstruction work but afterward moved elsewhere in Louisiana. One Mexican, a fifty-two-year-old man originally from Mexico City, came to New Orleans in November 2005 from Michigan. Other Mexicans, already in New Orleans, recruited him to join their demolition crew and arranged his accommodation. As demand for demolition work decreased, the crew shifted into roofing and house raising. As demand for that sort of work also decreased, he left New Orleans, first taking a job in Kentucky and then in Baton Rouge. Each time, he learned of the employment opportunity through social networks. By 2011 he was living in Gonzales, a suburban municipality on the southern margin of the Baton Rouge MSA. Together with some other Mexicans, all of whom had also originally come to Louisiana after Katrina to work in New Orleans, he rents a small house and works in a sugar refinery. Gonzales is only an hour's drive from North Kenner, but they prefer to live and work in the Baton Rouge metropolitan area rather than New Orleans to escape the dominance of the Honduran community. For them, Lake Pontchartrain demarcates the frontier between Honduran and Mexican Louisiana.[27]

UNTIL KATRINA, NEW ORLEANS HAD REMAINED relatively isolated from the networks that over the past century have brought so many Mexicans to the United States, including the New Latino South beginning in the 1990s. Katrina provided enough employment opportunity to nearly double the population of the Mexican community by 2010 and firmly establish it as one of the two largest Latino communities in the city. That history differs greatly from that of the city's other Hispanic and Latino groups and has therefore resulted in a different residential geography and relationship to the other communities. The population of the city's Honduran community, for example, has grown even more after Katrina than has that of the Mexican community, consolidating the Honduran sense of place and dominance over other Latino groups. That dominance is particularly strong on the northwestern side of the city. The dominance of Louisiana's Mexican community outside of New Orleans, however, provides much denser social networks to other places in the United States, including other cities in Louisiana. As a consequence, a frontier has emerged in the Latino geography of Louisiana: the Honduran community dominates in New Orleans, but the Mexican community dominates beyond Lake Pontchartrain.

5. BRAZILIANS

Hispanic or Latino. A person of Mexican, Puerto Rican, Cuban, South or Central American, or other Spanish culture or origin, regardless of race. The term, "Spanish origin," can be used in addition to "Hispanic or Latino."

—*White House Office of Management and Budget,*
"Revisions to the Standards for the Classification
of Federal Data on Race and Ethnicity," 1997

We Brazilians came here [to Nova Orleães] for the gold rush, and for a while there was plenty of work to be done.

—*Gerson, interview of August 6, 2010*

THE NETWORKS THAT BY THE NINETEENTH CENTURY linked New Orleans to ports around the Gulf of Mexico and the Caribbean also extended south of the equator—to Brazil. Rather than bananas and neocolonialism, however, the coffee trade has dominated that connection from the nineteenth century through to the present (fig. 37). While much of the coffee imported through New Orleans long came from the same Central American countries as bananas, none of the dozens of relatively small coffee importers ever attained the power and infamy of United Fruit. The term "coffee republic" therefore never became as prevalent as "banana republic."

Brazil became a major supplier of coffee beans to the New Orleans coffee industry in the nineteenth century, most of them exported through Rio de Janeiro and Santos, the port for São Paulo. Louisiana Coffee and Spice Mills, for example, guaranteed that its Lunch Bell brand contained "pure Rio," a reference to beans grown in the states of Minas Gerais and Rio de Janeiro, exported through the port of Rio de Janeiro (fig. 38). The wharf at the foot of Poydras

FIG. 37. "Men unloading coffee from a ship at the dock in New Orleans in the 1940s," object file name hp00935. Reproduced courtesy of the State Library of Louisiana.

Street, just downriver from the Banana Wharf, became known as the Coffee Wharf. The offices and warehouses of the coffee importers clustered nearby in an area called the Coffee District. As coffee consumption in the United States increased over the twentieth century, an ever-larger amount of that commodity entered through the Crescent City. By 1920, the three ports through which nearly all coffee entered the country were New York City, New Orleans, and San Francisco, respectively with 59, 25, and 12 percent of the total. By 1995 the United States had become the single largest consumer of coffee in the world, and 28 percent of all coffee imports entered through New Orleans, more than any other single port. Currently, about a quarter of all coffee imported from Brazil, which supplies nearly a third of the world's coffee, enters through the Crescent City. Many of those beans are roasted, ground, and packaged in the city by Folgers and more than a dozen other national and regional brands. When

FIG. 38. "Lunch Bell Ground Coffee label," accession number 1978.085.105. Reproduced courtesy of the Collections of the Louisiana State Museum, Gift of Mr. Thomas Favrot.

tourists in the French Quarter stop to order beignets and a *café au lait* at Cafe du Monde, the coffee likely grew in Brazil.[1]

That commercial connection provided much of the basis for a small community of Brazilians in New Orleans from the nineteenth century through Hurricane Katrina. While most of the nineteenth-century members of that community were involved in the coffee trade, a few might have been the repatriated children of the some two thousand southerners who emigrated to Brazil following the Civil War. Between 1865 and 1885, those *Confederados* left the South for Brazil. Their loss of lands, the abolition of slavery, and Reconstruction all encouraged them to emigrate. Affordable land and the legality of slavery in Brazil, not abolished there until 1888, attracted them to the states of São Paulo, Paraná, and others to grow cotton and sugarcane. While their settlements were more enduring than similar ones in British Honduras and elsewhere, some of the Confederados and their Brazilian-born children did return to the United States.[2]

Precise estimates of the changing population of the Brazilian community in New Orleans prove elusive but long remained much smaller than the Isleño, Cuban, Honduran, and Mexican communities. Census 1850 records 115 US residents born in Brazil, which had gained independence from Portugal in 1822. Only four of those 115 lived in Louisiana, however: all four in New Orleans, each with a different surname, each in a different neighborhood. Even by Census 1930, out of the nearly eight thousand US residents born in Brazil, only sixteen lived in New Orleans and ten others elsewhere in Louisiana.

The appearance of the Hispanic-origin question on the short form for Census 1980 began to generate precise population estimates for residents of Mexican, Cuban, and other Latin American origins but not for *brazucas,* as expatriate Brazilians call themselves. That question, beginning with the first version on the long form in 1970 and continuing through Census 1990, explicitly excluded non-Hispanic Latinos by asking whether the respondent identified as "of Spanish or Hispanic origin or descent." Censuses 2000 and 2010 added the term "Latino" and a write-in box to specify national origin, implying both that Brazilians could include themselves and, by emphasizing Spanish origins, that they should not.[3]

The Census Bureau's restrictive definition of "Latino" has emerged through a complex historical process. The civil rights legislation of the 1960s prompted Latinos to lobby for recognition and enumeration of residents of Latin American and Caribbean origin in order to benefit from new social programs. Some residents of Brazilian origin, however, believed that their inclusion in the same category as Hispanics would stigmatize them and lobbied to be excluded. In 1977, therefore, the White House's Office of Management and Budget defined Hispanics as persons of "Mexican, Puerto Rican, Cuban, South or Central American, or other Spanish culture or origin, regardless of race."[4] A revision in 1997 added the term "Latino" to the definition but continued to specify Spanish origin. Despite Brazil being Latin America's largest and most populous country, therefore, the US government does not consider Brazilians to be Latinos, and the decennial census reflects that position by excluding them from the question on Hispanic and Latino origins. At least some Brazilians continue to prefer that exclusion from the official definition of "Latino." Those that do respond affirmatively to the census question on Hispanic and Latino origins can indicate Brazil in the write-in box, but the Census Bureau does not code such responses, report the figure, or include it in the total Hispanic and Latino population estimate.[5]

The long form, sent to a 5 percent sample of the population each decennial census until the American Community Survey replaced it after Census 2000, does provide an estimate of the Brazilian-origin population commensurable with that for most other national-origin groups but not with Hispanics. While the foreign-born question on the long form provides some indication of the population of the Brazilian community in the United States, the ancestry question provides an estimate more comparable in meaning to the Hispanic-origin question. The ancestry question asks respondents to self-identify their ethnicity or descent, typically related to their country of birth or that of their ancestors. Some US residents born in Brazil or in the United States of parents born in Brazil might well consider their ancestry to be Portuguese, Italian, German, Japanese, Chinese, African, Kayapo, or some other, of course.[6] The same issue applies to the Hispanic-origin question, however, and does not render the two estimates incommensurable. The main issue that makes the estimates derived from the ancestry question quite different from those derived from the Hispanic-origin question involves the sample size. Estimates based on the long-form sample have large margins of error that become even larger for communities with small populations. Estimates of the population of Brazilian origin for the entire United States can therefore be roughly compared to, for example, the enumeration of the US Honduran-origin population derived from the short form. But estimates for an MSA with a small Brazilian community are imprecise compared to those for Hispanic-origin groups, even relatively small ones. And margins of error for individual census tracts with small Brazilian-origin populations preclude estimates entirely. While the decennial census thereby provides precise and spatially detailed estimates for Latinos with Hispanic origins, allowing mapping by census tracts, it cannot consistently do the same for those of Brazilian origin.

The difficulty inherent in quantitative analysis of the Brazilian community of New Orleans, in part a function of its exclusion from the official definition of "Latino" and in part of its small size, belies the significance of studying it. It contrasts with and provides different types of insights than study of the Isleño, Cuban, Honduran, and Mexican communities. The Isleños arrived in the eighteenth century and since then have not received any new members from the Canary Islands, becoming culturally distinct from the residents of that Spanish archipelago and suffering a demographic decline exacerbated by Katrina. The Cubans have achieved demographic stability amid social heterogeneity after several influxes over the twentieth century. The Honduran community became indisputably dominant, both demographically and socially, after Katrina and constitutes a cohesive transnational community with persistent linkages to Honduras and other catracho communities in the United States. The Mexican community has some of the same transnational characteristics as the Honduran one and also grew larger after Katrina, but Mexicans are part of a much larger US community that dominates in many cities while Hondurans dominate only in New Orleans. The Brazilian community, unlike any of those Hispanic communities, remained small through the nineteenth and twentieth centuries but grew rapidly in the immediate aftermath of Katrina to play a liminal role in the process through which the Latino side of New Orleans has since emerged, with brazucas presenting themselves as Latinos in some circumstances and non-Latinos in others. That characteristic sets them apart from the Hispanic groups of preceding chapters and demands detailed study.

Brazilians in the Twentieth Century

Brazilian emigration to the United States accelerated after the Second World War, particularly from the state of Minas Gerais. During the war, the US government established a mica mine near the city of Governador Valadares in order to ensure a secure supply of that mineral for use as an insulator in electrical equipment. When mine personnel returned home, some sponsored the immigration of their Brazilian household servants. As those immigrants in turn sponsored their relatives for residency, in a process known as chain migration, thousands of Brazilians from Governador Valadares ultimately came to the United States. They mainly settled in large cities such as Los Angeles and along the Atlantic coast from Boston to Miami. The remittances they sent to relatives in Governador Valadares became so critical to its economy that the municipal government erected a monument to honor the expatriates.[7]

Nonetheless, until the 1980s US residents of Brazilian origin remained few relative to other national groups. A debt crisis resulted in the collapse of Brazilian economic growth that decade and encouraged a dramatic increase in emigration, much of it to the United States. An overwhelming majority of the immigrants came from the middle class, motivated by stagnant wages, hyper-inflation, high unemployment and underemployment, and a lack of opportunities for their children. Many settled in the small, established brazuca communities that the immigrants from Governador Valadares had pioneered in Boston, other East Coast cities, and Los Angeles. As the Brazilian economy began to grow again in the late twentieth century, some of those brazucas returned home but maintained social and financial linkages to the United States, establishing a transnational community.[8]

The foreign-born and ancestry data sets of the decennial census quantify the history of Brazilian immigration during the late twentieth century (table 8). Between 1960 and 1970, the estimate of the Brazilian-born population more than doubled, from 13,988 to 27,069. So few of them and their US-born children and grandchildren claimed Brazilian ancestry, however, that the Census Bureau did not publish an estimate based on that question. Speculatively, many who claimed Brazilian birth must have indicated some other ancestry, such as Italian, German, or Portuguese. The number that claimed Brazilian birth in New Orleans, or even Louisiana, similarly remained too few to estimate a population. The size of the US Brazilian-born population increased more modestly over the 1970s, to 40,919 by Census 1980, but by then the New Orleans community had grown large enough to produce an estimate: 194 residents of Brazilian birth, 57 percent of all such Louisiana residents. The New Orleans brazuca community had therefore grown from sixteen in 1930 to 194 in 1980 and remained the largest in Louisiana but one of the smallest in the United States.

The surge in Brazilian immigration over the 1980s and 1990s increased the size of the US Brazilian-born population far more than that of Louisiana or New Orleans. Nationally, it doubled over the 1980s, to 82,489 by Census 1990, and more than doubled over the 1990s, to 212,428 by Census 2000. In Louisiana, in contrast, it remained static over the 1980s and nearly so in New Orleans, increasing from 194 to only 240. Over the 1990s, as the state's economy recovered from the decline in the oil sector, enough Brazilians settled in Louisiana to increase the Brazilian-born population from 339 to 701, more than double. New

TABLE 8. Population born in Brazil and of Brazilian ancestry resident in the United States, Louisiana, and New Orleans, 1960–2000

	UNITED STATES		LOUISIANA		NEW ORLEANS MSA[a]	
YEAR	Born in Brazil	Brazilian Ancestry	Born in Brazil	Brazilian Ancestry	Born in Brazil	Brazilian Ancestry
1960	13,988	no data	no data	no data	no data	no data
1970	27,069	no data	no data	no data	no data	no data
1980	40,919	27,640	341	239	194	no data
1990	82,489	65,875	339	290	240	no data
2000	212,428	181,076	701	689	450	409

[a]See note to table 4.

Orleans, however, lagged the nation, and even the state, in the rate of increase, growing from 240 to only 450. Nonetheless, in 1990 about 71 percent of Louisiana residents of Brazilian birth lived in the New Orleans MSA, and in 2000 the figure was 64 percent. Again, in all cases the Brazilian-ancestry estimates lagged behind the Brazil-born estimates. At least some of those born in Brazil and their US-born children seem to have claimed Portuguese ancestry: in 2000, thirty-one residents of the New Orleans MSA claimed to have been born in Portugal, but 1,109 claimed Portuguese ancestry; at the same time, 450 claimed Brazilian birth but only 409 claimed Brazilian ancestry.

The brazuca community concentrated in many of the same neighborhoods as Hispanic Latinos (fig. 39). In both 1990 and 2000, about half the Brazilian-born population resided in Jefferson Parish, mainly in North Kenner and Metairie north of Interstate 10. There, they could use Hispanic businesses such as international financial services that specialized in wiring money to South America and supermercados that stocked items common to both Brazilian and Hispanic cuisines: *picanha,* a particular cut of top sirloin; the *yerba mate* tea drunk in southern Brazil as well as Paraguay, Uruguay, and Argentina; and others. And they could communicate in Spanish, a Romance language like Portuguese, more easily than in English.

Census 2000 also reveals a more minor concentration in the Uptown neighborhood, highly constrained to the immediate vicinity of Tulane University. Tulane is a prominent center for research and teaching on Brazil, having offered Portuguese language courses since 1947. By 1999, enough faculty members specialized in Brazil that the university founded a Brazilian Studies degree program. While few of the faculty and students associated with that program are of Brazilian origin, the concentration likely includes some of them as well as faculty in entirely different disciplines and international students in a variety of majors.[9]

The relatively small size of the city's brazuca community did not prevent the establishment of at least some social institutions similar to the Isleño, Cuban, Honduran, and Mexican communities. Some were associated with the consulate that Brazil maintained in the city over the 1970s and 1980s to promote trade in coffee and other commodities. Consular staff organized the Brazilian-American Cultural Institute to host galas at which representatives of shipping companies like Lloyd Brasileiro could network with representatives of US businesses. The decline of the New Orleans economy over the 1980s, however, encouraged

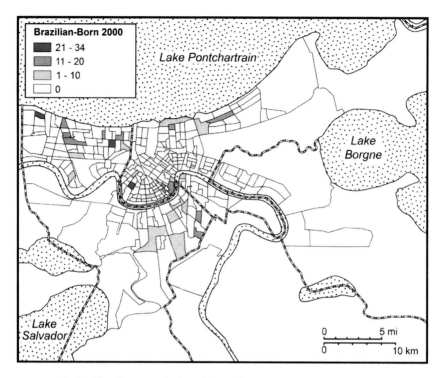

Lake Pontchartrain

Lake Borgne

Lake Salvador

0   5 mi

0   10 km

FIG. 39. The Brazilian-born population of New Orleans in 2000.

the Brazilian government to close the consulate. The Brazilian-American Cultural Institute has nonetheless remained somewhat active in efforts to promote Brazilian culture and the use of Portuguese among second-generation brazucas by employing performances and lectures to advance broader appreciation and community pride. Another institution also stands out: Casa Samba, a Brazilian samba school and performance troupe. Curtis Pierre, an African American from a small town near New Orleans, founded Casa Samba in 1987 to perform samba music and dance in the style of Rio de Janeiro. Casa Samba has performed in a range of city venues over its twenty-five years, mainly for audiences of tourists. The resulting hybridization of prominent elements of Brazilian culture—dance, music, and Carnival—with the architecture, cuisine, and other cultural elements of New Orleans has resulted in what Pierre refers to as an "Amerizilian" experience that compares and contrasts the legacy of the African diaspora in New Orleans and Rio de Janeiro.

Brazilians in the Twenty-first Century

On the eve of Katrina, the brazuca community of New Orleans remained small despite the surge of Brazilian immigration into the United States in the late twentieth century. Whether the 450 who claimed Brazilian birth or the 409 who claimed Brazilian ancestry, residents of Brazilian origin made up a small percentage of Latinos, broadly defined, in the Crescent City and a minuscule percentage of all residents.

But the city's brazuca community grew rapidly after Katrina. Over the first decade of the twenty-first century, the rate of increase for Brazilian-born residents in New Orleans surpassed, for the first time ever, the national rate. As of Census 2010, the Census Bureau no longer sends a long form to a sample of households during the decennial census. Instead, beginning in 2005, the bureau uses the American Community Survey to question a sample of households each month on a range of issues that include ancestry and foreign birth. While the American Community Survey thereby provides a more continuous measure of social change, the sample sizes have never amounted to 5 percent of the population and the estimates therefore remain subject to much larger margins of error than those based on the long form of the decennial census. While estimates based on the American Community Survey cannot be directly compared to those based on Census 2000, the rate of increase in the population of Brazilian-born US residents seems to have slowed considerably after more than doubling over the 1990s, increasing by only two-thirds between 2000 and 2010, from 212,428 to 339,613. Meanwhile, the number of Brazilian-born residents in the New Orleans MSA seems to have surged dramatically since Census 2000, increasing more than sixfold between 2000 and 2007, from 450 to 2,757 (table 9). Moreover, the vast majority, about 97 percent in 2007, of Louisiana residents born in Brazil lived in the New Orleans MSA. Small samples produce large inter-annual fluctuations and preclude estimates for individual census tracts and, therefore, a post-Katrina map to compare with figure 39.[10]

Although the American Community Survey's estimates are imprecise relative to the previous decennial estimates, the Brazilian consulate in Houston confirms that the Brazilian-born population of New Orleans increased by an order of magnitude, from the 100s into the 1,000s, over the first decade of the twenty-first century. That consulate serves Brazilian communities in Arkansas, Colorado, Kansas, New Mexico, Oklahoma, Texas, and Louisiana. Consular of-

TABLE 9. Population born in Brazil and of Brazilian ancestry resident in Louisiana and New Orleans, 2004–2010

| | LOUISIANA | | | | NEW ORLEANS MSA[a] | | | |
| | Born in Brazil | | Brazilian Ancestry | | Born in Brazil | | Brazilian Ancestry | |
YEAR	Estimate	Error	Estimate	Error	Estimate	Error	Estimate	Error
2004	1,190	± 1,272	766	± 1,103	424	± 695	0	± 485
2005	755	± 451	419	381	275	± 321	no data	n/a
2006	518	± 412	355	± 377	258	± 358	no data	n/a
2007	2,831	± 1,644	2,393	± 1,617	2,757	± 1,646	no data	n/a
2008	1,897	± 923	1,548	± 1,099	905	± 671	no data	n/a
2009	3,077	± 1,804	3,537	± 1,900	2,596	± 1,763	no data	n/a
2010	2,277	± 1,124	2,843	± 1,365	1,504	± 1,009	no data	n/a

[a] See note to table 4.

ficials travel to New Orleans every four months to provide a range of services to Brazilians in southern Louisiana, from renewals of national identity documents and passports to marriage licenses and visas. Based on the number of Brazilians who use those consular services, the vice-consul estimated their 2010 population throughout all of southern Louisiana to have reached "about five thousand."[11]

While the timing of the surge in the size of the city's brazuca community suggests that they came as part of the broader influx of post-Katrina reconstruction workers, interviews provide a deeper understanding of that complex process. Individual interviews and a focus group discussion indicate that many of the post-Katrina arrivals came to the United States from Brazil between 2005 and 2006. Initially they joined friends and families already established in the brazuca communities of various cities along the Atlantic coast but were unable to find steady employment. Moreover, unlike the middle-class professionals who dominated immigration from Brazil during the 1980s and 1990s, many of those who came in the early twenty-first century were manual laborers and undocumented, arriving via Mexico and crossing the border illegally or overstaying tourist visas. Despite renewed growth in the Brazilian economy and a return of some brazucas who had emigrated in the 1990s, neoliberal restructuring and associated austerity policies ensured high levels of poverty and landlessness that encouraged many to seek economic opportunities in the United States.

Even documented, let alone undocumented, immigration from Brazil doubled over the levels of the 1990s, to more than 9,000 in 2001. Not securing steady employment in Boston, Miami, or the other gateway cites they initially settled in, some of those newcomers moved on to other places. Chicago, Houston, the New Latino South, and, following Katrina, New Orleans all became destinations for Brazilians pioneering enough to seek opportunities beyond the established brazuca communities.[12]

The Boston area, in particular, became a source of Brazilians attracted to New Orleans by the reconstruction work. Of the seven Brazilians in the focus group, for example, five had come from Massachusetts, two from Los Angeles, and one from New York City. Nearly immediately after Katrina devastated New Orleans, enterprising Brazilians began recruiting work crews among the unemployed brazucas in the Boston area. The organizers promised jobs, housing, and transportation for a $500 fee. For a down payment on that amount, an unemployed Brazilian laborer could get into a van in Boston and expect—an expectation not always realized—to have a job and accommodation waiting on arrival in New Orleans two days later. The laborers lived together in abandoned houses without electricity until they had paid the fee and earned enough to rent their own apartments. Many eventually moved to the Uptown neighborhood around Tulane University because of the availability of unflooded rental housing and the pre-existing concentration of Brazilian residents. They socialized at *churrascos,* the Brazilian version of a barbecue, where they exchanged information about employment opportunities and housing availability, the two dominant concerns for Latinos in New Orleans immediately after Katrina. By networking for employment and housing mainly within their own community, they avoided exploitation suffered by many day laborers who congregated at pickup sites every morning—although Brazilian employees did report labor abuses by Brazilian employers.[13]

Many of the newcomers worked in specialized construction trades such as painting, flooring, roofing, dry walling, tiling, and window and countertop installation rather than as general laborers working in demolition and debris removal. Such specialization allowed them to negotiate higher wages and better working conditions than many other reconstruction workers. One leader of an all-Brazilian flooring crew that arrived in late 2005 commented on that advantage but also noted that by 2010 jobs had become scarcer and negotiations more difficult: "My crew is one of the few that can install floors quickly and with high quality. If a boss doesn't want to pay what we ask, we take other jobs. When we first arrived it was much easier to negotiate, but now there are fewer jobs available, and it's become more difficult. Now we are sometimes forced to take lower paying jobs, but people know we do good work so we don't go very long without work."[14]

The Brazilians who came in 2005 and 2006 included women as well as men. Some accompanied male partners who came for reconstruction work. But others came independently. As one recalled, "I heard there were many Brazilians here and that there was plenty of work, so I also came to New Orleans."[15] Those women who came in late 2005 and early 2006, however, found few opportunities. Some worked as translators and in restaurants, which were so desperate for employees at the time that they offered starting bonuses, but lack of documentation and English ability forced others into low-wage, hazardous jobs as debris removers. Many engaged in several roles at the same time: "I came back to New Orleans three months later in December [2005]. I came back to work with Casa Samba doing [dance] shows. I came back to work in my restaurant job. And I started construction work. I did demolition in the morning, and I worked at the restaurant at night."[16] As New Orleans regained population and brazuca women accumulated more social capital, many began to specialize in domestic services such as childcare and housecleaning. Of the seven interviews with women, six had worked in housecleaning.

Entrepreneurial opportunities attracted both men and women to New Orleans and encouraged them to remain. Two of the women, for example, had their own housecleaning businesses. They advertised their services with small yard signs throughout the city and gained a diverse clientele that included English-, Spanish-, and Portuguese-speaking households. One contrasted the possibilities for self-employment in post-Katrina New Orleans with the limitations of the Boston area: "Here there is opportunity. In Massachusetts the work was unreliable. There were lots of housecleaning services and they were always looking for new workers that would work for less pay. You couldn't start your own business. There was too much competition. That's why I came here, to start my own business."[17]

Census data, interviews, and landscape observation all suggest that the post-Katrina brazuca community occupies largely the same neighborhoods as in 2000, as mapped in figure 39, but with the addition of Chalmette, in northern St. Bernard Parish. Initially attracted to North Kenner and northern Metairie by the existing brazuca communities, the newcomers increased the demand for more specifically Brazilian goods and services. Consequently, in 2006 several Brazilians opened restaurants and small supermarkets on and near Williams Boulevard. One family from Framingham, in the Boston area, relocated their entire grocery store—merchandise, shelves, and all—to North Kenner in late 2005. Those *supermercados,* the same word in Portuguese as Spanish, offered items critical to Brazilian cuisine but not typically stocked in the Hispanic stores—for example, manioc flour and *dendê,* or palm oil.

Brazilians also founded their own Christian churches in North Kenner, and some churches in other neighborhoods began to offer a mass in Portuguese. The evangelical Assembleia de Deus Brasileira em Luisiana, the Brazilian Assembly of God, on West Esplanade near Williams Boulevard, became the largest Brazilian church in the city. As a social and spiritual center for the brazuca community, the Assembleia de Deus hosted the staff of the Brazilian consulate in Houston on their visits to provide consular services for southern Louisiana. The evangelical Revival Church for the Nations, headquartered in Boston and with congregations in brazuca communities from New England to Florida, is also located in North Kenner. More broadly across the city, Pentecostal and other evangelical Protestant churches began to offer services in Portuguese in North Kenner, Metairie, Mid-City, and Chalmette.

Brazilians have also established music bands that cater specifically to the brazuca community. The long-established Casa Samba has always been more oriented toward tourists than Brazilians; moreover, many of the post-Katrina arrivals do not come from Rio de Janeiro and have little interest in dance styles associated with that city's version of Carnival, which dominate performances by Casa Samba. Instead, some of the newcomers have established their own bands to perform at restaurants, weddings, birthdays, and churrascos. They favor music from Brazil's interior, emphasizing popular sertanejo, forró, and rock-and-roll over the *samba de enredo* of Rio de Janeiro performed by Casa Samba.[18]

Capoeira academies provide another opportunity for interaction among Brazilians as well as with residents of other backgrounds. Capoeira is a distinctively Brazilian martial art, albeit with African roots, that combines elements of dance and music. The main capoeira academy, Grupo Maculelê, moved to New Orleans from Atlanta in 2006 and began teaching capoeira classes six days a week. Most of the students are non-Brazilians interested in Brazilian culture, and Grupo Maculelê has thereby become a significant disseminator of Brazilian culture in New Orleans. The participants of Brazilian origin tend to be second-generation immigrants endeavoring to reinforce that element of their brazuca identity.[19]

Food trucks represent one of the most publicly visible elements of the brazuca community. A churrasco truck has augmented the many taco trucks that frequent Audubon and City parks, Saints football games, art and music festivals such as Jazz Fest, and Mardi Gras parade routes. The trucks that sell snowballs—cups of shaved ice flavored with a variety of syrups peculiar to New Orleans—have been joined by one specializing in fruit flavors popular among Brazilians, such as *açai*. The most successful Brazilian food truck entrepreneur, however, recognizes that the Mexican community far exceeds the Brazilian in number and that the Mexican taco remains far more familiar to non-Latinos than churrasco. He had lived in Connecticut for more than twenty years and operated a fleet of taco trucks there but moved to New Orleans in November 2005 with six trucks.[20]

By 2010, the post-Katrina "gold rush" in employment and entrepreneurial opportunities had ended, with a consequent decline in the size of the brazuca community. The Louisiana Workforce Commission reports that between June 2009 and 2010, the New Orleans MSA gained 4,800 nonfarm jobs but lost 1,400 in the construction sector. Consequently, some Brazilian men abandoned the uncertainty of construction work and joined their partners in expanding their housecleaning businesses. Others returned to Brazil or went elsewhere in the United States. Many of the Brazilian businesses that opened in 2005 and 2006 have closed or are barely surviving (fig. 40). The supermercado that relocated from the Boston area to North Kenner in 2005 has closed, and the owner of another that barely remains open lamented that sales had declined by 60 percent compared to a peak in 2008. The decline in the Brazilian-origin population of New Orleans partially explains the lower demand for products relatively unique to their cuisine, such as manioc flour and dendê, but so does competition from Hispanic supermercados that after Katrina began to stock those goods. Another factor might be the emergence of a secondary concentration in Chalmette, spatially dispersing the brazuca community across the city and diluting demand for Brazilian goods and services. The Chalmette concentration has grown so much that since 2011 the staff of the Brazilian consulate in Houston now sets up its visiting consular services in that neighborhood instead of North Kenner. Other supermercados that have closed include one in Village De

FIG. 40. Sign of a former Brazilian grocery store in Village De l'Est, one of the first to close. Photograph by A. Sluyter, February 22, 2007.

l'Est, another on St. Charles Avenue, and a third on Canal Street. Restaurants such as Taste of Brazil, Carnaval, and Suingue Brazil in Metairie and Mid-City have also closed. While the Brazilian business owners who remain prefer to employ other Brazilians, the reduction in the community's population forces them to hire Hispanics from Mexico and Central America.[21]

The brazucas who remained in 2010 recognized that the population of their community began to decline in 2008. They kept track of their friends and acquaintances that had left: "Some have gone back to other places in the US like Atlanta and Massachusetts, but many others have returned to Brazil."[22] Some thought about leaving themselves, citing the high crime rate as one motive: "I was thinking of moving to a more tranquil state. I don't want to raise my son here. I'm afraid he may get into trouble. Here I am a small business owner with lots of clients. Business is good, but sometimes I think we would all be better off in Florida. It's not safe here. Other times I think we should just stay and save money until we can go back to Brazil."[23]

Even those who planned to stay for the immediate future had concerns about underemployment, hoped to leave eventually, and shared return to Brazil as the ultimate goal: "I feel at home here. My daughter came here and we are excited about the future. But work has slowed and it's becoming harder to make money. Many people have already left. Brazilians always want to return to Brazil. There are many good things here. We have opportunities here. But Brazil is home. My daughter and I plan to be here for a while, but we long for Brazil and our friends and family there."[24] As children aged, however, parents worried that they would want to remain in the United States: "My son doesn't know Brazil. He wants to stay here."[25]

How many residents of Brazilian origin remained in New Orleans by 2010 is unclear. The American Community Survey that year recorded so few in the New Orleans MSA who claimed Brazilian birth or ancestry that the Census Bureau could not produce an estimate. The owner of the supermercado that remained open in 2010 despite a 60 percent reduction in sales since 2008 ventured, on the basis of receipts and daily interaction with many in the brazuca community, that in 2008 the population was 7,000–8,000 and that by 2010 it had dwindled to 1,000–1,500. Yet the owners of the Brasa Grill opened that *churrascaria,* a restaurant that specializes in churrasco, on Williams Boulevard in 2012 because they believed some 5,000–7,000 Brazilians remained in New Orleans. Although the success of the Brasa Grill seems to confirm that estimate, its clientele includes not only Brazilians, but Hispanics and many others. The anecdotal sources and range of such estimates only confirm the difficulty of determining the number of residents of New Orleans who consider themselves of Brazilian origin.

THE BRAZILIAN COMMUNITY GREW FROM the hundreds into the thousands during the post-Katrina reconstruction boom and then decreased somewhat but likely remains on the order of 2,000–3,000. While some considered New Orleans a boom town rather than a settlement frontier, those who have stayed continue to play a liminal role in creating a distinctive non-Hispanic Latino side to Nova Orleães. To some degree, the ability to identify as either Latino or non-Latino has allowed brazucas to create business opportunities among Hispanic Latinos, such as taco trucks, while avoiding discrimination against Latinos. That liminal social role cuts both ways, of course. Brazucas can choose to identify with Hispanic Latinos when to their advantage, for example, in business ventures. Yet they can have difficulty in establishing their own distinctive identity as non-Hispanic Latinos, such as when they need to converse in their native language to be absolutely clear when making a critical decision about treatment at a medical clinic and the staff cannot comprehend that any Latino speaks anything but Spanish and has no one but a Hispanic interpreter available. Despite such challenges, the Brazilians that have stayed are buying houses in Chalmette and North Kenner, establishing what seems to be a permanent Brazilian community in New Orleans. Moreover, they are involved more in construction and domestic services than in the long-standing coffee trade.[26]

6. OTHER COMMUNITIES

New Orleans is within the orbit of a Hellenistic world that never touched the North Atlantic. The Mediterranean, Caribbean and Gulf of Mexico form a homogenous, though interrupted, sea.

—A. J. Liebling, The Earl of Louisiana, 1961

The only real divisions were that you knew the Latinos that were from the Westbank and you knew which ones were from the Eastbank.... It's a big river that separates us. *—Alejandro, interview of January 15, 2011*

IN CONTRAST TO THE FOREGOING CHAPTERS, each of which focuses on one of the more prominent national-origin communities, this chapter treats a constellation of less conspicuous communities. While none is as populous as the Honduran, Mexican, or Cuban communities, as singular as the Brazilian, or as long-standing as the Isleño, each is of intrinsic interest and interacts with the others and the rest of the city in unique ways. Some have done so for decades, others mainly since Katrina. Some share with the Hondurans, Cubans, and Brazilians historic linkages between their countries of origin and New Orleans based on trade, in particular agricultural commodities such as coffee. Some share with the Mexicans and Cubans much larger, national communities and a relationship with the United States that has as much to do with geopolitics or labor as with commerce. And some reveal particularly well how ethnic, national, and racialized identities intersect in specific ways related to place.

Just as for the larger communities addressed so far, the populations of the smaller communities have fluctuated over time. Figure 6 illustrates how the total population of all those Hispanics and Latinos who did not self-identify as Honduran, Mexican, Cuban, or Spanish (Isleño) grew somewhat over the 1970s, from 29,778 to 33,401. Deterioration of the city's economy over the 1980s and stagnation over the 1990s prompted a dramatic decrease to 26,237 by Census 2000. The boom in post-Katrina reconstruction work reversed that decline, with an increase to 29,232 by 2010. Collectively, those self-identifying as of "All other Hispanic and Latino origins" made up nearly 80 percent of the total Hispanic and Latino population of Orleans, Jefferson, Plaquemines, and St. Bernard parishes in 1970, decreased somewhat to just over 71 percent by 1980, but thereafter declined dramatically: to about 55 percent in 1990, 51 percent in 2000, and 38 percent in 2010. That relative decline reflects the dramatically disproportionate growth of the city's Mexican and Honduran communities since Katrina.

With the appearance of the write-in box in Census 1990, population estimates for all the national-origin groups from Latin America began to accumulate (table 10).[1] Thereafter, those who self-identified as Hispanics or Latinos without writing in a more specific origin or checking one of the boxes for Mexican, Cuban, or Puerto Rican were reported in an "Unspecified" category. Two somewhat more specific categories, "Other Central American" and "Other South American," included those who wrote in a reference that the Census Bureau recognizes as associated with those two regions but not a specific national origin, for example, South American, Garínagu, Canal Zone, or Quechua. Moreover, the Census Bureau removes entirely from the count those who self-identify as Hispanics or Latinos but write in a country not included in its definition of Central or South America, namely Belize, Brazil, Guyana, French Guiana, or Suriname. In other words, the more respondents who fill in the write-in box with a national origin such as Honduran or Argentinean, the fewer are included in "Unspecified," "Other Central American," or "Other South American."

Figure 41 graphs the national-origin groups other than the Cubans, Hondurans, Mexicans, and Spaniards (Isleños), illustrating that most experienced the same decline in population over the 1990s and subsequent increase associated with the post-Katrina employment boom as evident in figure 6 for "All other Hispanic and Latino origins." Only the Puerto Ricans, Dominicans, Peruvians, Venezuelans, and Paraguayans increased in population over the 1990s. That said, a portion of the decline for the majority of the groups relates to the change in the instructions for the write-in box, with examples of what to write in appearing in Census 1990 but not Census 2000, resulting in many leaving the box blank and inflation of the "Unspecified," "Other Central American," and "Other South American" categories. With restoration of the examples in Census 2010,

TABLE 10. Population for all Latino- and Hispanic-origin groups in Censuses 1990, 2000, and 2010, ranked by 2010 population

Group	1990 (number)	2000 (number)	2010 (number)	2000–10 (percent change)
Honduran	9,282	7,503	22,335	198.7
Mexican	6,991	8,111	15,779	95.5
Unspecified	4,059	14,422	6,944	-52.9
Cuban	5,270	5,196	5,322	2.4
Nicaraguan	4,064	2,328	4,692	101.5
Puerto Rican	2,501	2,889	3,898	34.9
Guatemalan	1,956	1,527	3,768	146.8
Spanish (Isleño)	8,283	4,055	3,461	-14.6
Salvadoran	1,080	727	2,510	245.3
Dominican	291	623	2,282	266.3
Colombian	952	843	1,305	54.8
Costa Rican	675	422	686	62.6
Ecuadorian	477	313	605	93.3
Peruvian	141	243	535	120.2
Venezuelan	142	248	523	110.9
Panamanian	476	356	449	26.1
Argentinean	220	187	352	88.2
Other Central American (OCA)	96	778	207	-73.4
Chilean	227	141	198	40.4
Bolivian	95	45	147	226.7
Uruguayan	0	24	68	183.3
Other South American (OSA)	26	119	39	-67.2
Paraguayan	0	2	24	1,100.0
TOTALS:				
All categories	47,304	51,102	76,129	49.0
Mexican, Puerto Rican, and Cuban	14,762	16,196	24,999	54.4
Unspecified, OCA, and OSA	4,181	15,319	7,190	-53.1
All other categories	28,361	19,587	43,940	124.4

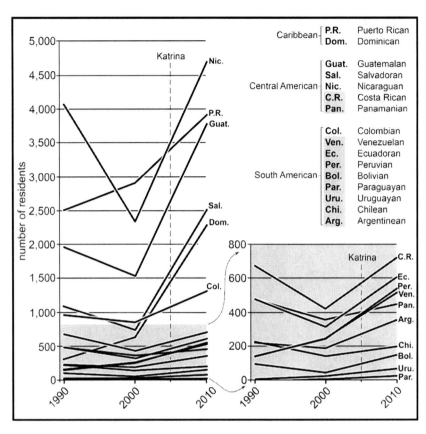

FIG. 41. Comparison of population of all Latino-origin groups other than Cuban, Mexican, and Honduran, 1990–2010.

those three generic categories declined as dramatically as they had increased in 2000. Since the combined growth between 2000 and 2010 of all the groups other than Mexicans, Cubans, and Puerto Ricans amounts to 24,353, more than half of that attributable to Hondurans alone, and since the reduction in the three generic categories comes to 8,129, as much as a third of the apparent growth in any of the groups other than Mexicans, Cubans, and Puerto Ricans could represent people who were already residents of New Orleans in 2000. If, in other words, they did not write in a specific origin for Census 2000 but did for Census 2010, some of the disproportionate growth between those two censuses of, for example, the Nicaraguan relative to the Puerto Rican population would be apparent rather than real. While not a major issue when examining a relatively large group such as Hondurans, such issues become more problematic for small groups in which minor changes in the number enumerated can appear as large percentage increases or declines, for example, the apparent near doubling of the Argentinean community on the basis of an additional 165 people between 2000 and 2010.[2]

Nonetheless, even recognizing the various undercounting biases that impact each national-origin group and the inflation of the generic categories in Census 2000, table 10 and figure 41 do reveal some patterns to organize this chapter. A majority of the five Central American groups, not including Hondurans, are notable for their apparent declines over the 1990s, rapid growth thereafter, and the number of Garínagu among them. The two Caribbean groups, Puerto Ricans and Dominicans, stand out as two of five communities, and the only relatively populous ones, that grew over the 1990s. And all of the South American groups are conspicuously small, with only Colombians exceeding a thousand by 2010 and the rest much smaller, down to the twenty-four Paraguayans enumerated in Census 2010. The small size of some of the communities has certainly been one of the factors contributing to the emergence of a pan-Latino identity in the city.

Central Americans

Between 1990 and 2010, the Nicaraguan, Guatemalan, and Salvadoran communities all more than doubled in population, similarly to the much larger Honduran one. The reasons for the parallels with the Honduran community involve similar transportation connections to New Orleans that developed through the trades in bananas and coffee. The factors pushing people to leave their homes also have similarities: periodic disasters such as hurricanes, earthquakes, and volcanic eruptions; extreme economic and social inequity; and political violence, sometimes related to US foreign policy. Over the early nineteenth century, for example, New Orleans entrepreneurs promoted filibuster campaigns in Central America, climaxing with occupation of Nicaragua from 1855 to 1857 by William Walker, formerly the editor of a New Orleans newspaper called the *Daily Crescent*. In 1903, President Theodore Roosevelt employed gunboat diplomacy to assist Panamanian oligarchs in gaining independence from Colombia in return for control of the Panama Canal, ushering in a century of dictatorship and US military interventions that culminated in the return of the Canal

Zone to Panama at the end of 1999. And in 1954, the United Fruit Company conspired with the CIA to overthrow Guatemala's democratically elected government because of plans to expropriate company land for redistribution to landless farmers.[3]

By 1990, small communities of Nicaraguans, Guatemalans, and Salvadorans lived in New Orleans, many of them political refugees from a century of violent conflict between oligarchies of Spanish descent and landless indigenous peoples. Between 1960 and 1996, various guerrilla groups fought against the series of military dictatorships that controlled Guatemala after the CIA-orchestrated coup that overthrew the government of President Jacobo Árbenz in 1954. In Nicaragua, the Sandinista National Liberation Front (FSLN) fought the dynasty of the Somoza family, its patriarch having been installed to head a puppet government following the US occupation of 1909–33. The Sandinistas overthrew the last of the dynasty, Anastasio Somoza, in 1979 and retained power in the democratic elections that followed in 1984, but the US-sponsored Contra war against Nicaragua and imposition of a trade embargo devastated the economy. And in El Salvador, the Farabundo Marti National Liberation Front (FMLN) battled a succession of US-supported dictatorships and nominally democratic governments between 1977 and 1992. The battles, assassinations, abductions, torture, state terrorism, and genocide that characterized those civil wars killed hundreds of thousands of people and forced many into exile. Following the wars, people continued to be displaced by earthquakes, hurricanes, and volcanic eruptions as well as violence and crime related to Central America's role as a transit route for narcotics from South American producers to markets in North America.[4]

Most of the Salvadorans, Guatemalans, and Nicaraguans who have come to the United States do not live in New Orleans, of course. Census 2010 enumerated about 1.65 million Salvadorans, a little over a million Guatemalans, and 348,202 Nicaraguans. All three groups experienced rapid growth after Census 2000, with the Salvadorans now the fourth-largest Latino-origin group in the United States and vying with Cubans to become the third-largest after Mexicans and Puerto Ricans. All three groups are concentrated in the Los Angeles metropolitan area, with other major concentrations of Salvadorans in Washington, DC, Guatemalans in New York City, and Nicaraguans in Miami.

Those who did settle in New Orleans have predominantly chosen to reside in Jefferson Parish in the same neighborhoods as Hondurans, particularly

North Kenner and Metairie north of Interstate 10. Before Katrina, many lived in the Redwood Park Apartments, near Williams Boulevard. Fat City, a neighborhood in northern Metairie with many modest apartment complexes, also became notable for its concentration of Central Americans. The rapid growth of their communities after Katrina did not much alter that residential geography. The majority of the nearly eleven thousand Salvadorans, Guatemalans, and Nicaraguans in New Orleans by 2010 continued to be concentrated in the same neighborhoods.

Proximity to the numerically greater Honduran community results in both clashes and support, as detailed in chapter 3. On the one hand, Hondurans own many of the businesses and dominate social interactions. On the other hand, those businesses provide services and products that support the other Central American communities, such as money transfer services and the pupusas shared among the region's cuisines but particularly central to Salvadoran identity. Nonetheless, each of the national-origin groups is actively attempting to increase its own social capital with community organizations such as the Nicaraguan Independent Committee for Assistance, Asociación Nicaragüense de Luisiana, Salvadoreños Unidos de Luisiana, and Asociación de Guatemala en Luisiana.

Transgressing categories based on national origins, the Garínagu form a community of Central Americans that provides a counter-narrative to the organization of this book and the census statistics. Touched on in the Introduction, Garínagu from the Caribbean coasts of Honduras, Guatemala, Nicaragua, and Belize originated in the expulsion of the so-called Black Caribs from the British colony of Saint Vincent in the late eighteenth century. Of the estimated 300,000 to 400,000 Garínagu worldwide, some 125,000 reside in Honduras; 100,000 in the United States, many undocumented; 15,000 in Belize; and the remainder in Nicaragua, Guatemala, and a variety of other countries. New York, Chicago, Los Angeles, Miami, Houston, and New Orleans have the largest Garifuna communities in the United States, with English-speakers from Belize mainly in Los Angeles. Unified by their mixed African and indigenous ancestry, the Garifuna language, and their transnational society, Garínagu do not fit well into any of the categories given on census forms. They might therefore choose to deny entirely Latino ethnicity, preferring instead to identify with one or more of the racialized categories, especially "Black or African American," "American Indian or Alaska Native," or "Some Other Race." Other Garínagu might well identify as Latinos and for their national origin write in Garifuna, Honduran, Guatemalan,

Nicaraguan, Belizean, or nothing at all. The Census Bureau eliminates those who write in Belize from the count of Hispanics and Latinos, counts those who write in any of the other national affiliations with those countries, and counts those who write in Garifuna or Garínagu as Latinos but as Other Central Americans. Their population in New Orleans therefore remains undetermined—and perhaps indeterminable given that their identities are so indefinite and malleable relative to those codified in the census.[5]

Nonetheless, estimates in the late 1990s placed the population of the New Orleans Garifuna community at 2,000–4,000. The push and the pull factors for leaving Central America, or some other US city, and settling in New Orleans would have been similar to those of Hondurans, Salvadorans, and Nicaraguans covered earlier. Garínagu have been coming to the United States through New Orleans since the banana trade established linkages to the Caribbean lowlands of Central America in the early twentieth century. Although some remained in New Orleans, most passed through on their way to the Garifuna community in New York City, which was not only larger but part of a broader Afro-Latino community of people from Puerto Rico and, later, the Dominican Republic and Cuba.[6]

After Katrina, as revealed through interviews with Garínagu, that community grew substantially. A large, albeit unknown, proportion of the 18,866 difference between the Honduran, Guatemalan, Nicaraguan, and Other Central American populations of 2000 and those of 2010 represents people who also self-identify as Garínagu. The transnational network that emerged over the twentieth century to connect Central America, New Orleans, and other US cities facilitated that post-Katrina influx.

The interviews also reveal the situational and relational character of Garifuna identity. In New York City, Garínagu tend to emphasize the African aspects of their identity because their residential concentrations make them the neighbors of many African Americans and other Afro-Latinos in Harlem and the Bronx: "In New York, there are people from everywhere, Jamaica, Puerto Rico, the Dominican Republic. There are bars, clubs, and stores where you can mix with these people."[7] When in New Orleans, in contrast, the same Garínagu tend to identify as Hondurans in order to capitalize on the dominance of that community in North Kenner and the stereotype of a Latino work ethic that emerged after Katrina: "In New Orleans you don't have that, people live separated: blacks, Latinos, whites. Here, I'm friends with Central Americans. I mean, I am the same person that I was. It's just different here."[8] Moreover, their identities change entirely and instantaneously according to the specific social situation and location, for example, work versus leisure situations and public versus private locations. And those identities are relational, as when Garínagu speak Spanish around Latinos and whites in order to identify as Latinos to secure employment: "In Honduras I am Garifuna first. In the United States I sometimes identify myself as Latina, and in New Orleans I always say Honduran among Latinos. . . . I consider myself Latina, it is part of me just as much as Garifuna. I grew up in Honduras and have a lot of friends that are not Garifuna. I have cousins that are mestizos."[9]

Yet the same Garínagu speak Garifuna around African Americans in New Orleans in order to sound African out of fear of being assaulted, for two main reasons. Latinos were commonly targeted by criminals of all kinds, including blacks, because they sometimes have all of their savings in cash rather than bank accounts due to their undocumented status and mobility. Also, a general "black-brown antagonism" emerged after Katrina because blacks characterized Latinos as newcomers who were competing for their traditional housing and employment as well as driving down wages. Which identity to use with police proved more problematic for Garínagu because of the city's long history of criminalizing blackness and poverty, with police forces that harbor corrupt officers who prey on both blacks and Latinos.[10]

> It's easier to tell people I'm Latino. In New Orleans, there are African Americans, Whites, Asians and there are Latinos. We are considered Latinos, especially to African Americans here in New Orleans. In New York, people are accustomed to other ethnic groups. You can say Garifuna, and they can distinguish you from other groups. Here, both African Americans and Whites are not familiar with Garínagu. If you speak Spanish, you are Latino and probably came after Katrina.[11]

> Yes, to people from here I look black. My skin is dark, but when I open my mouth, Americans know I am not a black person from here. After that, really nothing is similar. We are culturally different than African Americans; we have a different history. I don't have anything against them, but I don't consider myself one of them.[12]

In contrast to the other Central American groups, Costa Ricans and Panamanians are among the smallest of Latino-origin groups in both New Orleans and the United States as a whole. Nationally, each represented only about 0.3 percent of the total Hispanic and Latino population in 2010. And both concentrated in New York City. Their small communities in New Orleans are more similar in population to the South American groups, clustering near the bottom of figure 41 with fewer than a thousand each in 2010.

Puerto Ricans and Dominicans

Puerto Ricans and Dominicans are among the largest Latino groups in the United States and stand out as two of five communities in New Orleans that over the 1990s grew instead of declined. Yet by 2010, they both remained much smaller than the Honduran community. And the Puerto Rican community was being overtaken by the rapidly growing Nicaraguan and Guatemalan ones.

Nationally, residents of Puerto Rican origin are the second-largest group of Latinos, following those of Mexican origin. Census 2000 enumerated 3.4 million Puerto Ricans, not including those residing in Puerto Rico. While not growing as rapidly as many other groups, Puerto Ricans nonetheless reached 4.6 million by Census 2010. In New Orleans, though, Census 2000 enumerated only 2,889 Puerto Ricans. Rapid growth followed Katrina, with Census 2010 enumerating 3,898. Yet the city's Puerto Rican community remains substantially smaller than the Cuban one and an order of magnitude smaller than the Honduran and Mexican ones, even with the undercounting bias that impacts the enumerations of those groups. The Northeast has the most prominent communities of *boricuas,* as Puerto Ricans term themselves, yet their neocolonial relationship with the United States has shaped the small community in New Orleans as much as it has the large ones in New York City and Philadelphia.

Before Spain ceded Puerto Rico to the United States as a condition of the 1898 treaty that ended the Spanish-American War, only a few expatriate Puerto Ricans working in the cigar and shipping industries lived in New Orleans. Afterward, Puerto Rico became an unincorporated territory of the United States: its residents have elected their own legislature since 1900, been US citizens since 1917, begun to elect their governor in 1948, and enacted a constitution in 1952. Yet, because of Puerto Rico's territorial status, Puerto Ricans do not elect representatives to Congress or vote for the president. Periodic plebiscites since 1967 have posed three options regarding that status: to continue as a territory, to become a US state, or to become an independent country. None have received the sort of overwhelming support that would precipitate action by Congress. The status quo continues.[13]

New York and Philadelphia rather than New Orleans became major boricua communities because after the Spanish-American War, sugar refineries in Brooklyn and along the Delaware River became the principal importers of Puerto Rican raw sugar. The associated shipping and commercial linkages facilitated the settlement of large numbers of Puerto Ricans in the Northeast. While New Orleans, therefore, did not become directly involved in the neocolonial relationship, a small community of boricuas nonetheless became established there in the early twentieth century.[14]

The first members of that community were migrant workers on their way to Hawaiian sugar plantations. Between 1900 and 1901, more than five thousand Puerto Ricans landed at New Orleans, took trains to San Francisco, and then embarked ships to Hawaii for seasonal work in the cane fields. Some abandoned the journey along the route, however, dispirited by racism and harsh conditions, or attracted by opportunities in cities like New Orleans. Fifteen Puerto Ricans deserted their labor contracts and settled in New Orleans.[15]

Next, the First World War created a labor shortage, depressed European immigration to the United States, and increased demand for Latino workers. As part of the effort to secure additional workers, the 1917 Jones-Shafroth Act made Puerto Ricans US citizens and allowed them to work without visas, simultaneously subjecting them to military conscription. A parallel contract labor program subsidized their relocation to work in military industries, including the vast expansion of shipyards in New Orleans funded by the federal government. In 1918 alone, 2,774 Puerto Ricans relocated to New Orleans as part of the labor program. Ultimately that expansion of the city's Puerto Rican community proved temporary, ending with the war in 1919. When their labor contracts ended, they either returned to Puerto Rico or relocated to the Northeast, where the larger Puerto Rican communities provided support, not only culturally but in terms of employment and housing. Census 1920 revealed that while those of Puerto Rican birth in the United States had grown to 11,811, nearly three-quarters of them lived in New York, Pennsylvania, and New Jersey. Louisiana, in contrast, had only 217 residents born in Puerto Rico.[16]

Lacking strong commercial connections with Puerto Rico, the community in New Orleans remained relatively small throughout the twentieth century. After the Second World War, Puerto Rican migration to the United States escalated, driven by depression of the island's economy, affordable air connections, and other factors. By 1950, some 301,375 Puerto Ricans resided in the United States, increasing to nearly 1.4 million by 1970. The relatively small proportion that chose to settle in New Orleans rather than the large communities in the Northeast expanded and invigorated the city's small community enough to organize El Club de Puerto Rico de Nueva Orleans. Founded in 1960, that community organization continues to promote boricua cultural traditions through social gatherings every two months. Census 1990 enumerated 2,501 people in the city who self-identified as being of Puerto Rican origin, and modest growth continued over the 1990s to reach 2,889 by Census 2000.[17]

Despite this modest growth, a transient quality characterized the community throughout the twentieth century and stymied the accumulation of social capital. Many Puerto Rican migrant workers have passed through the city, but most later returned to Puerto Rico or settled in other parts of the United States. Likewise, the Puerto Ricans who come to New Orleans to study at Tulane, the University of New Orleans, and other universities typically leave after graduation, whether to return to Puerto Rico or relocate to a large boricua community in New York City or elsewhere: "There was a point when I was very involved with the Tulane and Loyola crowd. And yeah, over there, there is a bunch of them [Puerto Ricans] who are younger and they just come for a few years and then go back or somewhere else. They rarely stay. . . . Most Puerto Ricans come here to get their degrees and then they go home."[18]

The lack of residential concentration has also inhibited a prominent boricua community in the city. Those who have settled in New Orleans live dispersed throughout the city. As for many other groups, a progressive shift to Jefferson Parish has occurred, and concentrations occur in North Kenner and on the Westbank. Yet the majority of Puerto Ricans in the city are professionals, have broad social networks, and live throughout the city: "The very few Puerto Ricans that I know here, they have good jobs. They are doing well. Some are lawyers; others are teachers, doctors, some kind of corporate job."[19]

Just as for other Latinos, post-Katrina employment opportunities attracted Puerto Ricans. By Census 2010, the community had grown by a little over a third, to 3,898. That rate of growth, however, pales in comparison to nearly every other group. In fact, given the undercounting biases for all other Latino groups relative to Puerto Ricans, they have likely become less populous than not only Hondurans, Mexicans, Cubans, and Nicaraguans but Guatemalans and perhaps even Salvadorans and Dominicans. According to one Puerto Rican resident, most boricuas simply do not appreciate living in New Orleans: "Honestly, I don't really think this is a place that appeals to Puerto Ricans. Honestly, to me, the first five years it didn't appeal to me neither. Even though it was the closest thing to home, it didn't appeal as much. After Katrina, I kind of fell in love with the city."[20]

The community of Dominicans in New Orleans contrasts markedly with their Caribbean neighbors, in part due to the different commercial relationship New Orleans has had with the Dominican Republic than the one it has with Puerto Rico. Although the Dominican Republic achieved independence from Spain in the nineteenth century, the United States closely controlled its politics over the twentieth century. In the wake of a US occupation from 1916 through 1924, US corporations came to control most of the country's sugar production, and the dictatorship of Rafael Trujillo brutally repressed all opposition until his assassination in 1961. The next year, a democratic election coincided with the imposition of the US trade embargo on Cuba. With the close of shipping between US and Cuban ports, Santo Domingo suddenly became the principal Caribbean port for New Orleans at the same time that the new Dominican president began to threaten nationalization of foreign businesses. The United States first supported a series of military coups and then invaded, occupying the island from 1965 through 1966 to install one of Trujillo's former cronies as president.

One result was the flight of Dominicans who feared a return to the brutal repressions of the Trujillo dictatorship. That exodus continues to the present despite the establishment of democratic governments and peaceful transitions of power in the twenty-first century. Now mainly pushed to leave by a chronically poor economy, Dominicans are attracted to the United States by the established Dominican communities. Collectively, they had a population of 1.4 million in 2010 and formed the fifth-largest Latino group, mainly concentrating in the New York City metropolitan area.

A community of Dominicans also became established in New Orleans, albeit much smaller than the one in New York City. The embargo on trade with Cuba stimulated a boom in shipping between New Orleans and Santo Domingo, unlike Puerto Rico. Even now, only the ports of Miami and Houston handle more of the US-Dominican trade than New Orleans. With economic depression in the Dominican Republic through the 1970s while New Orleans had an expanding job market driven by growth of the petrochemical industry, an increasing number of Dominicans settled in the city. They concentrated in Gretna, on the Westbank near the petrochemical plants, and near related shipyards and fabrication shops along the southern and eastern margins of the city. Even with the city's decline in employment over the 1980s, economic conditions in the Dominican Republic continued to encourage Dominicans to move to New Orleans. Census 1990 counted just 291 Dominicans in New Orleans, but by 2000 that figure had more than doubled, to 623.[21]

Following Katrina, the population of the Dominican community in New Orleans nearly tripled, with 2,282 enumerated by Census 2010. Interviews reveal that while most of those who had arrived in the twentieth century came directly from the Dominican Republic, the post-Katrina influx also involved many from the Northeast, especially New York, New Jersey, and Boston. Though they all share a Dominican heritage, the post-Katrina arrivals differ in many ways from the twentieth-century arrivals and their descendants. The essence of those differences involves growing up in a small Dominican community that had to integrate with the city's broader society versus growing up in a large Dominican community that had enough social capital to sustain the ethnic identities of its members.

> Now there is a new division, not a real big one, it's not a political division, but you know who's been here pre-Katrina and post-Katrina. . . . The folks in New York, because my parents met in New York, that community is very different. You know, the way they organize themselves, they had proximity because of the density of the neighborhoods where they lived. Those folks are still very Dominican. Even if they are naturalized, in their minds they are still Dominicans. It's definitely different for us [being born in New Orleans of Dominican parents].[22]

The pre- and post-Katrina Dominicans do, however, share a residential concentration on the Westbank. That concentration and separation from the Central American community in North Kenner has resulted in cultural landscape elements that include barbershops and salons, restaurants, and a nightclub. Barbershops are prominent elements of the Dominican landscape in New York City as well as social spaces in which the community fosters social capital critical for developing and maintaining attachment to place and cultural identity. The post-Katrina proliferation of Dominican barbershops and hair salons in

Gretna indicates not only a vibrant and growing community, but also a connection to the communities in the Northeast, where those types of businesses serve to sustain the community. The Dominican establishments in New Orleans, like their counterparts in New York, are not insular, but serve a diverse clientele including Latinos of other national origins, Palestinians, African Americans, and others.[23]

That diversity signals the complex racialized and ethnic identities that Dominicans navigate within the black-white binary of the United States, made emphatically clear by the popular categorization of President Barack Obama as an African American despite having a white mother and a black father. In New Orleans, the malleable creole category necessitates adjustments for Dominicans more used to the black-white binary of New York City.

> I obviously had identity issues here because folks never knew what to make of me. Most folks, a lot of folks here just think I'm creole—local creole—because of my appearance. So that was always interesting. I always got to see race through peculiar angles. Because if folks just assumed that I was African American or Black Creole, I would find myself in situations where they would, for whatever reason, if Latinos came up, they would feel very free to start spreading anti-Hispanic, anti-Latino, anti-immigrant rhetoric. When folks were more correctly aware of what my actual background was, it was the opposite where they would feel for whatever reason when the topic came up that they could say rhetoric that was anti-Black. . . . It taught me a lot about people's perceptions. . . . Code switch is survival. I do it without even trying. I've talked to quite a few people that do it, and again, it's something that you don't even notice that you do. It depends on the crowd that you're with and how comfortable you are with yourself. I'm the same person no matter who I'm with. I may interact differently, but that's just communication.[24]

South Americans

Many of the countries of South America have had relationships with the United States somewhat similar to those of Mexico, Central America, and the Caribbean yet have relatively smaller communities in the United States, including New Orleans. The US military and CIA have become involved in every one of the South American republics over the twentieth century, although with fewer invasions and occupations compared to Mexico, the Central American republics, or the Caribbean. For example, the US Navy obstructed Colombian efforts to oppose separatist Panamanians in 1903. The CIA covertly supported the brutally repressive dictatorships of Chile, Argentina, Uruguay, Paraguay, Bolivia, and Brazil over the 1970s and 1980s. The Drug Enforcement Agency (DEA), sometimes with support from the US military, has long maintained counter narcotics operations in Bolivia, Peru, Ecuador, and Colombia. And United Fruit had banana plantations in Ecuador and Colombia, although it never controlled those countries to the same degree as Honduras.[25]

The rank order by population in 2010 of South American groups in New Orleans nearly perfectly reflects the national rank order. People of Colombian origin are the largest US group, with a population of 908,734, followed by Peruvians and Ecuadorians at about half a million each, Venezuelans and Argentinians at about a quarter of a million, and even smaller communities of Bolivians, Chileans, Uruguayans, and Paraguayans. Populations in New Orleans follow that same general order, from Colombians at 1,305 down to Paraguayans at 24. Some of the communities seem to have grown dramatically between 2000 and 2010 and others not, but the populations of most are so low in any case that interpreting the relative changes seems inappropriate, especially given the deflation of the "Unspecified" and "Other South American" categories in Census 2010 compared to Census 2000. Moreover, all the groups display relatively dispersed residential patterns, lacking notable concentrations in particular neighborhoods and thus further attenuating the small total populations.

Those South Americans in New Orleans, therefore, who want to sustain the cultural identities of their countries of origin must deploy different strategies than the larger or more residentially concentrated communities treated so far. Those groups can build identity through semi-fixed landscape elements and the frequent interactions that places such as barbershops facilitate. Interviews reveal that the smaller, more dispersed South American groups rely on the concentration of Latino supermarkets in North Kenner to maintain their cuisines as individuals and families. Argentineans, Uruguayans, and Paraguayans purchase *yerba mate* there, for example. As communities, though, they join together into a more populous "pan–South American" community.

While only the Argentineans maintain a formal social organization, others of South American origin participate in their activities. Founded in 1982, Casa Argentina organizes events such as an annual tango ball, picnics, and an *asado*.

The asado takes place outdoors and involves characteristic cuts of meat, sweet-breads, and *chorizos* grilled over charcoal and served with *chimichurri* sauce and red wine—quite unlike the Brazilian churrasco or North American bar-becue. Hundreds of people typically attend to enjoy the food and socialize. They include, however, not only some of the few hundred Argentineans living in New Orleans but others living in Baton Rouge and elsewhere in southern Louisiana and Mississippi. Moreover, Chileans, Uruguayans, Paraguayans, and others who feel they share somewhat similar cultural practices, such as asado or tango, also participate.[26]

Pan-Latinos

Consideration of the less populous Latino communities emphasizes that while each national-origin group attempts in various ways to maintain a distinct iden-tity while integrating into the broader New Orleans community, each also some-times adopts a pan-Latino identity. Argentineans, Uruguayans, Paraguayans, and Chileans certainly adopt a broader identity than one defined by national origins when they socialize at an asado, unifying around a shared cuisine, mu-sic, and history. Garínagu also adopt a pan-Latino identity in specific social situations and relations—in contrast to a pan-African, creole, or a more spe-cific Garifuna one in others. Interviews reveal that second-generation Latinos and their children in New Orleans tend to identify increasingly with a broader, pan-Latino identity, as do members of communities with small populations and people in relationships that include a mix of national origins.

That said, in other social contexts people might adopt identities at the sub-national scale. For example, a group of Argentineans will quickly identify, ex-plicitly or by inference from accents, which of them is a *porteño,* from Buenos Aires, and which from "the interior." A group of Cubans will just as quickly establish who came in the original exodus, who are Marielitos, and who are balseros. First-generation Latinos and members of more populous communities tend to focus on such subnational identities within their origin groups.

A pan-Latino identity emerges regularly in specific contexts. Organizations such as the Cervantes Fundación Hispano-Americana de Arte, the Hispanic Chamber of Commerce of Louisiana, and Puentes foster such an identity by sponsoring pan-Latino activities and addressing issues of broad concern for La-tinos. City-wide celebrations such as the Carnaval Latino music festival cultivate pan-Latino culture and creativity. But perhaps the most visible manifestation of a unified identity occurred on May 1, 2006, when thousands of Latinos marched together down Canal Street as part of the Gran Paro, the national strike in protest of the lack of progress on immigration reform as well as the exploitation of undocumented workers, a particularly acute issue in New Orleans in the immediate aftermath of Katrina.[27]

CONCLUSIONS

Instead of hybridity versus purity, this view suggests it is hybridity all the way down.   —*Renato Rosaldo, Foreword to* Hybrid Cultures, *1995*

A well-known scientist... described how the earth orbits around the sun and how the sun, in turn, orbits around the center of a vast collection of stars called our galaxy. At the end of the lecture, a little old lady at the back of the room got up and said: "What you have told us is rubbish. The world is really a flat plate supported on the back of a giant tortoise." The scientist gave a superior smile before replying, "What is the tortoise standing on?" "You're very clever, young man, very clever," said the old lady. "But it's tortoises all the way down!"

—*Stephen Hawking,* A Brief History of Time, *1988*

AS THE PROPORTION OF HISPANICS AND LATINOS in the United States has grown, the debate about immigration and national identity has become increasingly polarized between the advocates of purity versus those of hybridity. In *Who Are We? The Challenges to America's National Identity,* Samuel P. Huntington contends that Hispanics and Latinos are not assimilating to what he characterizes as the pure core of Anglo-Protestant culture. He argues that Latinos do not assimilate because they are able to maintain a strong ethnic identity through residential concentration in urban enclaves as well as in several regions: the Southwest, Texas, southern California, and southern Florida. Others counter that US immigrants assimilate at the same time as they contribute to a multicultural national identity. Sociological theories about the detailed processes involved do not support one side in that debate over the other. Contact theory suggests that residential integration of Latinos would indeed promote assimilation because the proximity of different groups supposedly results in greater interaction, intergroup mutual respect and cooperation, accumulation of social capital, and general prosperity that encourages assimilation to the putative national identity—Huntington's pure Anglo-Protestant core. Conflict theory suggests the opposite, namely that greater intergroup proximity and interaction actually result in more social competition and conflict, thus inhibiting assimilation to the pure, core identity.[1]

Such abstract generalizations, however, can only become concrete and meaningful through studies such as this one. This work combines mapping of modern census statistics, historical analysis that spans centuries, and contemporary interviews to explain the residential and cultural geographies of each group, its relationship to Katrina flooding, and interactions with other groups as played out in an actual place through the actions and thoughts of everyday life. It thereby reveals how Hispanics and Latinos in a particular place have over centuries established themselves and constructed community identities in relation to each other and the broader society. It also reveals the diversity involved in that process, both how different each community is from the others and how much diversity exists within each community. It demonstrates how the changes in the residential geography of each group have created different types of conflict and contact among them as well as the broader society in relation to their constructions of community and identity. It shows how critical transnational social networks have been to their identities and the disproportionate growth of some of the communities relative to others. And it reveals the dynamism of the processes involved, with major transformations associated with catastrophic events such as Katrina, economic change in New Orleans and elsewhere, and changes in trade and geopolitical relationships.

ONE OF THE CHIEF DISTINCTIONS AMONG those communities is the length of time each has been part of the city. The Isleños came during colonial times, and their identity formed and has persisted over many generations in relation to more demographically, socially, and culturally dominant non-Hispanic communities. The Cubans, Hondurans, Mexicans, and others from the Caribbean and Central America first became established as identifiable Latino communities during neocolonial times, many through commodity and labor connections established in the nineteenth and twentieth centuries due to US domination of those regions and many as political refugees from related oppression and conflict. The more recently arrived members of those communities, other Central Americans, and the small groups of South Americans, including Brazilians, reflect a more post-colonial, transnational process that fosters a pan-Latino, supranational identity. In general, second- and third-generation members of those communities embrace a broader, pan-Latino identity, as do members of communities with small populations, and people in relationships that include more than one national origin. First-generation Latinos, in contrast, as well as members of more populous communities, focus on the diversity within their communities related to subnational, class, political, and racialized categories.

Such diversity, moreover, refutes generalizations about any of the putative communities, or even their existence except as academic abstractions. Some groups encompass a great deal of social and racialized diversity, such as the Cuban community that became established in a series of mass departures from Cuba over half a century. Isleño settlement, in contrast, took place many generations ago over a brief period, ensuring relative community homogeneity but also no adoption of a pan-Latino identity despite a shared Hispanic heritage and language. The Brazilians also settled in New Orleans over a brief period and therefore relatively cohesively, albeit much more recently than the Isleños; they do not share a Hispanic heritage or the Spanish language yet in some situations and social relations nonetheless do adopt a pan-Latino identity. Other groups, such as the Garínagu, completely transgress the national-origin groups that structure this study, identifying in complex and malleable ways that depend on place, situation, and social relationship with Hondurans, other Latinos, African Americans, and creoles.

Moreover, the residential geography of each group has changed over time to create different degrees of segregation and integration as well as various types of conflict and contact in relation to the construction of community and identity formation. The incremental movement of Cubans, Hondurans, and other Latinos from Orleans to Jefferson Parish beginning in the 1970s not only decreased interactions with the African American community but spared many the persistent Katrina flooding that devastated the Isleño community on the eastern side of the city. Moreover, the resulting Honduran residential concentration on the northwestern side of the city has given rise to notable social cohesion, demographic and social dominance over other Latino groups concentrated there, and a landscape that reflects and reinforces the sense of place that imagines New Orleans as a Honduran city. The residential geography of the Mexican community, more focused on the southern side of the city, proximate to the petrochemical service industry, somewhat separated that group from the Honduran community so that, despite Mexican dominance among Latinos nationally, Hondurans are able to dominate New Orleans.

This study also demonstrates the significance of transnational social networks to some communities, to their identities as well as to their disproportionate growth relative to other groups. The lack of an active transnational network among the Isleños has resulted in a lack of continued immigration from Spain and an identity strongly related to a local place, especially St. Bernard Parish, rather than to a network of places that includes Spain and other US places with colonial Hispanic communities such as Santa Fe. The majority of Latino communities, in contrast, continue to become more populous due to new arrivals via their well-developed transnational networks connecting New Orleans to other sites in the United States and to Latin America and the Caribbean, especially the Hondurans and Mexicans but also other Central American and Caribbean groups. Also, the transnational spaces of mobility that connect the nodes of those networks relate to their identities as Latino communities in New Orleans, whether the historic memory of the banana freighters that once imported bananas from Honduras or personal memories of undocumented crossings of the US-Mexico border. The Cubans provide a striking counterexample due to the embargo that constrains development of their transnational network. Similarly, many of the South American groups, while engaged in transnational networks, lack the intricate connectivity characteristic of Central American and Caribbean groups that are rooted in more than a century of commercial and geopolitical interactions.

The dynamism of the processes involved, with major transformations triggered by hurricanes, revolutions, and other types of sudden events, has also become clear. The Isleños proved much more vulnerable to the devastation of Katrina than Latino communities, but an identity characterized by a deep attachment to place ensured that they returned to rebuild in disproportionate numbers. Katrina did have great indirect impact on the Latino communities, though, by catalyzing an influx of reconstruction workers that ensured the dominance of the existing Honduran community as well as establishing a nearly entirely new community of Brazilians. The internal heterogeneity of the Cuban community amid its relatively stagnant population is rooted in the episodic politics and economics of Cuba: the revolution that created a wave of political refugees in the late 1950s and 1960s, the trade embargo that ended a long-standing economic and cultural relationship with New Orleans, a second wave of political refugees precipitated by Cuban policy in the 1980s, and the collapse of Comecon in the 1990s that resulted in an influx of economic refugees. And the recent passage of Juan Crow laws in parts of the New Latino South encouraged some Mexicans to move to New Orleans.

SUCH DETAILED, COMPREHENSIVE TREATMENT of the several Hispanic and Latino sides of New Orleans has, most basically, demystified a major aspect of the city's ethnic history. No longer does anyone have any excuse to reduce the roles of so many Isleños and Latinos in the making of the Crescent City to Governor Gálvez, the Cabildo, and various plaques and monuments. And no longer can anyone bemoan being "overrun by Mexican workers" or celebrate that the city might become "a future San Antonio." By explicating the historical geography of each group and how they are related to each other and the broader city, this study makes clear their deep, intricately interwoven histories of participation in the creation of the city's distinctive landscapes, music, and culture. They variously concentrate in particular neighborhoods or disperse across the city, interacting with each other and the broader urban society to different degrees. And each incorporates aspects of the identities of other groups into their own at the same time that the city incorporates aspects of their identities. Revealing the diversity of the city's Hispanic and Latino communities, and even the diversity within some of them, renders nonsensical the debates about the assimilation of Hispanics and Latinos as some putatively homogenous group. Even more fundamentally, without the involvement of the communities addressed in this study, the identity of the city would be so different that debates over whether Hispanics and Latinos are assimilating to that identity or "overrunning" it become an exercise in circular reasoning.[2]

Instead of taking a side in the debate about whether a pure core or multiculturalism will define the future identity of New Orleans or the nation as a whole, then, this study forces the conclusion that "it is hybridity all the way down." The process through which identities emerge involves an ongoing integration of remembered and current performance of everyday life, modulated by place, networks connecting to other places, specific situations, and social relations. In contrast, attempts to define some sort of essential identity, a self-contained and timeless essence of what it *really* means to be American or Honduran or Latino, so remove identity from lived experience that such efforts become meaningless outside of the abstract debates of the academic experts. Reality, in other words, is more complex and alive than the degree of assimilation to a rehearsed definition of identity such as Huntington's Anglo-Protestant core.[3]

As this book details, Hispanics have been settling in New Orleans since the eighteenth century and Latinos since the nineteenth, but they form such a minor percentage of the population of New Orleans, not even 10 percent in 2010, that the city will not soon become majority Latino nor even join the New Latino South. Nor will it become anything like San Antonio, Miami, or Santa Fe. Instead, what has emerged is *pure New Orleans*. It is a place with an identity as difficult to define as the jazz that originated in the city. But, like that musical genre, it indubitably involves the hybridization of eclectic elements, including Hispanic and Latino ones. It changes through collaborative improvisation. It relishes extemporaneous performance. And it remains open to still unimagined possibilities.

NOTES

Introduction

1. Campo-Flores, "A New Spice in the Gumbo."

2. Waller, "El Sueño de Una Vida Mejor"; and Trujillo-Pagan, "From 'Gateway to the Americas' to the 'Chocolate City.'"

3. Sluyter, "(Post-)K New Orleans"; Sluyter, "The Role of Blacks in Establishing Cattle Ranching in Louisiana"; and Sluyter, *Black Ranching Frontiers*, 61–97.

4. Watkins and Hagelman, "Hurricane Katrina as a Lens for Assessing Socio-Spatial Change."

5. Chaney, "Uncovering Nodes."

6. A. Gibson, *Post-Katrina Brazucas.*

7. For thoughtful discussions of the terms "Hispanic" and "Latino," see Arreola, "Introduction," 1–12; and Passel and Taylor, *Who's Hispanic?* The word "Garifuna" is both the adjectival and the singular form of the noun "Garínagu."

8. C. Gibson and Jung, *Historical Census Statistics on Population Totals;* Lukinbeal, Price, and Buell, "Rethinking 'Diversity'"; Duany, "Reconstructing Racial Identity"; Benson, "Exploring the Racial Identities of Black Immigrants"; Levitt and Waters, *The Changing Face of Home;* Alba and Nee, *Remaking the American Mainstream;* Foner and Fredrickson, *Not Just Black and White;* Oropesa, Landale, and Greif, "From Puerto Rican to Pan-Ethnic"; Portes and Zhou, "The New Second Generation"; Bhabha, *The Location of Culture;* and Navarro, "For Many Latinos, Racial Identity Is More Culture than Color."

9. Brasseaux and Conrad, *The Road to Louisiana;* W. Davis, *The Pirates Laffite;* Mintz and Price, *An Anthropological Approach to the Afro-American Past;* Midlo Hall, *Africans in Colonial Louisiana;* Kein, "The Use of Louisiana Creole in Southern Literature"; Tregle, "Early New Orleans Society"; Hirsch and Logsdon, *Creole New Orleans;* C. Stewart, "Creolization"; and Dominguez, *White by Definition.*

10. Chaney, "Malleable Identities"; Palacio, *The Garifuna;* N. González, "Garifuna Settlement in New York"; N. González, *Sojourners of the Caribbean;* England, *Afro-Central Americans in New York;* England, "Afro-Hondurans in the Chocolate City"; Johnson, *Diaspora Conversations;* Kleyn, "Garífuna es Nuestra Manera de Ser"; Anderson, *Black Indigenous;* Gordon and Anderson, "The African Diaspora"; and Samers, *Migration.*

11. Szanton Blanc, Basch, and Glick Schiller, "Transnationalism," 684; and Basch, Glick Schiller, and Szanton Blanc, *Nations Unbound,* 7.

12. M. Davis, *Magical Urbanism,* 96.

13. Potter, "Transnational Spaces and Communal Land Tenure"; Mintz, "The Localization of Anthropological Practice"; Portes, Guarnizo, and Landolt, "The Study of Transnationalism"; and Foner, *From Ellis Island to JFK.*

14. For examples, see Maduell, *Spanish Citizens Entering New Orleans;* Euraque, "Honduran Memories"; Din, *The Canary Islanders;* Montero de Pedro, *The Spanish;* Caughey, *Bernardo de Gálvez;* and Henao, *The Hispanics.*

15. As mapped, the New Orleans of this study coincides with the vernacular conception of the city rather than the larger area that the Census Bureau refers to as the Metropolitan Statistical Area (MSA). For details of the method used to determine the extent of destructive flooding due to Hurricane Katrina, see Watkins and Hagelman, "Hurricane Katrina as a Lens for Assessing Socio-Spatial Change." The flood analysis employed a spatially enabled raster dataset depicting the extent and depth of floodwaters for September 2, 2005, based on LiDAR (Light-Imaging Detection and Ranging) imagery, available through the Louisiana State University GIS Information Clearinghouse at www.katrina.lsu.edu (accessed October 1, 2006) and developed by the US Geological Survey; see J. Smith and Rowland, "Temporal Analysis of Floodwater Volumes." For areas within the four parishes but outside of the built-up, leveed areas, the flood analysis employed polyline GIS shapefiles of Federal Emergency Management Agency surge contours (katrina_la_sec.shp), available at www .fema.gov (accessed January 12, 2010); and United States Department of Agriculture 1999 Digital Orthophoto MrSID Mosaics for Jefferson, Orleans, Plaquemines, and St. Bernard parishes, available at datagateway.nrcs.usda.gov (accessed January 12, 2010).

16. For overviews of the history of early New Orleans and Louisiana during the French and Spanish periods, see Giraud, *A History of French Louisiana;* and Din, *The Spanish Presence in Louisiana.*

17. Therrien and Ramirez, *The Hispanic Population;* Suro and Singer, *Latino Growth in Metropolitan America;* Campbell and Jung, *Historical Census Statistics on Population Totals;* and Ennis, Ríos-Vargas, and Albert, *The Hispanic Population.* Note that statistics for the United States relate to its fifty states and the District of Columbia; they do not include Puerto Rico. All population statistics used, unless otherwise stated, come from the decennial censuses and American Community Surveys available from the Census Bureau at www.census.gov, factfinder.cenus.gov, and factfinder2. census.gov (accessed October 6, 2011).

18. B. Smith, *The New Latino South;* H. Smith and Furuseth, *Latinos in the New South;* Odem and Lacy, *Latino Immigrants;* and Kochhar, Suro, and Tafoya, *The New Latino South,* 2–3.

19. Huntington, *Who Are We? The Challenges to America's National Identity;* Alba and Nee, *Remaking the American Mainstream;* Lukinbeal, Price, and Buell, "Rethinking 'Diversity,'" 111–13; Tropp and Petigrew, "Relationships between Intergroup Contact and Prejudice"; and Quillian, "Prejudice as a Response."

20. For examples, see Nostrand, *The Hispano Homeland;* Arreola and Curtis, *The Mexican Border Cities;* Levine and Asis, *Cuban Miami;* M. Davis, *Magical Urbanism;* Arreola, *Tejano South Texas;* Arreola, *Hispanic Spaces, Latino Places;* Kochhar, Suro, and Tafoya, *The New Latino South;* and James Chaney, "The Formation of a Hispanic Enclave."

21. The image derives from Landsat Mosaic Orthoimagery of June 2004, available from the US Geological Survey at www.usgs.com (accessed December 6, 2010). Parish boundaries and other

features derive from the US Geological Survey's National Atlas of the United States, available at www.nationalatlas.gov (accessed December 6, 2010); and Digital Raster Graphics of the following 1:24,000 US Geological Survey topographic quadrangles available at libremap.org (accessed December 6, 2010): Chalmette, 1994; Martello Castle, 1994; Belle Chase, 1994; Delacroix, 1994; and Yscloskey, 1994.

22. Colten, *An Unnatural Metropolis;* Colten, *Perilous Place, Powerful Storms;* Sluyter, "(Post-) K New Orleans"; Li, Airriess, Chen, Leong, and Keith, "Katrina and Migration"; Frey and Singer, *Katrina and Rita Impacts;* and Flaherty, *Floodlines.*

23. In 2000, the four parishes had 329 census tracts, which the Census Bureau usually sizes to contain 1,500 to 8,000 inhabitants, with 4,000 considered optimal. Figure 3 includes all or part of 325 of those 329 census tracts, the four excluded ones being located in sparsely populated southern Plaquemines Parish, stretching well downriver of the city along the bird's foot delta. In 2010 the four parishes had 331 census tracts, and figure 4 includes all or part of 324 of them, excluding seven in sparsely populated, coastal Plaquemines and Jefferson parishes.

24. The quotes are from Campo-Flores, "A New Spice in the Gumbo"; and Waller, "El Sueño de Una Vida Mejor." The Census Bureau's estimates for the US foreign-born population are 31,107,889 in 2000, with 82,858 of them born in Spain; and 39,955,673 in 2010, with 83,242 born in Spain.

25. Croxton, *Statistical Review of Immigration,* vol. 3, 289–92, table 27; and the Seventh (1850) US Census. The 1850 schedules for the City of New Orleans and St. Bernard, Jefferson, Plaquemines, and Orleans parishes are available as microfilm from the National Archives and Records Administration (Washington, DC): M432.232–239. The schedules are also available as a searchable database and page images at familysearch.org (accessed October 18, 2011), which is the source for the 1850 population statistics used throughout this book unless otherwise stated.

26. C. Gibson, *Population of the 100 Largest Cities;* Lewis, *New Orleans,* 57–58; Levander and Levine, *Hemispheric American Studies,* 140–65; Delgadillo, "A 'Spanish Element' in the New South"; and Kanellos and Martell, *Hispanic Periodicals in the United States.*

27. Karnes, *Tropical Enterprise;* and Striffler and Moberg, *Banana Wars.*

28. Ukers, *All about Coffee;* and Pendergrast, *Uncommon Grounds.*

29. Conrad and Lucas, *White Gold;* Pérez, *Cuba and the United States;* Rathbone, *The Sugar King of Havana;* Barnhart, *Southern Fried Football;* and Robins and Trujillo, "Normalized Trade Relations Between the United States and Cuba," 96–102.

30. Although figure 6 graphs statistics from Census 1970 through Census 2010, differences between those censuses render the figures only nominally commensurate. One difference involves changes to categories, such as the addition of the label "Latino" beginning with Census 2000, which potentially expanded the category to include non-Hispanic Latin Americans such as Brazilians. Another difference involves changes to collection methods, such as moving the Hispanic-origin question from the long form sent to a 5 percent sample of households to the short form sent to all households, which occurred with the main question in 1980, and changes to the write-in box for the "other" category in 1990, 2000, and 2010 that affected both the accuracy of the estimates and the minimal spatial unit reported, from regions and states through parishes and census tracts. Moreover, the pre-1990 Honduran estimates derive from entirely different questions, on foreign-birth and ancestry. Note that the "All other Latino and Hispanic origins" series includes specific groups such as Costa Rican and Argentinean as well as those in the "Unspecified" category, which

incorporates various categories and subcategories that have changed from census to census: "All other Spanish/Hispanic," "Not elsewhere classified," "All other Hispanic or Latino," "Other South American," "Other Central American," and so on.

31. US Census Bureau, *Measuring America*, 77–91; US Census Bureau, *1990 Census of Population: Persons of Hispanic Origin*, B-12; and Ennis, Ríos-Vargas, and Albert, *The Hispanic Population*, 1–4.

32. Bracken, *Hispanics in a Racially and Ethnically Mixed Neighborhood*; Romero, *Ethnographic Evaluation of Behavioral Causes of Census Undercount*; Duany, "Counting the Uncountable"; Guzmán, *Census 2000 Brief*; and US Congress, *The Statutes at Large of the United States*, vol. 39, pt. 1, 951–68.

33. Ennis, Ríos-Vargas, and Albert, *The Hispanic Population*, 3; Painter, "The Assimilation of Latino Americans"; Bracken, "Restructuring the Boundaries"; Ross, "Factors in Residence Patterns"; and Carballo, "A Socio-Psychological Study of Acculturation Assimilation."

34. Louisiana Public Health Institute, Louisiana Department of Health and Hospitals, and the Louisiana Recovery Authority, "2006 Louisiana Health and Population Survey," available from the Greater New Orleans Community Data Center at www.gnocdc.org (accessed February 10, 2007); Fletcher, Pham, Stover, and Vinck, *Rebuilding after Katrina*; Drever, "New Orleans"; Drever and Blue, "Surviving Sin Papeles in Post-Katrina New Orleans"; A. Gibson, "Immigrating to New Orleans Post-Katrina"; A. Gibson, "Brazuca in NOLA"; Fussell, "Hurricane Chasers in New Orleans"; Fussell, "Post-Katrina New Orleans"; and Sluyter, "(Post-)K New Orleans."

35. Interview materials are usually reported anonymously; in cases where a name is given, a pseudonym is used. All translations of interviews and written materials from Spanish and Portuguese into English are by the authors.

1. Isleños

1. Meinig, *The Shaping of America*, vol. 1, 267–88; Conrad, *New Iberia*; Weddle, *Changing Tides*, 91–99; Parsons, "The Migration of Canary Islanders to the Americas:"; Din, "Early Spanish Colonization Efforts in Louisiana"; Din, *The Canary Islanders*, 47–63; and Montero de Pedro, *The Spanish*, 170.

2. Archivo General de Indias, Papeles de Cuba (hereafter, AGI-PC) leg. 568, no. 3, ff. 1–111, "Libro maestro para sentar el cargo a las familias de la nueve población de Tierra de Bueyes"; AGI-PC leg. 689, ff. 137v–217, "Tierra de Bueyes, año de 1784"; and AGI-PC leg. 689, ff. 392–770, "Documentación relativa a las familias llegadas de las islas Canarias y Puerto Rico para repoblar Luisiana, años 1784 y 1786." In Louisiana the French *arpent*, a measure of both distance and area, had a length of 58.5 meters (192 feet) and an area of 0.342 hectares (0.846 acres); see Chardon, "The Linear League in North America."

3. The map is based on the original township plat maps for Louisiana's Southeastern District East of the Mississippi River, which date to 1831–59 and are archived at the State Land Office in Baton Rouge; see the plats for Township 13 South, Range 13 East; Township 13 South, Range 14 East; Township 13 South, Range 15 East; Township 14 South, Range 13 East; Township 14 South, Range 14 East; and Township 14 South, Range 15 East.

4. AGI-PC leg. 1425, ff. 88–90, Letter of 15 July 1789 by Eteban Rodríguez Miró to Domingo Cabello, inclosing a "Resumen general del padrón hecho en la Provincia de Luisiana, 1788."

5. AGI-PC leg. 121, ff. 211–26, Letter of 9 March 1790 by Pedro de la Ronde to Miró; AGI-PC leg. 188A, exp. 2, ff. 7–8, "Reglamentos de 18 febrero 1770"; Louisiana State University Special Collections, Louisiana and Lower Mississippi Valley Collections, Survey Collection, box 4, St. Bernard folder; and Historic New Orleans Collection, Louisiana Land Surveys, MF 1.1.30, 1.1.163–64, 1.1.168, 1.1.170–71, 1.1.73.

6. New Orleans Public Library, City Archives, manuscript AA840, Census of 1791; New Orleans Notarial Archives (hereafter, NONA), Notary Carlos Ximénez, book 15 (1798), ff. 413–15v, Last will and testament of Antonio González, notarized March 20, 1798; and book 19 (1803), ff. 217–23v, Last will and testament of Teresa de Flores, notarized November 25, 1803; and Din, *The Canary Islanders*, 61.

7. Coles, "The Confirmation of Foreign Land Titles in Louisiana"; Poret, "History of Land Titles in the State of Louisiana"; and Maduell, *Federal Land Grants*. GLO reports to Congress appear in US Congress, *American State Papers*. The GLO district offices in Louisiana retained much of the underlying documentation, and most of that spared by fires, inundations, pests, the Civil War, and numerous relocations as the district offices progressively finalized their work and consolidated had by the early twentieth century come to reside in the single remaining office in Baton Rouge, now the State Land Office.

8. US Congress, *American State Papers*, vol. 2, 258–439, "Land claims in the eastern district of the Orleans Territory communicated to the House of Representatives on 9 January 1812"; US Congress, *Bills Originating in the House*, House Bill no. 125, December 27, 1831, "A Bill for the Relief of the Inhabitants of Terre aux Boeufs"; US Congress, *US Congressional Serial Set*, House Report no. 62, December 27, 1831; US Congress, *Journal of the House*, March 28, 1832; US Congress, *Journal of the Senate*, June 8, 1832; and US Congress, *The Public Statutes at Large*, vol. 6, 498–501, "An Act for the Relief of the Inhabitants of Terre aux Boeufs."

9. Stoddard, *Sketches Historical and Descriptive*, 161; Darby, *The Emigrant's Guide*, 8; Darby, *A Geographical Description*, 71–72; King, *Creole Families of New Orleans*, 453; and US Congress, *The Public Statutes at Large*, vol. 6, 499–501. The original passenger lists are archived in AGI-PC leg. 1, ff. 754–54v, 797–97v, 875; AGI-PC leg. 689, ff. 397–98v, 676; AGI-PC leg. 1393, ff. 598–602v; Archivo General de Indias, Audiencia de Santo Domingo (hereafter, AGI-SD) leg. 2661, ff. 830–33, 942–46, 956–61v, 1000–1003v, 1073–78, 1133–38; and AGI-SD leg. 2662, ff. 835–40v, 850–51v, 893–93v. Genealogists have published and indexed those passenger lists: Hickey, *Canary Islands to Louisiana;* and Villeré, *The Canary Islands Migration to Louisiana*.

10. US Census Bureau, *Measuring America*, 473.

11. C. Gibson, *Population of the 100 Largest Cities*. Note that Plaquemines, St. Bernard, and Orleans parishes were established in 1807; Jefferson Parish was formed out of the western part of Orleans Parish in 1825; and the city of New Orleans and Orleans Parish became coterminous in 1874.

12. Guillotte, "Masters of the Marsh," 27–39; Quiñones, "Delacroix Island"; J. West, "Negotiating Heritage"; Jeansonne, *Leander Perez;* Perez, *The Isleños*, 67–74; and Montero de Pedro, *The Spanish*, 166.

13. Maduell, *Spanish Citizens Entering New Orleans*.

14. NONA, Almonester y Roxas, bk. 1 (1771), f. 155, notarization on July 29, 1771, of the last will and testament of Manuel Solís; Conrad and Lucas, *White Gold;* and Avequin, "The Sugar Cane in Louisiana."

15. Din, *The Canary Islanders,* 131–35; Barry, *Rising Tide;* and Gomez, "Perspective, Power, and Priorities."

16. R. West, *An Atlas of Louisiana Surnames,* 8, 114–15. By US law, census documents that identify individuals must remain confidential for seventy-two years after an enumeration, so Census 1930 was the most recent for which the detailed schedules were available in 2011, when we conducted this research; those Census 1930 schedules, like those for Census 1850, are available at familysearch.org (accessed October 21, 2011), which is the source for the 1930 population statistics used throughout this book unless otherwise stated. The schedules for Census 1940 were released in 2012, after we completed this phase of the project.

17. Lee, "The Land of the River"; Lipski, *The Language of the Isleños;* Armistead, *The Spanish Tradition in Louisiana;* Kaltenbaugh, "A Study of the Place Names of St. Bernard Parish"; MacCurdy, "Los Isleños de la Luisiana"; J. West, "Negotiating Heritage," 36–37; and Perez, *The Isleños,* 75–95.

18. For table 1, New Orleans refers to the sum of the four parishes named, not the MSA. Percent Hispanic and Latino refer to their proportion of the total population; percent Spanish origin refers to their proportion of the Hispanic and Latino population. The 1990 estimates of Spanish-origin populations derive from the long-form sample rather than the short-form enumeration and are therefore not strictly comparable to 2000 and 2010.

19. For figure 9, Spanish-Origin sums the three categories into which the Census Bureau coded the write-in responses: Spanish-American, Spanish, and Spaniard.

20. Ennis, Ríos-Vargas, and Albert, *The Hispanic Population,* 4; and US Census Bureau, *1990 Census of Population,* B-12.

21. Haverluk, "Hispanic Community Types."

22. The statistics derive from the Census 2000 enumerations for flooded and nonflooded census tracts in each parish, as determined in Watkins and Hagelman, "Hurricane Katrina as a Lens." For qualitative assessments of the destruction suffered by Isleños in St. Bernard Parish, see Marigny Hyland, Lopez Ramos, and Leblanc, "Report about the State of the Canarian Descendants"; and Perez, *The Isleños,* 97–100. The parish population losses due to Katrina and Rita come from Frey and Singer, *Katrina and Rita Impacts.*

23. For figure 10, Spanish-Origin sums the three relevant categories into which the Census Bureau coded the write-in responses on origin: Spanish-American, Spanish, and Spaniard. The only other tract in the city with a high proportion of Hispanics and Latinos of Spanish origin covered City Park, in northwestern Orleans Parish, and contained a total population of only four people, one of whom identified as Hispanic or Latino as well as of Spanish origin, resulting in a 100 percent figure.

24. Jeansonne, *Leander Perez,* 166.

25. Flaherty, *Floodlines,* 128–32.

26. Perez, *The Isleños,* 116–30.

2. Cubans

1. Dawdy, *Building the Devil's Empire;* Clark, *New Orleans, 1718–1812;* Guterl, *American Mediterranean;* and A. Carpenter, "Gateway to the Americas."

2. Post, "The Domestic Animals and Plants"; Dawdy, *Building the Devil's Empire;* and Cl
Orleans.

3. Din and Harkins, *The New Orleans Cabildo.*

4. Herbermann, Pace, Pallen, Shahan, Wynne, and MacErlean, *The Catholic Encyclopea*
9, 11; Din and Harkins, *The New Orleans Cabildo;* and Clark, *New Orleans,* 228.

5. Guanche Pérez, *Significación Canaria en el Poblamiento Hispánico de Cuba.*

6. Brasseaux and Conrad, *The Road to Louisiana;* and W. Davis, *The Pirates Laffite.*

7. Clark, *New Orleans,* 314; and Delgadillo, "A 'Spanish Element' in the New South."

8. Knight, *Slave Society in Cuba during the Nineteenth Century,* 67–68; Klein, *African Slavery in Latin America and the Caribbean,* 89–101; Murray, "Statistics of the Slave Trade to Cuba"; Bergad, Iglesias García, and Carmen Barcia, *The Cuban Slave Market;* Galloway, *The Sugar Cane Industry,* 162–67; Walker "Manufactures"; Campbell, "New Orleans at the Time of the Louisiana Purchase"; and Funes Monzote, *From Rainforest to Cane Field in Cuba,* 127–204.

9. Rehder, *Delta Sugar;* Watts, *The West Indies;* Avequin, "The Sugar Cane in Louisiana"; and Conrad and Lucas, *White Gold.*

10. Thrasher, "Cuban Annexation"; Thrasher, "Cuba and Louisiana"; Urban, "The Idea of Progress and Southern Imperialism"; Urban, "New Orleans and the Cuban Question"; Antón and Hernández, *Cubans in America;* and Guterl, *American Mediterranean.*

11. Kmen, *Music in New Orleans;* Loggins, *Where the Word Ends;* J. Stewart, "Cuban Influences on New Orleans Music"; Sublette, *Cuba and Its Music;* and Sublette, *The World that Made New Orleans.*

12. A. Carpenter, "Gateway to the Americas."

13. Sexton, *The Monroe Doctrine;* McCartney, *Power and Progress;* and Pérez, *Cuba and the United States.*

14. Quesada, *Cuba,* 147; Fortier, *The Spanish-American War of 1898;* and Bergeron, *Guide to Louisiana Confederate Military Units.*

15. Rathbone, *The Sugar King of Havana;* Conrad and Lucas, *White Gold;* Domestic Sugar Producers, "First Cuban Raws Arrive for Louisiana Factories"; and Barnhart, *Southern Fried Football.*

16. Robins and Trujillo, "Normalized Trade Relations"; and Jeansonne, *Leander Perez.*

17. Croxton, *Statistical Review of Immigration,* vol. 3, 289–92, table 27; Duany, "Cuban Communities in the United States"; and Carballo, "Socio-Psychological Study of Acculturation Assimilation."

18. Schafer, *Brass Bands and New Orleans Jazz;* McCusker, "The Onward Brass Band"; Lichtenstein and Dankner, *Musical Gumbo;* Roberts, *The Latin Tinge;* and Sublette, *Cuba and Its Music.*

19. Schoultz, *That Infernal Little Cuban Republic;* Pérez, *Cuba and the United States;* and Tulane University, Special Collections Library, Louisiana Research Collection, Winston Lill papers, box 2, folder 18, "Chep Morrison trip to Havana."

20. Duany, "Cuban Communities," fig. 1, table 1; Antón and Hernández, *Cubans in America;* and E. González, *Cuban Exiles on the Trade Embargo.*

21. The seventeen interviews with members of the Cuban community in New Orleans conducted over 2010–11 included men and women, a range of ages from 25 to 72, arrivals in New Orleans in each decade from the 1960s through 2000s, and occupations from domestic and construction workers to university professors and attorneys.

22. Interview of August 8, 2011.

23. A Cuban who arrived in New Orleans in the 1960s quoted in Montoya González, "Carnival, Feast Days, and House Parties," 3.

24. Figure 11 and all other maps in this book based on Census 1970 and Census 1980 employ the Neighborhood Change Database, 1970–2000 Tract Data developed by Geolytics and the Urban Institute, available at www.geolytics.com (accessed December 10, 2009), to map statistics using all or part of 325 of the 329 tracts across the four parishes used in Census 2000 because digitized tract boundaries remain unavailable for Census 1970 and Census 1980, the four excluded tracts being located in sparsely populated southern Plaquemines Parish. The same issues pertain to comparisons of maps of tract-level data based on Census 1970 through Census 2010 as to the graphs of parish-level data in figure 6: differences between those censuses render the maps only nominally commensurate because of changing categories, collection methods, and coding protocols. Moreover, data for all variables are not available for all years, for example, exclusion of the Cuban-origin statistics from the Geolytics database for 1970.

25. Flaherty, *Floodlines*, 197.

26. Lewis, *New Orleans*.

27. Flaherty, *Floodlines*, 18–19; Orleans Parish went from 54 percent white and 45 percent black in 1970 to 28 percent white and 67 percent black in 2000, with the remainder a small percentage of Asians and others. During the same period Jefferson Parish went from 87 percent white and 12 percent black to 70 percent white and 23 percent black while the relative proportions of the other two parishes remained fairly constant: St. Bernard, 88–95 percent white and 4–8 percent black; and Plaquemines, 70–77 percent white and 21–23 percent black.

28. In 1990, the four parishes had 327 census tracts, and figure 15 includes all or part of 320 of them, excluding seven in sparsely populated southern Plaquemines and Jefferson parishes and in eastern St. Bernard Parish.

29. Doss, *Let the Bastards Go;* and Antón and Hernández, *Cubans in America*.

30. Interview of July 15, 2011.

31. Antón and Hernández, *Cubans in America;* and interviews of July 15, August 8, August 10, and August 13, 2011.

32. Ackerman, "The Balsero Phenomenon"; and Fernández, *Adrift*.

33. Interview of August 10, 2011.

34. Montoya González, "Carnival, Feast Days, and House Parties," 4–5; LatiNOLA.com (accessed December 1, 2011); and CubaNOLA.org (accessed December 1, 2011). The acronym NOLA plays on the US Postal Service zip-code abbreviation for Louisiana, namely LA, and stands for New Orleans, Louisiana. Although the specific origin remains unknown, it likely began as slang when zip codes came into use in the 1960s before becoming the masthead of the biweekly *NOLA Express,* a countercultural newspaper published in New Orleans during the 1960s.

35. Fuente García, "La Virgen de la Caridad del Cobre"; and Tweed, *Our Lady of the Exile,* 49.

36. Interview of August 11, 2011.

37. Lukinbeal, Price, and Buell, "Rethinking 'Diversity,'" 111–13; Tropp and Petigrew, "Relationships between Intergroup Contact and Prejudice"; and Quillian, "Prejudice as a Response to Perceived Group Threat."

38. Baldwin and Childs, *2009/10 Rice Yearbook,* appendix table 7; US Congress, *Rice Programs,*

34–38, 51–58; and US Congress, *The Economic Relationship between the United States and Cuba After Castro,* 108–11.

39. Baldwin and Childs, *2009/10 Rice Yearbook,* appendix table 25; Varney, "Cuban Officials, Blanco Sign a $15 Million Deal"; Moran, "Lifting of Cuban Trade Embargo Could be Boon to Louisiana Ports"; Jervis, "U.S. Ports Set to Deal with Cuba"; Robins and Trujillo, "Normalized Trade Relations"; US Rice Producers Association, "Cuba Embargo"; Port of New Orleans, "Trade with Cuba"; and personal communication on July 21, 2011, by Robert M. Landry, Director of Marketing, Port of New Orleans.

40. Bahr, "Destination: Cuba"; and personal communication on July 15, 2011, by Romualdo González.

41. Personal communication on August 10, 2011, by Javier Olondo; Montoya González, "Music and Dance in South Louisiana's Cuban Community"; and personal communication on August 9, 2011, by Alexey Martí Soltero, which is the source of the quote.

3. Hondurans

1. Karnes, *Tropical Enterprise;* Dosal, *Doing Business with the Dictators,* 80–81; and Gruesz, "The Mercurial Space of 'Central' America."

2. Striffler and Moberg, *Banana Wars.*

3. Arreola, "Urban Ethnic Identity Landscape"; Tuan, *Space and Place;* Tuan, "Language and the Making of Place"; Proshansky, "The City and Self-identity"; Jorgensen and Stedman, "Sense of Place as an Attitude"; and J. Smith and Cartlidge, "Place Attachment among Retirees."

4. Croxton, *Statistical Review of Immigration,* vol. 3, 289–92, table 27; in addition to "Spanish-American," that table lists "Spanish," "Mexican," "Cuban," and "West Indian (except Cuban)" immigrants.

5. Simmons, *Confederate Settlements in British Honduras.*

6. Soluri, *Banana Cultures.*

7. US Census Bureau, *Measuring America,* 72–85. The detailed schedules for Census 1940 became available in 2012, after research on the Honduran community had been completed. Census 1980 contained a question for all households that asked, "Is this person of Spanish/Hispanic descent?" but did not provide an opportunity to be more specific except for those of Mexican, Puerto Rican, and Cuban origins; however, the census also contained a question for all households that asked respondents to fill in a blank to answer the question "What is this person's ancestry?" For Census 1970, the Hispanic-origin question was administered to a 5 percent sample of households but, as in 1980, did not provide an opportunity to specify Honduran origins; however, 20 percent of households were asked to fill in a blank to answer "Where was this person born?"; and 15 percent of households were asked to fill in blanks to answer "What country was his father born in?" and "What country was his mother born in?" While all three of those questions in Census 1970 generated ancestry statistics, they limited ancestry to first- and second-generation immigrants compared to the more open definition of Census 1980. Census 1960 did not include a Hispanic-origin question at all but did administer the same three ancestry questions contained in Census 1970 to a 25 percent sample of households.

8. Consolidated Metropolitan Statistical Areas are roughly comparable to Metropolitan Statistical Areas. Both consist of multiple counties or their equivalents, such as parishes in Louisiana, that according to the glossary at www.census.gov (accessed October 10, 2006) represent "core areas with a large population nucleus, together with adjacent communities that have a high degree of economic and social integration with that core." The Census Bureau differentiates MSAs and CMSAs on the basis of total population, with CMSAs generally having a population greater than 1 million. In 1990, the New Orleans MSA included Jefferson, Orleans, St. Bernard, St. Charles, St. John the Baptist, and St. Tammany parishes.

9. Euraque, "Honduran Memories."

10. Complex manager Jorge Picado quoted in Scallan, "In Damaged Apartments, the Poor Face Dilemma."

11. Euraque, "Honduran Memories."

12. In 2000, the New Orleans MSA included Jefferson, Orleans, St. Bernard, Plaquemines, St. Charles, St. John the Baptist, St. Tammany, and St. James parishes.

13. US Immigration and Naturalization Service, *1999 Statistical Yearbook,* 27, 87; and US Department of Homeland Security, *2003 Yearbook of Immigration Statistics,* 19, 150. Interviews of February 28 and March 5, 2010. The seventeen interviews referenced in this chapter were conducted during 2007 through 2011 and included two focus groups: one consisting of five longtime residents of the city from Colombia, Nicaragua, and Honduras on February 28, 2010; the other of nine post-Katrina arrivals from Honduras, Mexico, and El Salvador on March 5, 2010.

14. Ennis, Ríos-Vargas, and Albert, *The Hispanic Population,* 4; and US Census Bureau, *1990 Census of Population,* B-12.

15. Gershanik, "Ambassador of Honduras Loves N.O. for Work, Play."

16. US Congress, *The Congressional Record,* 10373.

17. Gruesz, "The Mercurial Space of 'Central' America," 140; and Donato, Trujillo-Pagán, Bankston, and Singer, "Reconstructing New Orleans after Katrina," 220.

18. In Census 1990, 82 percent of Hondurans enumerated in Florida lived in Miami; 98 percent of those in New York and New Jersey lived in New York City; 93 percent of those in Louisiana lived in New Orleans; and 84 percent of those in California lived in Los Angeles.

19. US Congress, *The Congressional Record,* 10373; and Gershanik, "Ambassador of Honduras."

20. Dirección General de Estadística y Censos, *Censo Nacional de Población y Vivienda;* Instituto Nacional de Estadística, *Censo Nacional de Población, 1988;* and Instituto Nacional de Estadística, *XVI Censo de Población y Vivienda.* The statistics are also available at www.citypopulation.de (accessed on September 20, 2010).

21. Gershanik, "Ambassador of Honduras."

22. Based on field surveys conducted in 2007 through 2012.

23. Benedict and Kent, "The Cultural Landscape of a Puerto Rican Neighborhood."

24. Census 2000 enumerated 8,792 residents in Louisiana who claimed Honduran origin and 462 in Mississippi, a total of 9,254 compared to the estimate of 50,000.

25. Interview of March 8, 2010.

26. Interview of March 1, 2010.

27. Interview of March 5, 2010.

28. Interview of September 17, 2009.

29. Scallan, "Amid Political Squabble, Few Residents Leave Damaged Kenner Apartments"; Swerczek, "Razing of Apartments Fuels Hispanic Concerns"; Watkins and Hagelman, "Hurricane Katrina as a Lens"; Sluyter, "(Post-)K New Orleans"; and Flaherty, *Floodlines*, 185–93.

30. Interview of March 8, 2010.

31. Frank, "In Honduras, a Mess made in the U.S."; and Cave and Thompson, "U.S. Rethinks Antidrug Efforts."

32. Sluyter, "(Post-)K New Orleans"; Li, Airriess, Chen, Leong, and Keith, "Katrina and Migration"; Airriess, Li, Leong, Chen, and Keith, "Church-Based Social Capital"; and Leong, Airriess, Li, Chen, and Keith, "Resilient History and the Rebuilding of a Community."

33. For Census 2010, the Census Bureau dropped "CMSA" and renamed and redefined the areas of some MSAs. The New Orleans MSA became the New Orleans–Metairie–Kenner MSA and included Jefferson, Orleans, St. Bernard, Plaquemines, St. Charles, St. John the Baptist, and St. Tammany parishes, the same as for Census 1990 except for dropping St. James Parish.

34. US Congress, *The Congressional Record*, 10373; and M. Davis, *Magical Urbanism*.

35. Gómez-Peña, *The New World Border*, 211–12.

4. Mexicans

1. Clark, *New Orleans, 1718–1812;* A. Carpenter, "Gateway to the Americas"; and Hoffman, *Luisiana*.

2. O'Sullivan, "Annexation"; Boyett, "Money and Maritime Activities in New Orleans"; Eisenhower, *So Far from God;* Miller, *New Orleans and the Texas Revolution;* and Gruesz, "The Gulf of Mexico System," 476–88.

3. Brian Hamnett, *Juárez*.

4. Alec-Tweedie, *The Maker of Modern Mexico: Porfirio Díaz;* and Garner, *Porfirio Díaz*.

5. J. Stewart, "The Mexican Band Legend"; and J. Stewart, "The Mexican Band Legend: Part 2."

6. Henderson, *Beyond Borders;* N. Carpenter, *Immigrants and Their Children*, 78; and Hutchinson, *Immigrants and Their Children*, 6–12.

7. Croxton, *Statistical Review of Immigration*, vol. 3, 289–92, table 27; and Painter, "The Assimilation of Latino Americans."

8. Cohen, *Braceros;* Hutchinson, *Immigrants and Their Children*, 220–21, 263–64; and Henderson, *Beyond Borders*.

9. Painter, "The Assimilation of Latino Americans." After completing his master's degree at Tulane University, Painter went on to do a doctoral degree at the University of Michigan, completing a dissertation on Costa Rica and later becoming a professor of sociology at the University of Illinois.

10. Cardullo, "The Blind Mexican Woman"; and Gruesz, "The Gulf of Mexico System," 488–90.

11. C. Gibson and Jung, *Historical Census Statistics on Population Totals by Race;* Guzmán, *Census 2000 Brief;* US Immigration and Naturalization Service, *1999 Statistical Yearbook,* 27, 87; US Department of Homeland Security, *2003 Yearbook of Immigration Statistics,* 19, 150; and Taylor and López, *The Mexican-American Boom*.

12. Donato and Bankston, "The Origins of Employer Demand for Immigrants in a New Destina-

tion"; Donato, Stainback, and Bankston, "The Economic Incorporation of Mexican Immigrants in Southern Louisiana"; and Donato, Bankston, and Robinson, "Immigration and the Organization of the Onshore Oil Industry."

13. Interview of November 11, 2011; the ten interviews referenced in this chapter were conducted in 2007–11 and include Mexicans who settled in New Orleans both before and after Katrina as well as a focus group of nine people made up of Hondurans, Mexicans, and Salvadorans who had arrived after Katrina.

14. Interview of November 9, 2011.

15. Interview of June 8, 2010.

16. Interview of June 8, 2010.

17. Campo-Flores, "A New Spice in the Gumbo"; Fletcher, Pham, Stover, and Vinck, *Rebuilding after Katrina;* and interviews of March 15, 2007 and June 8, 2010.

18. Taylor and Lopez, *The Mexican-American Boom,* 3–4; and Passel, Cohn, and Gonzalez-Barrera, *Net Migration from Mexico Falls to Zero,* 6–8.

19. Interviews of December 10 and November 20, 2011.

20. Interview of August 4, 2011; and "Matrículas Consulares de Alta Seguridad Expedidas en el Consulado de México en Nueva Orleans, 2010," available at www.ime.gob.mx/matriculas2010/consulado/nuevaorleans.html (accessed April 20, 2013).

21. Interview of November 20, 2011.

22. Interview of July 16, 2011.

23. Fausset, "Alabama's Immigration Law Prompts Alarm"; and interview of August 4, 2011.

24. Ray Nagin quoted in Campo-Flores, "A New Spice in the Gumbo."

25. McCarthy, "Riley, Nagin Push for Immigration Reform"; Weil, "Finding Housing"; Delp, Podolsky, and Aguilar, "Risk amid Recovery"; Faingold, "Official English in the Constitutions and Statutes of the Fifty States in the United States"; *Louisiana Constitution of 1974,* Article XII, Section 4, available at senate.legis.state.la.us (accessed September 16, 2012); and Wilkinson, Dunaway, and Goidel, "Rebuilding or Intruding?"

26. Ennis, Ríos-Vargas, and Albert, *The Hispanic Population,* 6, table 2; and Kochhar, Suro, and Tafoya, *The New Latino South,* 2–3.

27. Interview of December 10, 2011.

5. Brazilians

1. Ukers, *All About Coffee;* Pendergrast, *Uncommon Grounds;* Topik and Samper, "The Latin American Coffee Commodity Chain"; Port of New Orleans Overview, available at www.portno .com (accessed September 7, 2010); and US Department of Agriculture, Foreign Agriculture Service, Production, supply, and distribution database, available at www.fas.usda.gov (accessed August 20, 2010).

2. A. Gibson, "Immigrating to New Orleans Post-Katrina"; A. Gibson, "Brazuca in NOLA"; A. Gibson, *Post-Katrina Brazucas;* Dawsey and Dawsey, *The Confederados;* and Harter, *The Lost Colony of the Confederacy.*

3. US Census Bureau, *Measuring America,* 77–91.

4. US Office of the Federal Register, "Standards for the Classification of Federal Data on Race and Ethnicity," 29831–35.

5. US Office of the Federal Register, "Revisions to the Standards for the Classification of Federal Data on Race and Ethnicity," 58782–89; Beserra, *Brazilian Immigrants in the United States;* Margolis, *Little Brazil;* Marrow, "To Be or Not to Be (Hispanic or Latino)"; Martes, "Neither Hispanic, nor Black"; Marrow, "Who Are the Other Latinos and Why?"; and Marcus, "Becoming Brazuca."

6. The Kayapo are a native group that lives in the Brazilian Amazon. Significant numbers of immigrants came to Brazil from Portugal, Africa, Italy, Germany, Japan, China, and other countries over the colonial period, nineteenth century, and twentieth century.

7. Margolis, *Little Brazil.*

8. Falconi and Mazzotti, *The Other Latinos;* Beserra, *Brazilian Immigrants in the United States;* Marrow, "To Be or Not to Be"; Margolis, *Little Brazil;* A. Gibson, "Immigrating to New Orleans"; A. Gibson, "Brazuca in NOLA"; A. Gibson, *Post-Katrina Brazucas;* Jouët-Pastré and Braga, *Becoming Brazuca;* Marcus, *An Invisible Minority;* Marcus, "Brazilian Immigration to the United States and the Geographical Imagination"; Marcus, "(Re)creating Places and Spaces in Two Countries"; Marcus, "Brazilians and the 1990 United States Census"; Marcus, "Becoming Brazuca"; Teresa Sales, *Brazilians Away From Home;* Jackiewicz and Sun, "The Ties That Bind, or Not?"; and Goza, "Brazilian Immigration to North America."

9. "Spanish and Portuguese," available at tulane.edu/liberal-arts/spanish-portuguese (accessed September 12, 2012).

10. The Census Bureau conducts the American Community Survey on a monthly basis by mailing questionnaires in English and Spanish to a sample of 250,000 households throughout the nation and requesting that participants complete and return them in a self-addressed, stamped envelope. Nonresponders receive follow-up phone calls and, eventually, if necessary, a visit from bureau personnel. The bureau compiles the monthly returns to produce annual estimates.

11. Personal communication (e-mail) of August 24, 2010, from Claudio Teixeira, vice-consul, Consulado-Geral do Brasil em Houston.

12. The twenty-two interviews referenced in this chapter were conducted over 2010. The focus group took place at a Latino health fair in June 2010. A. Gibson, "Immigrating to New Orleans Post-Katrina"; A. Gibson, "Brazuca in NOLA"; Marcus, *An Invisible Minority;* B. Smith, *The New Latino South;* H. Smith and Furuseth, *Latinos in the New South;* Martin Kaste, "For Poor Brazilians, a Perilous, Illegal Journey to US," Reporter's Notebook, National Public Radio, April 14, 2006, available at http://www.npr.org (accessed September 13, 2014); Nolan, "Many Brazilians Settling in N.O."; US Immigration and Naturalization Service, *1999 Statistical Yearbook,* 27; and US Department of Homeland Security, *2003 Yearbook of Immigration Statistics,* 19.

13. Weil, "Finding Housing"; Delp, "Risk amid Recovery"; and A. Gibson, "Immigrating to New Orleans Post-Katrina."

14. Interview of June 15, 2010.

15. Interview of June 13, 2010.

16. Interview of July 25, 2010.

17. Interview of June 13, 2010.

18. *Samba-enredo* is the specific style of samba that samba schools perform during the Carnival parades of Rio de Janeiro.

19. Assunção, *Capoeira.*

20. Waller, "New Rules Eliminate Taco Trucks."

21. Interview of June 13, 2010; and Louisiana Workforce Commission, "June Employment Numbers Show Job Gains," July 23, 2010, news release, available at laworks.net (accessed September 13, 2012).

22. Interview of June 13, 2010.

23. Interview of August 14, 2010.

24. Interview of June 15, 2010.

25. Interview of August 14, 2010.

26. Portuguese renders "New Orleans" as either "Nova Orleães" or "Nova Orleans."

6. Other Communities

1. Brazilians do not appear in table 10 due to a lack of comparable data but seem to have grown from the hundreds in 1990 to the thousands in 2010, with a population trajectory similar to that of the Dominicans.

2. Ennis, Ríos-Vargas, and Albert, *The Hispanic Population,* 4; and US Census Bureau, *1990 Census of Population,* B-12.

3. Moore, "Pierre Soulé"; Collin, *Theodore Roosevelt's Caribbean*; and Striffler and Moberg, *Banana Wars.*

4. LaFeber, *Inevitable Revolutions*; Menchú, *I, Rigoberta Menchú*; and Steinberg, Hobbs, and Mathewson, *Dangerous Harvest.*

5. Chaney, "Malleable Identities"; Palacio, *The Garifuna*; N. González, "Garifuna Settlement in New York"; N. González, *Sojourners of the Caribbean*; England, *Afro-Central Americans in New York*; England, "Afro-Hondurans in the Chocolate City; Johnson, *Diaspora Conversations*; Kleyn, "'Garífuna es Nuestra Manera de Ser'"; Anderson, *Black Indigenous*; and Gordon and Anderson, "The African Diaspora."

6. Ferguson, "Many Garifuna Moving Families to New Orleans."

7. Interview of May 22, 2010.

8. Interview of May 22, 2010.

9. Interview of October 13, 2009; *mestizo* designates people who are westernized but of mixed indigenous and white parentage, more often used in Mexico than in Central America, where *ladino* is similarly but more commonly used.

10. Flaherty, *Floodlines,* 160–64, 213–16.

11. Interview of June 11, 2010.

12. Interview of June 15, 2010.

13. Whalen, "Colonialism, Citizenship, and the Making of the Puerto Rican Diaspora."

14. Vázquez-Hernández, "From Pan-Latino Enclaves to a Community."

15. Whalen, "Colonialism, Citizenship, and the Making of the Puerto Rican Diaspora," 8–11.

16. US Employment Service, "To Increase Common Labor Supply with Porto Ricans"; US Census Bureau, *Fourteenth Census of the United States,* vol. 2, 626–30, table 17; and Whalen, "Colonialism, Citizenship, and the Making of the Puerto Rican Diaspora," 8–11.

17. El Club de Puerto Rico de Nueva Orleans maintains a Web site at www.puertoricoclub.net (accessed May 27, 2014).

18. Interview of April 6, 2013.

19. Interview of April 6, 2013.

20. Interview of April 6, 2013.

21. Interview of January 15, 2011; Interview of July 21, 2011 with Robert M. Landry, director of marketing, Port of New Orleans; and Foreign Trade Division of the Census Bureau, statistics available at www.usatradeonline.gov (accessed June 5, 2013).

22. Interview of January 15, 2011.

23. Interview of February 14, 2013; and Candelario, *Black behind the Ears;* Duany, "Reconstructing Racial Identity."

24. Interview of January 15, 2011; although "code switching" is a formal concept used by linguists, it has entered popular usage to mean, quite broadly, the alternation between cultural modes as well as languages, as in "Spanglish."

25. Collin, *Theodore Roosevelt's Caribbean;* Striffler and Moberg, *Banana Wars;* Brands, *Latin America's Cold War;* McSherry, *Predatory States;* Stokes, *America's Other War;* and Steinberg, Hobbs, and Mathewson, *Dangerous Harvest.*

26. "Casa Argentina," available at ga.lsu.edu/blog/andrewsluyter/2013/11/13/casa-argentina/ (accessed June 3, 2014); and interviews of November 10, 2013.

27. Flaherty, *Floodlines,* 217.

Conclusions

1. Huntington, *Who Are We? The Challenges to America's National Identity;* Alba and Nee, *Remaking the American Mainstream;* Lukinbeal, Price, and Buell, "Rethinking 'Diversity,'" 111–13; Tropp and Petigrew, "Relationships between Intergroup Contact and Prejudice"; and Quillian, "Prejudice as a Response to Perceived Group Threat."

2. Campo-Flores, "A New Spice in the Gumbo," 5.

3. García Canclini, *Hybrid Cultures;* Appadurai, *Modernity at Large;* and Bhabha, *The Location of Culture.*

WORKS CITED

Ackerman, Holly. 1996. "The Balsero Phenomenon, 1991–1994." *Cuban Studies* 26: 169–200.

Airriess, Christopher A., Wei Li, Karen J. Leong, Angela Chia-Chen Chen, and Verna M. Keith. 2008. "Church-Based Social Capital, Networks and Geographical Scale: Katrina Evacuation, Relocation, and Recovery in a New Orleans Vietnamese American Community." *Geoforum* 39: 1333–46.

Alba, R., and V. Nee. 2003. *Remaking the American Mainstream: Assimilation and Contemporary Immigration.* Cambridge, MA: Harvard University Press.

Alec-Tweedie, Ethel. 1906. *The Maker of Modern Mexico: Porfirio Díaz.* New York: John Lane Company.

Anderson, M. 2009. *Black Indigenous: Garifuna Activism and Consumer Culture in Honduras.* Minneapolis: University of Minnesota Press.

Antón, Alex, and Roger E. Hernández. 2002. *Cubans in America: A Vibrant History of a People in Exile.* New York: Kensington Books.

Appadurai, Arjun. 2008. *Modernity at Large: Cultural Dimensions of Globalization.* Minneapolis: University of Minnesota Press.

Armistead, Samuel G. 1992. *The Spanish Tradition in Louisiana: Isleño Folk Literature.* Newark, DE: Juan de la Cuesta.

Arreola, Daniel D. 1995. "Urban Ethnic Identity Landscape." *Geographical Review* 42: 518–34.

———. 2002. *Tejano South Texas: A Mexican-American Cultural Province.* Austin: University of Texas Press.

———. 2004. "Introduction." In *Hispanic Spaces, Latino Places,* edited by Daniel D. Arreola, 1–12. Austin: University of Texas Press.

Arreola, Daniel D., and James R. Curtis. 1993. *The Mexican Border Cities: Landscape Anatomy and Place Personality.* Tucson: University of Arizona Press.

Assunção, Matthias Röhrig. 2005. *Capoeira: The History of an Afro-Brazilian Martial Art.* New York: Routledge.

Avequin, J. B. 1857. The Sugar Cane in Louisiana. *Debow's Review: Agricultural, Commercial, Industrial Progress and Resources* 22 (6): 615–19.

Bahr, Emilie. 2009. "Destination Cuba: New Orleans Pursues Status as Port of Entry to Island Nation." *New Orleans City Business,* August 3.

Baldwin, Katherine, and Nathan Childs. 2011. *2009/10 Rice Yearbook.* Washington, DC: US Department of Agriculture.

Barnhart, Tony. 2000. *Southern Fried Football: The History, Passion, and Glory of the Great Southern Game.* Chicago: Triumph Books.

Barry, John M. 1997. *Rising Tide: The Great Mississippi Flood of 1927 and How It Changed America.* New York: Simon & Schuster.

Basch, Linda, Nina Glick Schiller, and Cristina Szanton Blanc, eds. 1994. *Nations Unbound: Transnational Projects, Postcolonial Predicaments, and Deterritorialized Nation-States.* Amsterdam: Gordon & Breach.

Benedict, Albert, and Robert B. Kent. 2004. "The Cultural Landscape of a Puerto Rican Neighborhood in Cleveland, Ohio." In *Hispanic Spaces, Latino Places,* edited by Daniel Arreola, 187–205. Austin: University of Texas Press.

Benson, J. 2006. "Exploring the Racial Identities of Black Immigrants in the United States." *Sociological Forum* 21: 219–47.

Bergad, Laird W., Fe Iglesias García, and María del Carmen Barcia. 1995. *The Cuban Slave Market, 1790–1880.* Cambridge: Cambridge University Press.

Bergeron, Arthur. 1989. *Guide to Louisiana Confederate Military Units, 1861–1865.* Baton Rouge: Louisiana State University Press.

Beserra, Bernadete. 2003. *Brazilian Immigrants in the United States: Cultural Imperialism and Social Class.* New York: LFB Scholarly Publishing.

Bhabha, Homi K. 2004. *The Location of Culture.* London: Routledge.

Boyett, Gene W. 1976. Money and Maritime Activities in New Orleans during the Mexican War. *Louisiana History* 17: 413–29.

Bracken, Mary K. 1992. *Hispanics in a Racially and Ethnically Mixed Neighborhood in the Greater Metropolitan New Orleans Area.* Washington, DC: US Census Bureau.

———. 1992. "Restructuring the Boundaries: Hispanics in New Orleans, 1960–1990." PhD dissertation, University of New Mexico.

Brands, Hal. 2012. *Latin America's Cold War.* Cambridge, MA: Harvard University Press.

Brasseaux, Carl A., and Glenn R. Conrad, eds. 1992. *The Road to Louisiana: The Saint-Domingue Refugees, 1792–1809.* Lafayette: Center for Louisiana Studies, University of Southwestern Louisiana.

Bunner, E. 1855. *History of Louisiana: From Its Discovery and Settlement to the Present Time.* New York: Harper.

Campbell, Edna F. 1921. "New Orleans at the Time of the Louisiana Purchase." *Geographical Review* 11: 414–25.

Campo-Flores, Arian. 2005. "A New Spice in the Gumbo: Will Latino Day Laborers Locating in New Orleans Change Its Complexion?" *Newsweek* 147 (23): 46.

Candelario, Ginetta E. B. 2007. *Black behind the Ears: Dominican Racial Identity from Museums to Beauty Shops.* Durham, NC: Duke University Press.

Carballo, Manuel. 1970. "A Socio-Psychological Study of Acculturation Assimilation: Cubans in New Orleans." PhD dissertation, Tulane University.

Cardullo, Bert. 1983. "The Blind Mexican Woman in Williams' *A Streetcar Named Desire*." *Notes on Modern American Literature* 7 (2): 15–17.

Carpenter, Arthur E. 1987. "Gateway to the Americas: New Orleans's Quest for Latin American Trade, 1900–1970." PhD dissertation, Tulane University.

Carpenter, Niles. 1927. *Immigrants and Their Children, 1920*. Washington, DC: Bureau of the Census.

Caughey, John W. 1998. *Bernardo de Gálvez in Louisiana, 1776–1783*. Gretna, LA: Pelican.

Cave, Damien, and Ginger Thompson. 2012. "U.S. Rethinks Antidrug Efforts after Deadly Turn in Honduras." *New York Times*, October 13, A1.

Chaney, James. 2010. "The Formation of a Hispanic Enclave in Nashville, Tennessee." *Southeastern Geographer* 50: 17–38.

———. 2012. "Malleable Identities: Placing the Garínagu in New Orleans." *Journal of Latin American Geography* 11: 121–44.

———. 2013. "Uncovering Nodes in the Transnational Social Networks of Hispanic Workers." PhD dissertation, Louisiana State University.

Chardon, Roland. 1980. "The Linear League in North America." *Annals of the Association of American Geographers* 70: 129–53.

Clark, John G. 1970. *New Orleans, 1718–1812: An Economic History*. Baton Rouge: Louisiana State University Press.

Cohen, Deborah. 2011. *Braceros: Migrant Citizens and Transnational Subjects in the Postwar United States and Mexico*. Chapel Hill: University of North Carolina Press.

Coles, Harry L. 1955. "The Confirmation of Foreign Land Titles in Louisiana." *Louisiana Historical Quarterly* 38: 1–22.

Collin, Richard H. 1990. *Theodore Roosevelt's Caribbean: The Panama Canal, the Monroe Doctrine, and the Latin American Context*. Baton Rouge: Louisiana State University Press.

Colten, Craig E. 2005. *An Unnatural Metropolis: Wresting New Orleans from Nature*. Baton Rouge: Lousiana State University Press.

———. 2009. *Perilous Place, Powerful Storms: Hurricane Protection in Coastal Louisiana*. Jackson: University of Mississippi Press.

Conrad, Glenn R., ed. 1979. *New Iberia: Essays on the Town and Its People*. Lafayette: University of Louisiana Press.

Conrad, Glenn R., and Ray F. Lucas. 1995. *White Gold: A Brief History of the Louisiana Sugar Industry*. Lafayette: Center for Louisiana Studies, University of Southwestern Louisiana.

Croxton, Frederick C. 1911. *Statistical Review of Immigration, 1820–1910*. 3 vols. Washington, DC: US Government Printing Office.

Darby, William. 1817. *A Geographical Description of the State of Louisiana*. 2nd ed. New York: James Olmstead.

———. 1818. *The Emigrant's Guide to the Western and Southwestern States and Territories.* New York: Kirk & Mercein.

Davis, Mike. 2001. *Magical Urbanism: Latinos Reinvent the U.S. Big City.* New York: Verso.

Davis, William C. 2005. *The Pirates Laffite: The Treacherous World of the Corsairs of the Gulf.* Orlando, FL: Harcourt.

Dawdy, Shannon L. 2008. *Building the Devil's Empire: French Colonial New Orleans.* Chicago: University of Chicago Press.

Dawsey, Cyrus B., and James M. Dawsey, eds. 1995. *The Confederados: Old South Immigrants in Brazil.* Tuscaloosa: University of Alabama Press.

Delgadillo, Rafael E. 2009. "A 'Spanish Element' in the New South: The Hispanic Press and Community in Nineteenth-Century New Orleans." MA thesis, University of New Orleans.

Delp, L., L. Podolsky, and T. Aguilar. 2009. "Risk amid Recovery: Occupational Health and Safety of Latino Day Laborers in the Aftermath of the Gulf Coast Hurricanes." *Organization Environment* 22: 479–90.

De Quesada, Gonzalo. 1905. *Cuba.* Washington, DC: Government Printing Office for the International Bureau of the American Republics.

Din, Gilbert C. 1972. Early Spanish Colonization Efforts in Louisiana. *Louisiana Studies* 11: 31–49.

———. 1988. *The Canary Islanders of Louisiana.* Baton Rouge: Louisiana State University Press.

———, ed. 1996. *The Spanish Presence in Louisiana, 1763–1803.* Lafayette: University of Louisiana Press.

Din, Gilbert C., and John E. Harkins. 1996. *The New Orleans Cabildo: Colonial Louisiana's First City Government, 1769–1803.* Baton Rouge: Louisiana State University Press.

Dirección General de Estadística y Censos. 1976. *Censo Nacional de Población y Vivienda, 1974.* 3 vols. Tegucigalpa, Honduras: Dirección General de Estadística y Censos.

Domestic Sugar Producers, Inc. 1921. "First Cuban Raws Arrive for Louisiana Factories." *Facts about Sugar* 12: 266, 273.

Dominguez, Virginia. 1994. *White by Definition: Social Classification in Creole Louisiana.* New Brunswick, NJ: Rutgers University Press.

Donato, Katherine M., and Carl L. Bankston. 2008. "The Origins of Employer Demand for Immigrants in a New Destination: The Salience of Soft Skills in a Volatile Economy." In *New Faces in New Places: The Changing Geography of American Immigration,* edited by Douglas S. Massey, 124–48. New York: Russell Sage Foundation.

Donato, Katharine M., Carl L. Bankston, and Dawn T. Robinson. 2001. "Immigration and the Organization of the Onshore Oil Industry: Southern Louisiana in the Late 1990s." In *Latino Workers in the Contemporary South,* edited by Arthur D. Murphy, Colleen Blanchard, and Jennifer A. Hill, 104–13. Athens: University of Georgia Press.

Donato, Katherine M., Melissa Stainback, and Carl L. Bankston. 2005. "The Economic Incorporation of Mexican Immigrants in Southern Louisiana: A Tale of Two Cities." In *New Destinations of Mexican Immigration in the United States: Community Formation, Local Responses and Inter-Group Relations,* edited by Víctor Zúñiga and Rubén Hernández-León, 76–100. New York: Russell Sage Foundation.

Donato, Katharine M., Nicole Trujillo-Pagán, Carl L. Bankston, and Audrey Singer. 2007. "Reconstructing New Orleans after Katrina: The Emergence of an Immigrant Labor Market." In *The Sociology of Katrina: Perspectives on a Modern Catastrophe,* edited by David L. Brunsma, David Overfelt, and J. Steven Picou, 217–33. Lanham, MD: Rowman & Littlefield.

Dosal, Paul J. 1993. *Doing Business with the Dictators: A Political History of United Fruit in Guatemala, 1899–1944.* Lanham, MD: Rowman & Littlefield.

Doss, Joe Morris. 2003. *Let the Bastards Go: From Cuba to Freedom on God's Mercy.* Baton Rouge: Louisiana State University Press.

Drever, Anita I. 2008. "New Orleans: A Re-emerging Latino Destination City." *Journal of Cultural Geography* 25: 287–303.

Drever, Anita I., and Sarah A. Blue. 2011. "Surviving *Sin Papeles* in Post-Katrina New Orleans: An Exploration of the Challenges Facing Undocumented Latino Immigrants in New and Re-emerging Latino Destinations." *Population, Space and Place* 17: 89–102.

Duany, Jorge. 1996. "Counting the Uncountable: Undocumented Immigrants and Informal Workers in Puerto Rico." *Latino Studies Journal* 7 (2): 69–107.

———. 1998. "Reconstructing Racial Identity: Ethnicity, Color, and Class among Dominicans in the United States and Puerto Rico." *Latin American Perspectives* 25:147–72.

———. 1999. "Cuban Communities in the United States: Migration Waves, Settlement Patterns and Socioeconomic Diversity." *Pouvoirs dans la Caraïbe* 11: 68–103.

Eisenhower, John S. D. 1989. *So Far from God: The U.S. War with Mexico, 1846–1848.* New York: Random House.

England, Sarah. 2006. *Afro-Central Americans in New York City: Garifuna Tales of Transnational Movements in Racialized Space.* Gainesville: University of Florida Press.

———. 2010. "Afro-Hondurans in the Chocolate City: Garifuna, Katrina, and the Advantages of Racial Invisibility in the Nuevo New Orleans." *Journal of Latino-Latin American Studies* 3 (4): 31–55.

Ennis, Sharon R., Merarys Ríos-Vargas, and Nora G. Albert. 2010. *The Hispanic Population: 2010.* Washington, DC: US Census Bureau.

Euraque, Samantha. 2004. "Honduran Memories: Identity, Race, Place and Memory in New Orleans." MA thesis, Louisiana State University.

Faingold, Eduardo D. 2012. "Official English in the Constitutions and Statutes of the Fifty States in the United States." *Language Problems and Language Planning* 36: 136–48.

Falconi, José L., and José A. Mazzotti, eds. 2007. *The Other Latinos: Central and South Americans in the United States.* Cambridge, MA: Harvard University Press.

Fausset, Richard. 2011. "Alabama's Immigration Law Prompts Alarm." *Los Angeles Times,* October 8.

Ferguson, H. 1997. "Many Garifuna Moving Families to New Orleans." *Times-Picayune,* April 6, A4.

Fernández, Alfredo. 2000. *Adrift: The Cuban Raft People.* Houston: Arte Público Press.

Flaherty, Jordan. 2010. *Floodlines: Community and Resistance from Katrina to the Jena Six.* Chicago: Haymarket Books.

Fletcher, Laurel E., Phuong Pham, Eric Stover, and Patrick Vinck. 2006. *Rebuilding after Katrina: A Population-Based Study of Labor and Human Rights in New Orleans.* Berkeley and New Orleans: International Human Rights Law Clinic and Human Rights Center, University of California at Berkeley; Payson Center for International Development and Technology Transfer, Tulane University.

Foner, Nancy. 2000. *From Ellis Island to JFK: New York's Two Great Waves of Immigration.* New Haven, CT: Yale University Press.

Foner, Nancy, and George M. Fredrickson, eds. 2004. *Not Just Black and White: Historical and Contemporary Perspectives on Immigrant, Race and Ethnicity in the United States.* New York: Russell Sage Foundation.

Fortier, James J. A., ed. 1939. *The Spanish-American War of 1898: Liberty for Cuba and World Power for the United States.* New Orleans: Louisiana State Museum.

Frank, Dana. 2012. "In Honduras, a Mess Made in the U.S." *New York Times,* January 27, A27.

Frey, William H., and Audrey Singer. 2006. *Katrina and Rita Impacts on Gulf Coast Populations: First Census Findings.* Washington, DC: US Census Bureau.

Fuente García, José de la. 1999. "La Virgen de la Caridad del Cobre: Estudio de la Imagen y el Mito de su Aparición." *Revista de los Ciencias Sociales* 6: 99–122.

Funes Monzotes, Reinaldo. 2008. *From Rainforest to Cane Field in Cuba: An Environmental History since 1492.* Translated by Alex Martin. Chapel Hill: University of North Carolina Press.

Fussell, Elizabeth. 2009. "Hurricane Chasers in New Orleans." *Hispanic Journal of Behavioral Sciences* 31: 375–94.

———. 2009. "Post-Katrina New Orleans as a New Migrant Destination." *Organization and Environment* 22: 458–69.

Galloway, Jock H. 2005. *The Sugar Cane Industry: An Historical Geography from Its Origins to 1914.* Cambridge: Cambridge University Press.

García Canclini, Nestor. 1995. *Hybrid Cultures: Strategies for Entering and Leaving Modernity.* Minneapolis: University of Minnesota Press.

Garner, Paul. 2001. *Porfirio Díaz: Profiles in Power.* White Plains, NY: Longman Publishing.

Gershanik, Ana. 1993. "Ambassador of Honduras Loves N.O. for Work, Play." *Times-Picayune,* March 28.

Gibson, Annie M. 2008. "Brazuca in NOLA: A Cultural Analysis of Brazilian Immigration to New Orleans Post-Katrina." *Studies in Latin American Popular Culture* 27: 103–28.

———. 2010. "Immigrating to New Orleans Post-Katrina: An Ethnographic Study of a Brazilian Enclave." PhD dissertation, Tulane University.

———. 2012. *Post-Katrina Brazucas: Brazilian Immigrants in New Orleans.* New Orleans: University of New Orleans Press.

Gibson, Campbell. 1998. *Population of the 100 Largest Cities and Other Urban Places in the United States: 1790 to 1990.* Washington, DC: US Census Bureau.

Gibson, Campbell, and Kay Jung. 2002. *Historical Census Statistics on Population Totals by Race, 1790 to 1990, and by Hispanic Origin, 1970 to 1990, for the United States, Regions, Divisions, and States.* Washington, DC: US Census Bureau.

Giraud, Marcel. 1974–91. *A History of French Louisiana.* 5 vols. Baton Rouge: Louisiana State University Press.

Gomez, Gay. 2000. "Perspective, Power, and Priorities: New Orleans and the Mississippi River Flood of 1927." In *Transforming New Orleans and Its Environs: Centuries of Change,* edited by Craig E. Colten, 109–20. Pittsburgh, PA: University of Pittsburgh Press.

Gómez-Peña, Guillermo. 1996. *The New World Border: Prophecies, Poems, and Loqueras for the End of the Century.* San Francisco: City Lights.

González, Edward J. 2007. *Cuban Exiles on the Trade Embargo: Interviews.* Jefferson, NC: McFarland.

González, N. 1979. "Garifuna Settlement in New York: A New Frontier." *International Migration Review* 13: 255–63.

———. 1988. *Sojourners of the Caribbean: Ethnogenesis and Ethnohistory of the Garifuna.* Chicago: University of Illinois Press.

Gordon, E., and M. Anderson. 1999. "The African Diaspora: Toward an Ethnography of Diasporic Identification." *Journal of American Folklore* 112: 282–96.

Goza, Franklin. 1994. "Brazilian Immigration to North America." *International Migration Review* 28: 136–52.

Gruesz, Kirsten Silva. 2006. "The Gulf of Mexico System and the 'Latinness' of New Orleans." *American Literary History* 18: 468–95.

———. 2008. "The Mercurial Space of 'Central' America: New Orleans, Honduras, and the Writing of the Banana Republic." In *Hemispheric American Studies,* edited by Caroline F. Levander and Robert S. Levine, 140–65. New Brunswick, NJ: Rutgers University Press.

Guanche Pérez, Jesús. 1992. *Significación Canaria en el Poblamiento Hispánico de Cuba: Los Archivos Parroquiales, 1690–1898.* Tenerife: Ayuntamiento de La Laguna Centro de la Cultura Popular Canaria.

Guillotte, Joseph V. 1982. "Masters of the Marsh: An Introduction to the Ethnography of the Isleños of Lower St. Bernard Parish." Unpublished report, Jean Lafitte National Historical Park.

Guterl, Matthew Pratt. 2008. *American Mediterranean: Southern Slaveholders in the Age of Emancipation*. Cambridge, MA: Harvard University Press.

Guzmán, Betsy. 2001. *Census 2000 Brief: The Hispanic Population*. Washington, DC: US Census Bureau.

Hall, Gwendolyn Midlo. 1995. *Africans in Colonial Louisiana: The Development of Afro-Creole Culture in the Eighteenth Century*. Baton Rouge: Louisiana State University Press.

Hamnett, Brian. 1993. *Juárez*. London: Longman Publishing.

Harter, Eugene C. 1985. *The Lost Colony of the Confederacy*. Jackson: University Press of Mississippi.

Haverluk, Terrence W. 1998. "Hispanic Community Types and Assimilation in Mex-America." *Professional Geographer* 50: 465–80.

Hawking, Stephen. 1988. *A Brief History of Time*. New York City: Bantam.

Henao, Luis Emilio. 1982. *The Hispanics in Louisiana*. New Orleans: Apostolado Latinoamericano.

Henderson, Timothy J. 2011. *Beyond Borders: A History of Mexican Migration to the United States*. Malden, MA: Wiley-Blackwell.

Herbermann, Charles George, Edward Aloysius Pace, Condé Bénoist Pallen, Thomas Joseph Shahan, John Joseph Wynne, and Andrew Alphonsus MacErlean, eds. 1907–12. *The Catholic Encyclopedia: An International Work of Reference on the Constitution, Doctrine, Discipline, and History of the Catholic Church*. 15 vols. New York: Robert Appleton.

Hickey, John. 2002. *Canary Islands to Louisiana, 1778–1783*. Baton Rouge: Canary Islanders Heritage Society of Louisiana.

Hirsch, Arnold R., and Joseph Logsdon, eds. 1992. *Creole New Orleans: Race and Americanization*. Baton Rouge: Louisiana State University Press.

Hoffman, Paul E. 1992. *Luisiana*. Madrid: Editorial Mapfre.

Huntington, Samuel P. 2004. *Who Are We? The Challenges to America's National Identity*. New York: Simon & Schuster.

Hutchinson, E. P. 1956. *Immigrants and Their Children, 1850–1950*. New York: John Wiley & Sons.

Instituto Nacional de Estadística. 1989–90. *Censo Nacional de Población, 1988*. 5 vols. Tegucigalpa: Instituto Nacional de Estadística.

———. 2002. *XVI Censo de Población y Vivienda, 2001*. 10 vols. Tegucigalpa: Instituto Nacional de Estadística.

Jackiewicz, E. L., and Y. Sun. 2003. "The Ties That Bind, or Not? The Assimilation of Brazilian Migrants in South Florida." *North American Geographer* 5: 114–28.

Jeansonne, Glen. 1977. *Leander Perez: Boss of the Delta*. Baton Rouge: Louisiana State University Press.

Jervis, Rick. 2009. "U.S. Ports Set to Deal with Cuba; Embargo Remains, but Cities Float Trade Ideas." *USA Today*, June 18.

Johnson, B. C. 2007. *Diaspora Conversations: Black Carib Religion and the Recovery of Africa.* Berkeley: University of California Press.

Jorgensen, Bradley S., and Richard C. Stedman. 2001. "Sense of Place as an Attitude: Lakeshore Property Owners' Attitudes toward Their Properties." *Journal of Environmental Psychology* 21: 233–48.

Jouët-Pastré, Clémence, and Leticia J. Braga, eds. 2008. *Becoming Brazuca: Brazilian Immigration to the United States.* Cambridge, MA: Harvard University Press.

Kaltenbaugh, Louise P. 1970. "A Study of the Place Names of St. Bernard Parish." MA thesis, University of New Orleans.

Kanellos, Nicolás, and Helvetia Martell. 2000. *Hispanic Periodicals in the United States, Origins to 1960: A Brief History and Comprehensive Bibliography.* Houston: University of Houston Press.

Karnes, Thomas L. 1978. *Tropical Enterprise: The Standard Fruit and Steamship Company in Latin America.* Baton Rouge: Louisiana State University Press.

Kein, Sybil. 2000. "The Use of Louisiana Creole in Southern Literature." In *Creole: The History and Legacy of Louisiana's Free People of Color,* edited by Sybil Kein, 117–56. Baton Rouge: Louisiana State University Press.

King, Grace E. 1921. *Creole Families of New Orleans.* New York: MacMillan.

Klein, Herbert S. 1986. *African Slavery in Latin America and the Caribbean.* New York: Oxford University Press.

Kleyn, T. 2008. "'Garífuna es Nuestra Manera de Ser, es lo que Somos': Enfoque de Identidades e Hibridaciones en la Transculturación." In *Escrituras, Polimorfías e Identidades,* edited by F. Nájera and P. Viturro, 63–85. Buenos Aires: Libros del Rojas.

Kmen, Henry A. 1966. *Music in New Orleans: The Formative Years, 1791–1841.* Baton Rouge: Louisiana State University Press.

Knight, Franklin W. 1970. *Slave Society in Cuba during the Nineteenth Century.* Madison: University of Wisconsin Press.

Kochhar, Rakesh, Roberto Suro, and Sonya Tafoya. 2005. *The New Latino South: The Context and Consequences of Rapid Population Growth.* Washington, DC: Pew Research Center.

LaFeber, Walter. 1993. *Inevitable Revolutions: The United States in Central America.* 2nd ed. New York: W. W. Norton.

Lee, Douglas. 1983. "The Land of the River." *National Geographic* 164 (2): 226–52.

Leong, Karen J., Christopher A. Airriess, Wei Li, Angela Chia-Chen Chen, and Vera M. Keith. 2007. "Resilient History and the Rebuilding of a Community: The Vietnamese American Community in New Orleans East." *Journal of American History* 94: 770–79.

Levander, Arthur E., and Robert S. Levine, eds. 2008. *Hemispheric American Studies.* New Brunswick, NJ: Rutgers University Press.

Levine, R., and M. Asis. 2000. *Cuban Miami.* New Brunswick, NJ: Rutgers University Press.

Levitt, P., and M. Waters, eds. 2002. *The Changing Face of Home: The Transnational Lives of the Second Generation*. New York: Russell Sage Foundation.

Lewis, Peirce F. 2003. *New Orleans: The Making of an Urban Landscape*. 2nd ed. Charlottesville: University of Virginia Press.

Li, Wei, Christopher Airriess, Angela Chia-Chen Chen, Karen Leong, and Verna Keith. 2010. "Katrina and Migration: Evacuation and Return by African Americans and Vietnamese Americans in an Eastern New Orleans Suburb." *Professional Geographer* 62: 1–16.

Lichtenstein, Grace, and Laura Dankner. 1993. *Musical Gumbo: The Music of New Orleans*. New York: W. W. Norton.

Liebling, A. J. 1961. *The Earl of Louisiana*. Baton Rouge: Louisiana State University Press.

Lipski, John M. 1990. *The Language of the Isleños: Vestigial Spanish in Louisiana*. Baton Rouge: Louisiana State University Press.

Loggins, Vernon. 1958. *Where the Word Ends: The Life of Louis Moreau Gottschalk*. Baton Rouge: Louisiana State University Press.

Lukinbeal, Christopher, Patricia L. Price, and Cayla Buell. 2012. "Rethinking 'Diversity' through Analyzing Residential Segregation among Hispanics in Phoenix, Miami, and Chicago." *Professional Geographer* 64: 109–24.

MacCurdy, Raymond R. 1975. "Los Isleños de la Luisiana: Supervivencia de la Lengua y Folklore Canario." *Anuario de Estudios Atlánticas* 21: 471–591.

Maduell, Charles R. 1975. *Federal Land Grants in the Territory of Orleans: The Delta Parishes*. New Orleans: Polyanthos Press.

——. 1980. *Spanish Citizens Entering New Orleans from 1820–1865*. Cecilia, LA: Hébert Publications.

Marcus, Alan P. 1995. "Brazilians and the 1990 United States Census: Immigrants, Ethnicity, and the Undercount." *Human Organization* 54: 52–59.

——. 2007. "Becoming Brazuca: Brazilian Identity in the United States." In *The Other Latinos: Central and South Americans in the United States,* edited by José L. Falconi and José A. Mazzotti, 213–30. Cambridge, MA: Harvard University Press.

——. 2009. *An Invisible Minority: Brazilians in New York City*. 2nd ed. Gainesville: University Press of Florida.

——. 2009. "Brazilian Immigration to the United States and the Geographical Imagination." *Geographical Review* 99: 481–98.

——. 2009. "(Re)creating Places and Spaces in Two Countries: Brazilian Transnational Migration Processes." *Journal of Cultural Geography* 26: 173–98.

Margolis, Maxine L. 1994. *Little Brazil: An Ethnography of Brazilian Immigrants in New York City*. Princeton, NJ: Princeton University Press.

Marigny Hyland, William de, Sergio Lopez Ramos, and Chad J. Leblanc. 2007. "Report about the State of the Canarian Descendants in St. Bernard Parish, New Orleans, 2005." Unpublished report, Canary Islanders Heritage Society of Louisiana.

Marrow, Helen. 2003. "To Be or Not to Be (Hispanic or Latino): Brazilian Racial and Ethnic Identity in the United States." *Ethnicities* 3: 427–64.

———. 2007. "Who Are the Other Latinos and Why?" In *The Other Latinos: Central and South Americans in the United States,* edited by José L. Falconi and José A. Mazzotti, 39–77. Cambridge, MA: Harvard University Press.

Martes, Ana Cristina Braga. 2007. "Neither Hispanic, nor Black: We're Brazilian." In *The Other Latinos: Central and South Americans in the United States,* edited by José L. Falconi and José A. Mazzotti, 231–56. Cambridge, MA: Harvard University Press.

McCarthy, Brendan. 2009. "Riley, Nagin Push for Immigration Reform." *Times-Picayune,* September 9.

McCartney, Paul T. 2006. *Power and Progress: American National Identity, the War of 1898, and the Rise of American Imperialism.* Baton Rouge: Louisiana State University Press.

McCusker, John. 1999. "The Onward Brass Band in the Spanish American War." *Jazz Archivist* 13: 24–35.

McSherry, J. Patrice. 2005. *Predatory States: Operation Condor and Covert War in Latin America.* Lanham, MD: Rowman & Littlefield.

Meinig, Donald W. 1986–2004. *The Shaping of America: A Geographical Perspective on 500 Years of History.* 4 vols. New Haven, CT: Yale University Press.

Menchú, Rigoberta. 1987. *I, Rigoberta Menchú, An Indian Woman in Guatemala.* New York: Verso.

Miller, Edward L. 2004. *New Orleans and the Texas Revolution.* College Station: Texas A&M University Press.

Mintz, Sidney W. 1998. "The Localization of Anthropological Practice: From Area Studies to Transnationalism." *Critique of Anthropology* 18: 117–33.

Mintz, Sidney W., and Richard Price. 1976. *An Anthropological Approach to the Afro-American Past: A Caribbean Perspective.* Philadelphia: Institute for the Study of Human Issues.

Montero de Pedro, José. 2000. *The Spanish in New Orleans and Louisiana.* Translated by Richard E. Chandler. Gretna, LA: Pelican.

Montoya González, Tomás. 1999. "Carnival, Feast Days, and House Parties: Cuban Celebrations in Louisiana after 1960." Unpublished paper, Louisiana Division of the Arts.

———. 1999. "Music and Dance in South Louisiana's Cuban Community." Unpublished paper, Louisiana Division of the Arts.

Moore, J. Preston. 1955. "Pierre Soulé: Southern Expansionist and Promoter." *Journal of Southern History* 21: 203–23.

Moran, Kate. 2009. "Lifting of Cuban Trade Embargo Could Be Boon to Louisiana Ports, Panelists Say." *Times-Picayune,* May 29.

Murray, David R. 1971. "Statistics of the Slave Trade to Cuba, 1790–1867." *Journal of Latin American Studies* 2: 131–49.

Navarro, Mireya. 2012. "For Many Latinos, Racial Identity Is More Culture Than Color." *New York Times,* January 14, A11.

Nolan, Bruce. 2008. "Many Brazilians Settling in N.O., But for How Long?" *Times-Picayune,* January 19, A1.

Nostrand, Richard L. 1992. *The Hispano Homeland.* Norman: University of Oklahoma Press.

Odem, Mary E., and Elaine Lacy, eds. 2009. *Latino Immigrants and the Transformation of the U.S. South.* Athens: University of Georgia Press.

Oropesa, R. S., N. L. Landale, and M. J. Greif. 2008. "From Puerto Rican to Pan-Ethnic in New York City." *Ethnic and Racial Studies* 31: 1315–39.

O'Sullivan, John. 1845. "Annexation." *United States Magazine and Democratic Review* 17 (1): 5–10.

Painter, Norman W. 1949. "The Assimilation of Latino Americans in New Orleans." MA thesis, Tulane University.

Palacio, J., ed. 2005. *The Garifuna,* a *Nation across Borders: Essays In Social Anthropology.* Belize City: Cubola Press.

Parsons, James J. 1983. "The Migration of Canary Islanders to the Americas: An Unbroken Current since Columbus." *The Americas* 39: 447–81.

Passel, Jeffrey, D. Vera Cohn, and Ana Gonzalez-Barrera. 2012. *Net Migration from Mexico Falls to Zero—and Perhaps Less.* Washington, DC: Pew Research Center.

Passel, Jeffrey, and Paul Taylor. 2009. *Who's Hispanic?* Washington, DC: Pew Research Center.

Pendergrast, Mark. 1999. *Uncommon Grounds: The History of Coffee and How It Transformed Our World.* New York: Basic Books.

Pérez, Louis. 2003. *Cuba and the United States: Ties of Singular Intimacy.* 3rd ed. Athens: University of Georgia Press.

Perez, Samantha. 2011. *The Isleños of Louisiana: On the Water's Edge.* Charleston, SC: The History Press.

Poret, Ory G. 1973. "History of Land Titles in the State of Louisiana." *Publications of the Louisiana Historical Society* 1: 25–42.

Portes, Alejandro, Luis E. Guarnizo, and Patricia Landolt. 1999. "The Study of Transnationalism: Pitfalls and Promise of an Emergent Research Field." *Ethnic and Racial Studies* 22: 217–37.

Portes, Alejandro, and Min Zhou. 1993. "The New Second Generation: Segmented Assimilation and Its Variants." *Annals of the American Academy of Political and Social Science* 530: 74–96.

Port of New Orleans. No date. "Trade with Cuba." Unpublished paper, Port of New Orleans.

Post, Lauren C. 1933. "The Domestic Animals and Plants of French Louisiana as Mentioned in the Literature with Reference to Sources, Varieties and Uses." *Louisiana Historical Quarterly* 16: 554–86.

Potter, Amy. 2011. "Transnational Spaces and Communal Land Tenure in a Caribbean Place: 'Barbuda is for Barbudans.'" PhD dissertation, Louisiana State University.

Proshansky, Harold M. 1978. "The City and Self-identity." *Environment and Behavior* 10: 147–69.

Quillian, Lincoln. 1995. "Prejudice as a Response to Perceived Group Threat: Population Composition and Anti-immigrant and Racial Prejudice in Europe." *American Sociological Review* 60: 586–611.

Quiñones, Mark A. 1955. "Delacroix Island: A Sociological Study of a Spanish American Community." MA thesis, Louisiana State University.

Rathbone, John Paul. 2010. *The Sugar King of Havana: The Rise and Fall of Julio Lobo, Cuba's Last Tycoon.* New York: Penguin.

Rehder, John B. 1999. *Delta Sugar: Louisiana's Vanishing Plantation Landscape.* Baltimore: Johns Hopkins University Press.

Roberts, John Storm. 1979. *The Latin Tinge: The Impact of Latin American Music on the United States.* New York: Oxford University Press.

Robins, Nicholas A., and Maria F. Trujillo. 1999. "Normalized Trade Relations between the United States and Cuba: Economic Impact on New Orleans and Louisiana." In *Cuba in Transition: Papers and Proceedings of the Ninth Annual Meeting of the Association for the Study of the Cuban Economy,* edited by Jorge F. Pérez-López and José F. Alonso, 96–102. Coral Gables, FL: Association for the Study of the Cuban Economy.

Romero, Mary. 1992. *Ethnographic Evaluation of Behavioral Causes of Census Undercount of Undocumented Immigrants and Salvadorans in the Mission District of San Francisco, California.* Washington, DC: US Census Bureau.

Rosaldo, Renato. 1995. Foreword. In *Hybrid Cultures: Strategies for Entering and Leaving Modernity,* edited by Néstor García Canclini, x–xvii. Minneapolis: University of Minnesota Press.

Ross, Elmer L. 1973. "Factors in Residence Patterns among Latin Americans in New Orleans: A Study in Urban Anthropological Methodology." PhD dissertation, University of Georgia.

Sales, Teresa. 2004. *Brazilians Away from Home.* New York: Center for Immigration Studies of New York.

Samers, M. 2010. *Migration.* New York: Routledge.

Scallan, Matt. 2005. "In Damaged Apartments, the Poor Face Dilemma: Asked to Leave, No Place to Go." *Times-Picayune,* September 16.

Schafer, William. 1977. *Brass Bands and New Orleans Jazz.* Baton Rouge: Louisiana State University Press.

Schoultz, Lars. 2009. *That Infernal Little Cuban Republic: The United States and the Cuban Revolution.* Chapel Hill: University of North Carolina Press.

Sexton, Jay. 2011. *The Monroe Doctrine: Empire and Nation in Nineteenth-Century America.* New York: Hill & Wang.

Sierra, Justo. 1895. *En Tierra Yankee: Notas a Todo Vapor.* Mexico City: Timbre.

Simmons, Donald C. 2001. *Confederate Settlements in British Honduras.* Jefferson, NC: McFarland, 2001.

Sluyter, Andrew. 2008. "(Post-)K New Orleans and the Hispanic Atlantic: Geographic Method and Meaning." *Atlantic Studies* 5: 383–98.

———. 2012. *Black Ranching Frontiers: African Cattle Herders of the Atlantic World, 1500–1900.* New Haven, CT: Yale University Press.

———. 2012. "The Role of Blacks in Establishing Cattle Ranching in Louisiana in the Eighteenth Century." *Agricultural History* 86: 41–67.

Smith, Barbara E. 2001. *The New Latino South: An Introduction.* Atlanta: Southern Regional Council.

Smith, Heather A., and Owen J. Furuseth, eds. 2006. *Latinos in the New South.* Burlington, VT: Ashgate.

Smith, Jeffrey S., and Matthew R. Cartlidge. 2011. "Place Attachment among Retirees in Greensburg, Kansas." *Geographical Review* 101: 536–55.

Smith, Jodie, and James Rowland. 2007. "Temporal Analysis of Floodwater Volumes in New Orleans after Hurricane Katrina." In *Science and the Storms: The USGS Response to the Hurricanes of 2005,* edited by G. S. Farris, G. J. Smith, M. P. Crane, C. R. Demas, L. L. Robbins, and D. L. Lavoie, 57–61. Reston, VA: US Geological Survey.

Soluri, John. 2005. *Banana Cultures: Agriculture, Consumption, and Environmental Change in Honduras and the United States.* Austin: University of Texas Press.

Steinberg, Michael, Joseph J. Hobbs, and Kent Mathewson, eds. 2004. *Dangerous Harvest: Drug Plants and the Transformation of Indigenous Landscapes.* Oxford: Oxford University Press.

Stewart, Charles. 2007. "Creolization: History, Ethnography, Theory." In *Creolization: History, Ethnography, Theory,* edited by Charles Stewart, 1–25. Walnut Creek, CA: Left Coast Press.

Stewart, Jack. 1991. "The Mexican Band Legend." *Jazz Archivist* 6 (2): 1–14.

———. 1994. "The Mexican Band Legend: Part 2." *Jazz Archivist* 9 (1): 1–17.

———. 1999. "Cuban Influences on New Orleans Music." *Jazz Archivist* 13: 14–23.

Stoddard, Amos. 1812. *Sketches Historical and Descriptive of Louisiana.* Philadelphia: Mathew Carey.

Stokes, Doug. 2005. *America's Other War: Terrorizing Colombia.* London: Zed Books.

Striffler, Steve, and Mark Moberg, eds. 2003. *Banana Wars: Power, Production, and History in the Americas.* Durham, NC: Duke University Press.

Sublette, Ned. 2004. *Cuba and Its Music: From the First Drums to the Mambo.* Chicago: Chicago Review Press.

———. 2008. *The World That Made New Orleans: From Spanish Silver to Congo Square.* Chicago: Lawrence Hill Books.

Suro, Robert, and Audrey Singer. 2002. *Latino Growth in Metropolitan America: Changing Patterns, New Locations.* Washington, DC: Center on Urban and Metropolitan Policy, Brookings Institution, and Pew Research Center.

Swerczek, Mary. 2006. "Razing of Apartments Fuels Hispanic Concerns." *Times-Picayune*, August 15.

Szanton Blanc, Cristina, Linda Basch, and Nina Glick Schiller. 1995. "Transnationalism, Nation-States, and Culture." *Current Anthropology* 36: 683–86.

Taylor, Paul, and Mark Hugo López. 2011. *The Mexican-American Boom: Births Overtake Immigration*. Washington, DC: Pew Research Center.

Therrien, Melissa, and Roberto R. Ramirez. 2000. *The Hispanic Population in the United States*. Washington, DC: US Census Bureau.

Thrasher, John S. 1854. Cuba and Louisiana. *New Orleans Picayune*, May 7.

———. 1854. "Cuban Annexation: Influence of Annexation on the Sugar Interest." *New York Times*, May 23.

Topik, Steven, and Mario Samper. 2006. "The Latin American Coffee Commodity Chain: Brazil and Costa Rica." In *From Silver to Cocaine: Latin American Commodity Chains and the Building of the World Economy, 1500–2000*, edited by Steven Topik, Carlos Marichal, and Zephyr L. Frank, 118–46. Durham, NC: Duke University Press.

Tregle, Joseph G. 1952. "Early New Orleans Society: A Reappraisal." *Journal of Southern History* 18: 20–36.

Tropp, Linda R., and Thomas F. Petigrew. 2005. "Relationships between Intergroup Contact and Prejudice among Minority and Majority Status Groups." *Psychological Science* 16: 951–57.

Trujillo-Pagan, Nicole. 2007. "From 'Gateway to the Americas' to the 'Chocolate City': The Racialization of Latinos in New Orleans." In *Racing the Storm: Racial Implications and Lessons Learned from Hurricane Katrina*, edited by Hillary Potter, 95–114. New York: Lexington Books.

Tuan, Yi-Fu. 1977. *Space and Place: The Perspective of Experience*. Minneapolis: University of Minnesota Press.

———. 1991. "Language and the Making of Place: A Narrative-Descriptive Approach." *Annals of Association of American Geographers* 81: 684–96.

Tweed, Thomas. 1997. *Our Lady of the Exile: Diasporic Religion at a Cuban Catholic Shrine in Miami*. New York: Oxford University Press.

Ukers, William Harrison. 1922. *All about Coffee*. New York: Tea and Coffee Trade Journal Company.

Urban, Chester S. 1939. "New Orleans and the Cuban Question during the Lopez Expeditions of 1849–1851: A Local Study in 'Manifest Destiny.'" *Louisiana Historical Quarterly* 22: 1095–1167.

———. 1943. "The Idea of Progress and Southern Imperialism: New Orleans and the Caribbean, 1845–1861." PhD dissertation, Northwestern University.

US Census Bureau. 1922. *Fourteenth Census of the United States, 1920, Population*, vol. 2, *General Report and Analytical Tables*. Washington, DC: Government Printing Office.

———. 1993. *1990 Census of Population: Persons of Hispanic Origin in the United States*. Washington, DC: US Census Bureau.

——. 2002. *Measuring America: The Decennial Censuses from 1790 to 2000.* Washington, DC: US Census Bureau.

US Congress. 1831. *Bills Originating in the House of Representatives during the 1st Session of the 22nd Congress.* Washington, DC: Duff Green.

——. 1832. *Journal of the House of Representatives during the 1st Session of the 22nd Congress.* Washington, DC: Duff Green.

——. 1832. *Journal of the Senate during the 1st Session of the 22nd Congress.* Washington, DC: Duff Green.

——. 1832. *US Congressional Serial Set.* Washington, DC: Government Printing Office.

——. 1832–1861. *American State Papers,* series on *Public Lands.* 8 vols. Washington, DC: Gales & Seaton.

——. 1845–67. *The Public Statutes at Large of the United States of America, From the Organization of the Government in 1789, to March 3, 1845.* 8 vols. Boston: Charles C. Little & James Brown.

——. 1917. *The Statutes at Large of the United States of America, from December, 1915 to March, 1917,* vol. 39, pt. 1. Washington, DC: Government Printing Office.

——. 1975. *Rice Programs: Hearing before the Subcommittee on Agricultural Production, Marketing, and Stabilization of Prices of the Committee on Agriculture and Forestry, United States Senate, Ninety-fourth Congress, First Session, November 14, 1975.* Washington, DC: US Government Printing Office.

——. 1995. *The Economic Relationship between the United States and Cuba after Castro: Hearing before the Subcommittee on Trade of the Committee on Ways and Means, House of Representatives, One Hundred Fourth Congress, First Session July 30, 1995.* Washington, DC: US Government Printing Office.

——. 1999. *The Congressional Record: Proceedings and Debates of the 1st Session of the 106th Congress.* Washington, DC: US Government Printing Office.

US Department of Homeland Security. 2004. *2003 Yearbook of Immigration Statistics.* Washington, DC: US Government Printing Office.

US Employment Service. 1918. "To Increase Common Labor Supply with Porto Ricans." *U.S. Employment Service Bulletin,* 1 (17): 1.

US Immigration and Naturalization Service. 2000. *1999 Statistical Yearbook of the Immigration and Naturalization Service.* Washington, DC: US Government Printing Office.

US Office of the Federal Register. 1994. "Standards for the Classification of Federal Data on Race and Ethnicity." *Federal Register* 59 (110): 29831–35.

——. 1997. "Revisions to the Standards for the Classification of Federal Data on Race and Ethnicity." *Federal Register* 62 (210): 58782–89.

US Rice Producers Association. 2010. "Cuba Embargo: 50 Years and Counting." *Rice Advocate* 7 (October 22): 1–2.

Varney, James. 2005. "Cuban Officials, Blanco Sign a $15 Million Deal—They Hail the Revival of Old Relationship." *Times-Picayune,* March 10.

Vázquez-Hernández, Victor. 2005. "From Pan-Latino Enclaves to a Community: Puerto Ricans in Philadelphia, 1910–2000." In *The Puerto Rican Diaspora: Historical Perspectives,* edited by Carmen Teresa Whalen and Victor Vázquez-Hernández, 88–105. Philadelphia: Temple University Press.

Villeré, Sidney L. 1971. *The Canary Islands Migration to Louisiana, 1778–1783: The History and Passenger Lists of the Isleños Volunteer Recruits and Their Families.* New Orleans: Genealogical Research Society.

Walker, Norman. 1900. "Manufactures." In *Standard History of New Orleans, Louisiana,* edited by Henry Rightor, 511–37. Chicago: Lewis Publishing Company.

Waller, Mark. 2006. "El Sueño de Una Vida Mejor: The Dream of a Better Life." *Times-Picayune,* October 8.

——. 2007. "New Rules Eliminate Taco Trucks." *Times-Picayune,* June 21.

Watkins, Case, and Ronald R. Hagelman III. 2011. "Hurricane Katrina as a Lens for Assessing Socio-Spatial Change in New Orleans." *Southeastern Geographer* 51: 110–32.

Watts, David. 1990. *The West Indies: Patterns of Development, Culture, and Environmental Change since 1492.* Cambridge: Cambridge University Press.

Weddle, Robert S. 1995. *Changing Tides: Twilight and Dawn in the Spanish Sea, 1763–1803.* College Station: Texas A&M University Press.

Weil, J. H. 2009. "Finding Housing: Discrimination and Exploitation of Latinos in the Post-Katrina Rental Market." *Organization and Environment* 22: 491–502.

West, Jonathan J. 2009. "Negotiating Heritage: Heritage Organizations amongst the Isleños of St. Bernard Parish; Louisiana and the Use of Heritage Identity to Overcome the Isleños/Tornero Distinction." MA thesis, University of New Orleans.

West, Robert C. 1986. *An Atlas of Louisiana Surnames of French and Spanish Origin.* Baton Rouge: Geoscience Publications.

Whalen, Carmen Teresa. 2005. "Colonialism, Citizenship, and the Making of the Puerto Rican Diaspora: An Introduction." In *The Puerto Rican Diaspora: Historical Perspectives,* edited by Carmen Teresa Whalen and Victor Vázquez-Hernández, 1–42. Philadelphia: Temple University Press.

Wilkinson, Betina, Johanna Dunaway, and Robert Goidel. 2009. "Rebuilding or Intruding?" Paper presented at the Annual Meeting of the Southern Political Science Association, New Orleans, January 7–10.

ABOUT THE AUTHORS

JAMES P. CHANEY received his PhD from Louisiana State University and now teaches at Middle Tennessee State University in the Global Studies and Cultural Geography Program. His research interests include cultural geography, Latin America, transnational approaches to migration scholarship, the role of place in identity formation, landscape transformation, and postcolonial studies. Before returning to his hometown of Nashville, he lived in New Orleans and worked as an associate director of a Latino-focused nonprofit organization advocating for southeast Louisiana's post-Katrina immigrant population. At the same time, he conducted research on the identity formation of Garifuna transmigrants living in New Orleans. He has published articles on the Garifuna community in New Orleans as well as the Latino community of Nashville, Tennessee. More recently, he has extended his scholarly focus to include Kurdish, Laotian, and Somali communities in Tennessee.

ANNIE M. GIBSON is an administrative assistant professor in the Department of Global Education at Tulane University. Her areas of specialization include Cuban and Brazilian performance cultures and Latin American immigration to the United States. Her first book, *Post-Katrina Brazucas: Brazilians in New Orleans* (2012), is an ethnographic study of the Brazilian immigrants who relocated to New Orleans during post-Katrina reconstruction. Her research contextualizes Brazilian imaginings of their place in New Orleans in theoretical debates about transnationality, hybridity, and performances of the everyday. She has also published articles about Brazilian and Cuban immigration and performance in academic journals such as *Studies in Latin American Popular Culture, Latin American Music Review, Brasil/Brazil,* and the *Delaware Review of Latin American Studies.* Her travels and research have been supported by two Foreign Language Area Studies Fellowships, the Tinker Foundation, and the

Research Group for the Study of the Global South. Beyond teaching a diverse range of courses in the Spanish and Portuguese languages, literatures, and cultures, she administers and directs Tulane Abroad programs in Costa Rica, Cuba, and Brazil.

ANDREW SLUYTER received his PhD from the University of Texas at Austin and currently teaches at Louisiana State University. His major interests involve the environmental history and historical ecology of the colonization of the Americas, and he has made various contributions to the theorization of colonialism and landscape, the critique of neo-environmental determinism, the understanding of precolonial and colonial agriculture and environmental change in Mexico, and the discovery of African contributions to the establishment of cattle ranching in Louisiana, the Caribbean, and Latin America. He is the author of dozens of journal articles as well as the books *Colonialism and Landscape: Postcolonial Theory and Applications* (2003) and *Black Ranching Frontiers: African Cattle Herders of the Atlantic World, 1500–1900* (2012). He is the recipient of a fellowship from the American Council of Learned Societies and serves as the executive director of the Conference of Latin Americanist Geographers.

CASE WATKINS received his PhD in geography and anthropology from Louisiana State University. He studies human-environmental interaction and development in the global South using a political ecology approach to analyze historical, cultural, and ecological transformations, especially in Latin America. His current focus is the development of African oil palm landscapes and economies in Bahia, Brazil, from the early colonial period through the present. Drawing on ethnography, archival research, and GIScience, the project connects environmental histories of colonialism and the African diaspora with contemporary politics of agricultural development, biofuels, and environmental governance. His previous work has appeared in *Environment and History, Journal of Latin American Geography,* and *Southeastern Geographer.*

Carnival, Brazilian-origin population and, 125, 130

Casa Argentina, 150–51

Casa Samba, 125, 129, 130

Castro, Fidel, 48, 59

Catholic Church: anti-Latino legislation opposed by, 113; Diocese of San Cristobal de la Habana, 41; and La Virgen de la Caridad del Sobre, 58–59; settling Cuban immigrants, 49

census (US): American Community Survey (replacing long form), 126, 133, 171n10; Brazilians and, 120–22; census tracts, 171n23; Consolidated Metropolitan Statistical Areas, 71, 168n8; differentiation of Hispanic and Latino origins, changing nature of, 17–20, 33–35, 70–71, 76–77, 78, 120–21, 136–39, 137–38, 161–62n30, 164nn18,19,23, 167n7; ethnicity of Hispanic or Latino vs. racialized categories, 4–5; identification of individuals on, 32, 164n16; Metropolitan Statistical Areas, 71, 168n8; as source for study, 160n17. *See also censuses for specific years; undercounting*

Census 1850, 14, 28, 29, 30, 31, 42, 45, 67–68, 96, 99, 119

Census 1870, 98

Census 1920, 145

Census 1930, 14, 32, 47, 68, 98, 99, 102, 120, 167n7

Census 1940, 99; and differentiation of Hispanic and Latino origins, 70

Census 1950, and differentiation of Hispanic and Latino origins, 70

Census 1960, 99; and differentiation of Hispanic and Latino origins, 70

Census 1970, *51*, *52*, 101–2, 103, 136; and differentiation of Hispanic and Latino origins, 17–18, 33, 50, 70, 78, 167n7

Census 1980, 51, *52–53*, 78, 103–4, 136; and differentiation of Hispanic and Latino origins, 18, 70, 120, 167n7

Census 1990, 9, 33, 33–35, 36, 73, 78, 81, 102, 136, 146, 148; census tracts of, 166n28;

and differentiation of Hispanic and Latino origins, 18–19, 19, 33, 35, 71, 76–77, 120, 136, *137*, 161n30, 164n18; New Orleans MSA defined by, 168n8

Census 2000, 9, 10, 12, 20, 33–36, 38, 52, 56, 73, 81, 86, 88, 101, 102, 104–5, 106, 115, 124, 126, 146, 148, 150, 168n24; and differentiation of Hispanic and Latino origins, 19, 33, 35, 76, 76–77, 120, 136, *137*, 138–39, 161–62n30, 164nn18–19; New Orleans MSA defined by, 168n12

Census 2010, 9, 12–14, 19, *35*, 37–38, 38, 60, 89, 92, *93*, 108, 109, 115, 140, 146, 148, 150; and differentiation of Hispanic and Latino origins, 5, 19–20, 35, 120, 136, *137*, 138–39, 161n30, 164nn18,23

Center for Latin American Studies (Tulane), 17

Central America (region): banana trade and, 66, 142; as birthplace, 67–68; smaller groups from, 139–44; and transnational networks, 156. *See also* Spanish colonies, independence movements of

Central City neighborhood, 90, *91*

Central Intelligence Agency (CIA), 48, 140, 149–50

Cervantes Fundación Hispano-Americana de Arte, 56, 58, 151

chain migration, 122

Chalmette, LA, 31, 75; Brazilian-origin population, 129, 130, 131, 134

Chaney, James, 3

Chicago, IL: Brazilian-origin population, 128; Garínagu and, 141; transnational communities and, 7

Chile and Chilean-origin population, 150, 151

churrascos, 128, 130, 131, 133

Churros Cuban Café, 53, 58

CIA. *See* Central Intelligence Agency (CIA)

Citizenship and Immigration Service, US, 75

Ciudad Juárez, Mexico, 105

Civil War: and attempts to annex Cuba, 45; *Confederados* in Brazil, 119; expatriate Louisianans in British Honduras (Belize), 68,

cuisine: of Argentinean-origin population, 150–51; of Brazilian-origin population, 124, 128, 130, 131; Brazilian supermercados, 130, 131–32, *132;* creole, 5–6; Honduran-owned supermercados, 82–83, 87, 112, 150; of Mexican-origin population, 108, *109,* 111–12; Salvadoran, 87, 141

Cuyamel Fruit Company, 65, 66

cypress lumber, 43–44

Daily Crescent, 139

De Boré, Etienne, 44

Deepwater Horizon oil spill, 38

Delacroix, LA, 29

Delisle, John Baptiste, 48

Díaz, Porfirio, 97–98

diversity: of community identity formation, 154; focus on, by first generation and members of more populous groups, 155; hybridity of identity and, 157–58; range of dimensions of, 4; within Cuban-origin population, 56–58, 61, 121, 151, 155, 156–57

Dominican-origin population: Afro-Latino community and, 142; as creoles, 149; in New Orleans, 147–49; oil and gas industry and, 148; residential concentration, 148–49; sense of place within, 66; social capital and, 148–49; statistics, 20, 136, *137,* 148

Dominican Republic, US intervention in, 147

Drug Enforcement Agency (DEA), 150

drug trade: violent crime and, 89, 108, 140

drug war, 89, 150

dynamism of community processes, 156–57

economic slowdown, of 1980s New Orleans: and closure of Brazilian consulate, 124–25; and Cuban-origin population, 75; and Dominican-origin population, 148; and Honduran-origin population, 75, 78, 85; and isolation from New Latino South, 10; oil industry decline and, 10, 54, 55, 102

Ecuador and Ecuadorian-origin population, 150

Eisenhower, Dwight D., 48

El Club de Puerto Rico de Nueva Orleans, 146

El Latin American (nightclub), 50

El Loco, 50

El Lucero Latino, 16

El Mercurio, 16

El Misisipi, 16, 43

El Pulpo ("The Octopus"), 16. *See also* United Fruit Company

El Salvador, 67–68, 69; civil war of, 69, 75, 140 —Salvadoran-origin population, 20, 140–41; and Honduran-origin population, 87, 141

El Tiempo, 58

El Tranvia (nightclub), 50

English Turn, 29–30

enslaved population, 43, 119; eighteenth-century statistics, 24, 26; nineteenth-century statistics, 28, 29, 43. *See also* African Americans

Estelle, LA, 73, 75, 89

Estrampes y Gómez, Francisco, 45

ethnic identity. *See* assimilation of immigrants

Europe, immigration from, 98

Farabundo Marti National Liberation Front (FMLN), 140

Fat City (neighborhood), 141

Faubourg Marigny, 55

Flood of 1927, 31–32

Flores, Carlos Roberto, 85

Flores, Mary Flake, 85

Florida: Catholic Church and, 41; Cuban-origin population, 47, 48, 49, 54, 55, 56, 60, 62; Honduran-origin population, 70, *71,* 78, 168n18; immigration from Spain, 14; residential concentration in, 153; and trade with French Louisiana, 41

France, 42–43, 96

free people of color, 5, 24, 26, 28, 29

French and Indian War (1754–63), 22

French Guiana, 136

French Louisiana: ceded to Spain, 22; and contraband trade, 40, 41, 95; founding of, 22

French Quarter (Vieux Carré), 26

(demographic component), 66, 67–68; overestimation of population and, 76–79, 85–86; relative size of population and, 79–81, 92, 94

Honduran-origin population statistics: after Katrina, 76, *80,* 89–90; before Katrina, 20; in twentieth century, 68–69, 76, 77, 78–79, *82;* in twenty-first century, 114

Honduras: banana trade and, 65–66, 69; as birthplace, 70, 78; and civil wars in neighboring countries, 69, 75; coups in, 65–66, 69; Garínagu from, 6, 141; hurricanes and, 69, 75, 78, 85; patron saint of, 73; political repression in, 65–66, 69, 75, 78; population of places in, 78–79, *80;* similarities with New Orleans, 69, 86, 89; and Soccer War with El Salvador, 69; undocumented immigration from, 75

housecleaning businesses, 129, 131

Houston, TX: Brazilian-origin population, 126, 128; Garínagu and, 141; Honduran-origin population, *72, 74,* 75, 78, 92, *93;* Mexican-origin population, 102, 112; surpassing New Orleans as major metropolis of Gulf Coast, 15, 40–41, 62

Hurricane Betsy, 32

Hurricane Fifi (1974), 69

Hurricane Hattie (1959), 69

Hurricane Katrina: Brazilian-origin population and, 122, 126–27, 128–29, 156; Cuban-origin population and, 59–61; extent of flooding and wind damage, *8,* 10–11, 20, 37; flood analysis of, 160n15; Garínagu and, 142; Honduran-origin population, 88–94; Isleños and, 20, 36–38, 155, 156; Mexican-origin population and, 108; population after, 11–14, *12–13,* 36–38, *37,* 76, *80,* 89–90, 108–9, 114, 126, 127; population before, 20, 38, 126; Puerto Rican–origin population, 146; residential concentrations of populations and differential effects of, 20, 37, 59, 88, 108, 155, 156; shipping channel storm surges, 32

—cleanup and reconstruction work following: abuse of undocumented workers and, 112–14, 128, 152; affordable housing and, 109–11, 128; and black-brown antagonism, 143; Brazilian-origin population and, 122, 126–27, 128–29, 156; Central American–origin population and, 141; Cuban-origin population and, 60, 61; Dominican-origin population, 148; effect on pre-existing Hispanic and Latino communities, 20–21; and Honduran dominance in region, 88–91, 112, 113, 156; Mexican-origin population and, 108–15; Puerto Rican–origin population and, 146; reactions of politicians and media to influx of Latinos, 2, 12, 95, 108, 113–14, 157; recognition of Latino contributions to, 113–14; and social capital, 20; specialized construction trades, 128–29

Hurricane Mitch (1998), 69, 75, 76, 78, 85

Hurricane Rita, 11

Illinois, 71

immigration reform, 152

integration of immigrants. *See* assimilation of immigrants

interview methodology, 85, 162n35, 165n21, 168n13, 170n13, 171n12

Intracoastal Waterway (ICWW), 32

Irish Channel neighborhood, 71. *See also* Lower Garden District neighborhood

Irish-Italian-Isleño Parade, 33

Irish-origin population, 31

Isleños: and Civil War, 29; Cuba sojourn of, 25, 28, 42; in eighteenth century, 22–26; First and Second Settlements of, 24–25, 29; and Hurricane Katrina, 20, 36–38, 155, 156; immigration to New Orleans, 22, 24, 28, 29, 121; initial support from Spain, 24; integration of non-Isleño Hispanics and Latinos into community of, 31, 32, 42; and lack of transnational community, 156; land grants of, 24–28, *25,* 31, 36, 38; and length of time as community in city, 154; livelihoods of,

national "white Protestant" identity. *See* assimilation of immigrants
neocolonialism, US: Cuban Revolution and, 48; and establishment of Hispanic and Latino communities, 154–55; Spanish-American War and, 46, 144. *See also* military intervention
Neville, Art, 48
New Iberia, LA, 22
New Jersey: Honduran-origin population, 70, 71, 78, 168n18; Puerto Rican–origin population, 145
New Latino South: Brazilian-origin population and, 128; defined as term, 9, 114–15; Juan Crow laws and, 157; and literature on Hispanic and Latino communities, 10; Louisiana not part of, 114; New Orleans not part of, 10, 20; population growth of, 9, 102, 114–15
New Mexico: Brazilian-origin population, 126; Hispanos, 10, 36, 156
New Orleans: defined in terms of study, 7–8, *8, 11;* founding of, 7–8; as "Gateway to the Americas," 46, 94, 95; as major immigration reception port in nineteenth century, 30; NOLA as acronym for, 166n34; racial segregation increase, 52–53, 166n27. *See also* cuisine; diversity; economic slowdown, of 1980s New Orleans; Hurricane Katrina; New Orleans Metropolitan Statistical Area (MSA); residential concentration; sense of place; social capital; transnational communities; *specific parishes, places, and people*
New Orleans East neighborhood: Cuban-origin population, 52, 53; Honduran-origin population, 90, *91;* Mexican-origin population, 103, 104, 108, 109
New Orleans Metropolitan Statistical Area (MSA): Brazilian-origin population, 123–24, *123,* 126, 133; defined, 168nn8, 12; Honduran-origin population, 71, 92; jobs reports, 131; vs. vernacular conception of city used in study, 160n15

New Orleans Picayune, 44
New Spain, 36, 41
New York: Honduran-origin population, 70, *71,* 75, 78; immigration from Spain, 14
New York City: Brazilian-origin population, 128; Cuban-origin population, 45, 47, 48, 49, 50; Dominican-origin population, 66, 147, 148, 149; Garínagu and, 6, 141, 142, 143; Guatemalan-origin population, 140; Honduran-origin population, 68, 71, *72, 74,* 75, 78, 79, 92, 93, 168n18; literature on Latino communities, 10; Puerto Rican-origin population, 66, 144, 145; sense of place of, 66; Spanish American–origin population, 68; transnational communities and, 7
New York Times, 44
Nicaragua: civil war of, 69, 75, 140; and dissolution of United Provinces, 67–68; Garínagu and, 141; occupation by US, 139, 140; trade embargo imposed on, 140
Nicaraguan Independent Committee for Assistance, 141
Nicaraguan-origin population, 20, 140–41, 144
NOLA Express, 166n34
Nortenización, 7. *See also* transnational communities
North Carolina, population growth of, 9, 114, 115
North Kenner: Brazilian-origin population, 124, 129–30, 131, 134; Central American–origin population, 140–41; Cuban-origin population, 51–52, 56, 60–61, 107; Garínagu, 142; Honduran-origin population, 73, 81–84, 94; Mexican-origin population, 104; Puerto Rican–origin population, 146. *See also* Williams Boulevard corridor (North Kenner)

Obama, Barack, 62
Ocampo, Melchor, 96
oil and gas industry: Deepwater Horizon oil spill, 38; Dominican-origin population and, 147–48; Isleños and, 31; Mexican-origin population and, 102, 105, 156; and 1980s economic slowdown, 10, 54, 55, 102

sawmills, 43–44

Scott, Winfield, 96

second-line parades, music of, 45, 63

Second Louisiana Regiment, 46

self-identification, 4–5, 7

sense of place: Cuban-origin population, 50–51; Dominican-origin population, 66; identity and, 66–67; Isleños and, 156; literature on, 9–10; Mexican-origin population, 105, 106–8, 111–12; music/jazz and, 45; Puerto Rican–origin population, 66; as term, 66–67; Vietnamese-origin population, 90–91. *See also under* Honduran-origin population

Seven Years' War (1754–63), 22

Shell Beach, LA, 29

shipping channels, 31, 32

ships and shipping: banana trade, 66; Cuban trade embargo and easing of, 61–62; and Dominican Republic, 147; Spanish, and port of New Orleans, 40, 41–42, 43

slaves. *See* enslaved population

snowballs, 131

"Sobre las Olas" ("Over the Waves"), 97

social capital: Brazilian-origin population and, 124–25, 128–33; Central American–origin population and, 141; Cuban-origin population and, 50–51, 53, 55, 56, 58–59, 60–61; development of, following Katrina, 20; Dominican-origin population and, 148–49; Honduran-origin population and, 71, 73, 79, 82–85, 86–88, 94; Isleños and, 32–33, 38; Mexican-origin population and, 99–100, 102, 106–8, 109, 111–12, 115; Vietnamese-origin population and, 90–91

Solís, Joseph, 31, 44

Solís, Juan, 28, 31

Solís, Manuel, 28, 31

Solís, Manuel (grandfather), 31

Solís family, 42

Soltero, Alexey Martí, 63

Somoza, Anastasio, 140

South (region): Honduran-origin population, 70, 78; population growth of, 9, 115. *See also* New Latino South

South America (region): banana trade and, 66; smaller groups from, 139, 149–51; transnational networks and, 156. *See also* Spanish colonies, independence movements of

South Carolina: Juan Crow laws, 113; population growth of, 9, 114, 115

Southwest (region): residential concentration of Hispanics and Latinos in, 153

Soviet Union, 56, 157

Spain: as birthplace of immigrants, 29, 30, 31, 161n24; immigration from, 14; Napoleonic Wars and, 42–43

Spanish-America, defined, 68

Spanish-American War (1898), 40, 46, 47, 48, 144, 145

Spanish colonies, independence movements of: and *criollo* as term, 5; and Cuba, US relationship with, 44, 45–46; monuments to heroes of, 1, 17, 85, 100, *100;* and New Orleans/Latin America interaction, 14–15

Spanish Honduras, 68. *See also* Honduras

Spanish language: *criollo* as term, 5; and *Hispanic* as term, 4; idiom of, and Honduran social dominance, 106; masses said in, 59, 91; signage in, 83–84, *84;* spoken by Brazilian-origin population, 124

Spanish-language periodicals, 16, 43, 58

Spanish Louisiana (colony): and Acadians, 22; and Cuba, 40, 41–42, 46; immigration encouraged, 22, 24; integration with majority-French community, 26; map of, *23;* and Mexico, 95; population, 24, 26. *See also* Isleños

Spanish-origin population statistics: in twentieth century, 14, 33–35, *34;* in twenty-first century, *34–35,* 35, 36–38, *37,* 161n24

"Spanish tinge" in music, 48

Standard Fruit and Steamship Company, 16

stereotypes, 2, 101

CPSIA information can be obtained
at www.ICGtesting.com
Printed in the USA
FFOW03n2053071215
19320FF

9 780807 160879